Language and Globalization

Series Editors: **Sue Wright**, Universit   's,
University of Limerick, Ireland.

In the context of current political a
group is not so clearly defined and c
dominant in every domain, and cr
than a small elite, new patterns of lai   ...s to
provide a framework for reporting on   ...stic outcomes of
globalization and localization.

Titles include:

David Block
MULTILINGUAL IDENTITIES IN A GLOBAL CITY
London Stories

Diarmait Mac Giolla Chríost
LANGUAGE AND THE CITY

Julian Edge (*editor*)
(RE)LOCATING TESOL IN AN AGE OF EMPIRE

Roxy Harris
NEW ETHNICITIES AND LANGUAGE USE

Clare Mar-Molinero and Patrick Stevenson (*editors*)
LANGUAGE IDEOLOGIES, POLICIES AND PRACTICES
Language and the Future of Europe

Clare Mar-Molinero and Miranda Stewart (*editors*)
GLOBALIZATION AND LANGUAGE IN THE SPANISH-SPEAKING
WORLD
Macro and Micro Perspectives

Ulrike Hanna Meinhof and Dariusz Galasinski
THE LANGUAGE OF BELONGING

Leigh Oakes and Jane Warren
LANGUAGE, CITIZENSHIP AND IDENTITY IN QUEBEC

Colin Williams
LINGUISTIC MINORITIES IN DEMOCRATIC CONTEXT

Forthcoming titles:

John Edwards
LANGUAGE AND SOCIAL LIFE

Language and Globalization
Series Standing Order ISBN 978–1–4039–9731–9
(*outside North America only*)

You can receive future titles in this series as they are published by placing a
standing order. Please contact your bookseller or, in case of difficulty, write to us
at the address below with your name and address, the title of the series and the
ISBN quoted above.

Customer Services Department, Macmillan Distribution Ltd, Houndmills,
Basingstoke, Hampshire RG21 6XS, England

Multilingual Identities in a Global City

London Stories

David Block

Institute of Education, University of London

First published in hardback 2006

First published in paperback 2008 by
PALGRAVE MACMILLAN
Houndmills, Basingstoke, Hampshire RG21 6XS and
175 Fifth Avenue, New York, N.Y. 10010
Companies and representatives throughout the world

PALGRAVE MACMILLAN is the global academic imprint of the Palgrave Macmillan division of St. Martin's Press, LLC and of Palgrave Macmillan Ltd. Macmillan® is a registered trademark in the United States, United Kingdom and other countries. Palgrave is a registered trademark in the European Union and other countries.

ISBN-13: 978–1–4039–3964–7 hardback
ISBN-10: 1–4039–3964–0 hardback
ISBN-13: 978–0–230–55434–4 paperback
ISBN-10: 0–230–55434–2 paperback

This book is printed on paper suitable for recycling and made from fully managed and sustained forest sources. Logging, pulping and manufacturing processes are expected to conform to the environmental regulations of the country of origin.

A catalogue record for this book is available from the British Library.

Library of Congress Cataloging-in-Publication Data
Block, David, 1956–
    Multilingual identities in a global city : London stories / David Block.
        p.   cm. — (Language and globalization)
    Includes bibliographical references (p.) and index.
    ISBN 1–4039–3964–0 (cloth) ISBN 0–230–55434–2 (pbk)
    1. London (England)—Ethnic relations.   2. Globalization—Social aspects—England—London.   3. London (England)—Emigration and immigration.   4. Multilingual persons—England—London.   5. Visitors, Foreign—England—London.   6. Multiculturalism—England—London.   7. Immigrants—England—London.   I. Title.   II. Series.
DA686.9.A1B58 2005
305.8′009421—dc22   2005049194

Printed and bound in Great Britain by
CPI Antony Rowe, Chippenham and Eastbourne

Contents

List of Tables and Figure

Tables

Figure

Preface

Introduction

I am sitting on a bus on my way from my house in Finchley, North London, to Bloomsbury in Central London. I am speaking to my partner in Catalan, the language we brought with us when we moved from Barcelona to London nearly a decade ago. A man talking on his mobile telephone is sitting two seats back. He is speaking rather loudly in Spanish. Two rows in front of us are two teenagers who are conversing in Russian. The bus stops. Among the many people getting on are two elderly men. As they pass us, I hear Greek spoken. My linguistic radar by now more than activated, I begin to listen more intently to the conversations around me. I hear two people conversing, half in what I think is Gujarati, half in English. I hear Spanish again. And I hear Arabic, but from where I really do not know. And I hear English. One conversation is between an older woman, speaking with a Caribbean accent, and a younger woman (her daughter?), who speaks with a London accent. There are the children of South Asian immigrants, the children of the refugees from the ex-Yugoslavia and there are the children of white Londoners, who can trace their Englishness back six generations. They are all speaking their varieties of London English – a little Estuary, a little cod Jamaican – complete with the all purpose tag question: 'innit?'

I begin to look around the bus. I see people of every possible racial phenotype associated with an area of the world – African, European, South Asian, North African, East Asian – and a few people who would qualify as 'mixed race'. I see different forms of dress: teenage boys in rap attire, two young women with veils, a man in a pin striped suit, a woman in a sari, a group of university students informally dressed in jeans and sweaters and a man who looks to be wearing a dressing gown and slippers. I cannot tell from physical appearance, but I wonder how many of these people were born in London or Britain. How many have British nationality? How many have dual nationality? More importantly, how many of them see themselves as English? As British? I also wonder about social class. How many of these people come from deprived backgrounds? How many of these people would be classified as middle class?

This is the multilingual, multiethnic and multicultural London I live in. Like so many of today's Londoners, I am a relatively recent arrival to the city, having spent most of my life elsewhere. I am also like a lot of today's Londoners in that I do not live here as a classic immigrant, settling into a new home. Indeed, I often feel as though I am living in somewhat of a limbo in London, with one foot in what I consider my home, Barcelona, and the other just about touching the ground somewhere between Bloomsbury – where I work – and Finchley – where I live. I came to London in 1996, at the age of 40, to take up a lectureship at the Institute of Education, University of London. Prior to my arrival in London, my life could roughly be split into two significant parts. I spent my first 22 years in the United States, in Houston, Texas for the most part, which makes me an American (and a Texan) by birth and upbringing. However, at the age of 22, I migrated to Europe and soon afterwards settled in Barcelona, capital of Catalonia, in Spain. I lived in Barcelona for 18 years, during which time I behaved more as an immigrant than an expatriate American: I became a Catalan speaker and tried my best to adapt to local belief and value systems and lifestyles, while making no effort whatsoever to maintain American norms and customs. Importantly, it was in Barcelona where I did most of the important adult-type things in my life, such as developing a professional career, setting up friendship networks and having a family. In a sense, I now feel as though Houston is the place where I grew up and Barcelona is the far more important place where I became an adult. London takes the consolation prize of being where I am currently reconciling what my historical baggage means to my sense of self. Ultimately it is my reflections on this process which have led me to write this book, which is about the multilingual, multicultural, multiethnic global city that is London.

Multilingual Identities in a Global City: London Stories focuses on the stories told by some of my fellow denizens of London at the beginning of the 21st century. At one level, it simply tells these stories back to the reader, focusing on who these people are as regards their language identity, their national identity, their gendered identity and so on. However, there is also an attempt to relate the stories to the historical events and sociological phenomena that preceded them and surround them, respectively. These historical events and sociological phenomena are obviously much bigger than the stories being told, but they are nonetheless inextricably intertwined with them, providing a casing for them. From this point of view, Lise's story in Chapter 6 could be understood as that of a well-educated, peripatetic, English-speaking French national, passing through London for a few years. However, it may also be seen as representative of the massive increase in the number of French nationals who have come to London over the past 12 years, since the passing of the Maastricht treaty, which allowed for the free movement of all European Union citizens across all member state borders. Similarly, Javier's story in Chapter 7 can be understood on its own, as that of a Spanish-speaking Latino migrant living a marginalized existence in London. However, it comes to life far more when seen as just one of several different ways of articulating what it is like to be a member of one of the fastest growing migrant groups in London.

The book comprises nine chapters. In Chapters 1–3, my aim is to provide the reader with some theoretical background to the stories told in Chapters 5–8. I attempt to provide a comprehensive answer to the question: What is the sociohistorical backdrop to the stories told in this book and what are the conceptual frameworks drawn on to make sense of them? In Chapter 1, I discuss globalization in detail, as a system of forces and flows, and the different ways of conceptualizing and studying migration, the global flow of people. In Chapter 2, I consider issues such as culture, multiculturalism and identity, in a sense, the human consequences of migration as a global phenomenon. Finally, in Chapter 3, I turn to the idea of London as global city and I present a brief account of the city's multi-ethnic and multilingual history.

Chapter 4 is a link between the theoretical discussion in Chapters 1–3 and the London stories in Chapters 5–8. In this chapter, I briefly discuss the main issues relevant to the research behind Chapters 5–8.

In Chapters 5–7, the aim is to answer two key questions about three migrant groups in London. The first question is, what is the history of this migrant group in London? The answer to this question gives the reader an idea of how long the migrant group in question has existed as such in London. It also provides the reader with some idea about the degree to which the group is more classically immigrant in its settlement patterns and practices or more transnational. The second key question answered by the stories moves from the more general sociohistorical background to the individual level: Who are these people? Here there is a move to the life stories of individual members of migrant groups, examining in detail the different subject positions they adopt as denizens of London. The focus here is on who they are as regards their ethnic, racial, national, gendered, social class, and above all, language identities. There is also an interest in how they 'do being' a Londoner, and to what extent they do this as expatriates, classic immigrants or transnationals, that is as migrants who maintain strong social, political and economic contacts with their countries of origin while forging new identities in London.

In Chapter 5, I examine the past and present of Japanese migrants in London, before focusing specifically on the lives of five graduate students. In Chapter 6, I examine the past and present of French migration to London, before retelling the stories of four French nationals working as foreign-language teachers in London schools. In Chapter 7, I examine the past and present of Spanish-speaking Latinos in London, before examining the London experiences of two Colombians and one Cuban, living and working in London.

Chapter 8, written by Siân Preece, presents somewhat of a departure from the pattern set in Chapters 5–8. Preece focuses on the English and home language affiliations and practices of three British Asian university students: two of Punjabi/Urdu-speaking, Pakistani origin, and one of Gujarati-speaking, Kenyan origin. Unlike Chapters 5–7, this chapter does not begin with a historical survey of this ethnolinguistic group in London (this is covered in Chapter 3); rather, it focuses on the here and now of individuals who are not migrants, but the children of migrants.

The four migrant/ethnolinguistic groups discussed in Chapters 5–8 by no means exhaust the human and linguistic diversity of London. However, they are very distinct and vivid examples of this human and linguistic diversity. First, they are migrants who come from very different geographical areas: the Japanese graduate students represent East Asia; the French foreign-language teachers represent the European Union; the Spanish-speaking Latinos represent South America and the Caribbean; and the British Asian students represent South Asia and Africa. In addition, these four geographical regions offer a good balance between the well-developed and less-developed world, with the Japanese and French migrants representing the former and the Spanish-speaking Latinos and the parents of the British students representing the latter. These individuals also represent a range of settlement patterns, as they cover an array of options ranging from fixed-term sojourners to second-generation immigrants. Finally, the migrant groups considered in this book have not appeared to any significant degree in publications focusing on migration and multilingualism in London. Thus, as we will see in the coming chapters, not much has been published on Japanese, French and Spanish-speaking Latino migrants in London and what has been published about different migrant groups from South Asia (e.g. Robinson, 1986; Brah, 1996; Anwar, 1998; Visram, 2002; Raj, 2003) has not focussed sufficiently on the language practices of second generation young adults.

The book concludes with Chapter 9. In this chapter, I return to the theoretical frameworks and concepts introduced in Chapters 1–3 in an attempt to answer the following question: What do the stories tell us about migration as a global phenomenon; multiculturalism and multi-lingualism; migrant identities in the early 21st century; and London as a global city?

Acknowledgements

During the process of writing the book, I have benefited from different kinds of help from different people. I would like to thank: Amos Paran for reading all but one draft chapter of the book and making extremely helpful comments; Celeste Kinginger for reading a large proportion of this book in draft form and making helpful comments; Cathie Wallace for providing helpful feedback on an early draft of Chapter 7; Siân Preece for taking time out while finishing the final draft of her PhD thesis to write Chapter 8; series editor Sue Wright for asking me to write this book and for providing feedback on several early draft chapters; and Jill Lake and Melanie Blair at Palgrave Macmillan for their patience and professionalism throughout the entire process. Finally, I am grateful to my family, Adrià and Vicky, for letting me have a room in the house where I could shut myself in and write.

1
Globalization and Migration

Introduction

In this chapter and the next two, my aim is to introduce some of the key concepts and background information necessary to the presentation and discussion of the different London stories in Chapters 5–8. Here, I begin by defining globalization before going on to discuss the main issues and options related to it. I then move to talk about one particular aspect of globalization: migration. I consider different theories of migration, coming down on the side of one which takes into account events happening at levels ranging from the macro, global level to the micro, local level. I end this discussion of migration models with some mention of policies enacted by governments to accommodate migrants. However, I conclude that independently of what governments do, a new settlement option for migrants has arisen in recent years, which calls into question attempts to assimilate migrants to local host cultures. This option is transnationalism, to which I devote some space, as it is crucial to understanding how different migrant groups live in London today.

What is globalization?

Over the past three decades and in particular from 1990 onwards, there has been an exponential increase in the number of academics focusing on the topic of globalization. However, the term has been around for somewhat longer. In an historical account preceding the current boom by some 20 years, Modelski (1972) offered the following definition:

> The process by which a number of historical societies were brought together into one global system might be referred to as globalization. (Modelski, 1972, cited in Held and McGrew, 2000: 49)

Modelski's argument is that globalization has been going on for millennia. He cites as early examples of the phenomenon the city states of Mesopotamia six thousand years ago, the Roman Empire of two thousand years ago and the expansion of India and China at more or less the same time. However, for Modelski, the first truly global political entity was that which resulted from the spread of Islam from the 7th century until the 15th century. This empire, which at its high point in about AD 1000 stretched from Spain to the Northern India, is described as 'the true seat of civilization' (Modelski, 1972, cited in Held and McGrew, 2000: 50). Nevertheless, from the 15th century, it 'was strategically out-flanked by European naval operations and its vitality continued to decline' (Modelski, 1972, cited in Held and McGrew, 2000: 50).

The decline of the Moslem world described by Modelski is the starting point of globalization for a good number of social scientists writing during the past 30 years. Thus, while authors such as Robertson (1995), Held *et al.* (1999) and Friedman (2004) acknowledge that globalization is perhaps a pre-modern phenomenon with beginnings well before the 15th century, they take the view that the birth of the modern nation state in Europe at this time marked the beginnings of international economics and politics. In addition, at this time, the Catholic Church began to spread worldwide and thus became a global religion to a greater extent than Islam previously had. Finally, the 15th century was when the European superpowers, such as Portugal, Spain and England, began to spread outwards and colonize the world.

Convincing as these views about the beginnings of globalization might be, they do not hold sway among all globalization theorists. Indeed, many take a more here-and-now position, seeing as turning points in the history of the world the first major fuel crisis of 1973 and more importantly, the decline of traditional modes of industrial production and the subsequent move towards demand-led economies (Bell, 1973). As Cox (1996) argues, it was in the early 1970s that the developed capitalist states began to abandon the 'Fordist mode of production... which had been based on a well-paid labor force able to buy its own products and protected by institutionalized collective bargaining and by redistributative state policies acting as an economic stabilizer...' (Cox, 1996: 22). There was, at this time, a move towards 'strategies [which] emphasized a weakening of trade union power, cutting of state budgets (especially for social policy), deregulation, privatization, and priority to international competitiveness' (Cox, 1996: 22).

While authors might differ as to whether it is better to take a more historical view or situate globalization in the past 35 years, they do agree about the general characteristics of the phenomenon. In his oft-cited book *The Consequences of Modernity*, Anthony Giddens sees globalization as

> the intensification of worldwide social relations which link distant localities in such a way that local happenings are shaped by events occurring many miles away and vice versa. (Giddens, 1990: 64)

A more elaborate definition, taken from Held *et al.* (1999), looks as follows:

> Globalization can be located on a continuum with the local, national and regional. At the one end of the continuum lie social and economic relations and networks which are organized on a local and/or national basis; at the other end lie social and economic relations and networks which crystallize on the wider scale of regional and global interactions. Globalization can be taken to refer to those spatio-temporal processes of change which underpin a transformation in the organization of human affairs by linking together and expanding human activity across regions and continents. Without reference to such expansive spatial connections, there can be no clear or coherent formulation of the term. (Held *et al.*, 1999: 15)

Finally, more recently, Nederveen Pieterse offers the following definition:

> Globalization is an objective, *empirical process* of increasing economic and political connectivity, a subjective process unfolding in consciousness as the collective *awareness* of growing global interconnectedness, and a host of globalizing *projects* that seek to shape global conditions. (Nederveen Pieterse, 2004: 16–17)

In these three definitions, there is a consensus view of globalization as the observable ongoing process of the increasing and ever-more intensive interconnectedness of communications, events, activities and relationships taking place at the local, national or international level. However, while Giddens (1990) and Held *et al.* (1999) frame globalization exclusively from a social scientific point of view, Nederveen Pieterse (2004) acknowledges in his definition that this is but one of three general ways that the term might be used. First, there is globalization as an *empirical process*, the view of the phenomenon from a sociologist's perspective. Second, there is a self-reflective, self-conscious globalization, whereby people are aware of their global human condition. Third and finally, there is a policy driven globalization, which has spawned organizations such as the World Bank, Amnesty International, and of course, the anti-globalization movement.

While globalization specialists seem to agree on the general parameters of globalization, they nevertheless have tended to focus on it from particular ideological standpoints, situated in particular academic disciplines. They have, therefore, set out to focus on one particular dimension or feature of globalization to the exclusion of others. Nederveen Pieterse (2004) discusses what this actually means as regards partiality of discussions and analyses. In Table 1.1, I outline Nederveen Pieterse's list of disciplines and how they have tended to frame globalization.

A perusal of publications on globalization published in the last decade or so reveals a picture similar to the one presented by Nederveen Pieterse. Thus, there have been what appear on the surface to be mono-thematic discussions of globalization and the economy (e.g. Hirst and Thompson, 1999; Gilpin, 2001; Stiglitz, 2002; Perrons, 2004); globalization, culture and identity (e.g. Mathews, 2000; Benhabib, 2002; Vertovec and Cohen, 2002; Croucher, 2004; Nederveen Pieterse, 2004); globalization and American imperialism (Ritzer, 1998; Petras and Veltmeyer, 2001); globalization and consumerism (Ritzer, 1998, 1999, 2004; Flusty, 2004); globalization and sex (Binnie, 2004); globalization and politics (e.g. Hoogvelt, 2001; Held and McGrew, 2002; Held and Koenig-Archibugi,

Table 1.1   How different social science disciplines focus on globalization

Discipline	Main focus
Economics	Global corporations, the new economy and global capitalism in general
Cultural studies	The global village and processes such as McDonaldization and hybridization
Political science/international relations	International relations and movements.
Geography	The relativization of space, time and distance
Sociology	The nation state, world capitalism and post-industrial societies
Philosophy	World ethics, universal human rights
Political economy	Capitalism and the world market
History/anthropology	Evolution and development of international capitalism, war, world religions
Ecology	Global environmentalism

Source: Based on Nederveen Pieterse (2004: 16).

2003; Held, 2004); globalization and migration (e.g. Cohen, 1995; Faist, 2000; Papastergiadis, 2000; Jordan and Düvell, 2003; Friedman and Randeria, 2004) and globalization and technology (e.g. Castells, 2000). However, as Nederveen Pieterse and most of the above-cited authors explicitly acknowledge, it is practically impossible to discuss any one aspect of globalization in complete isolation from others. Therefore, discussions of the global economy often bleed into discussions of global governance (e.g. Hirst and Thompson, 1999); discussions of American imperialism must consider not only economic factors but also political and cultural factors (e.g. Ritzer, 1998); discussions of globalization and migration are also about culture and identity, and vice versa (e.g. Papastergiadis, 2000; Jordan and Düvell, 2003; Nederveen Pieterse, 2004); and discussions of global technology overlap with issues such as the transmission of culture around the world and new economies based on new technologies (e.g. Castells, 2000).

To capture the plurality of potential angles on globalization, some authors have elaborated frameworks which are meant to take on glob-alization in its totality. This has been the chief labour of David Held and his colleagues at the London School of Economics over the past 15 years and Held *et al.* (1999) and Held and McGrew (2002) are two examples of books approaching globalization in an all-encompassing manner. For Held and his colleagues, globalization can be examined from at least eight different angles. These angles are reflected in the chapter titles of Held *et al.* (1999), which read as follows: 'Global politics and the nation state'; 'Organized violence and military globalization'; 'Global trade and markets'; 'Global finance'; 'Multinational corporations and production networks'; 'Globalization and migration'; 'Cultural globalization'; and 'Globalization and the environment'. Held and com-pany's attempt at an all-encompassing model has echoes of an earlier, more modest framework, developed by Arun Appadurai (1990), often cited in the globalization literature published in the past 15 years. Appadurai defines globalization as a 'complex, overlapping and disjunc-tive order' made up of five dimensions of cultural flows, which he calls 'scapes'. These scapes are listed, glossed and exemplified in Table 1.2.

Globalization as the 'spatio-temporal processes of change which under-pin a transformation in the organization of human affairs by linking together and expanding human activity across regions and continents' (Held *et al.*, 1999: 15), globalization as 'the intensification of worldwide social relations which link distant localities in such a way that local happenings are shaped by events occurring many miles away and vice versa' (Giddens, 1990: 64) and globalization as the 'complex, overlapping

Table 1.2 Appadurai's (1990) scapes

Scape	Gloss	Examples
Ethnoscapes	Flows of people	Migrants, asylum seekers, exiles, tourists
Technoscapes	Flows of technology	Hardware components, technical know-how
Financescapes	Flows of money	National stock exchanges, commodity speculations
Mediascapes	Flows of information	Newspapers, magazines, satellite television channels, websites + the images and symbols they create and provide
Ideoscapes	Flows of ideas	Human rights, environmentalism, free trade movements, fear of terrorism

and disjunctive order' of ethnoscapes technoscapes, financescapes, mediascapes and ideoscapes (Appadurai, 1990) together form the backdrop to this book about London as a global city and some of the migrant groups that inhabit it. However, while all of the different aspects of globalization are important in the stories presented in this book, it is the processes and flows of people around the world, that is migration, which is the key area of focus. It is to migration that I now turn.

What is migration?

Migration may be defined as 'the movement of people across borders, both by choice and under economic and political forces, which involves stays of over a year' (Jordan and Düvell, 2003: 5). There is a long history of migration in the world, dealt with from different angles, in surveys such as Castles and Miller (2003), Sowell (1996), Cohen (1997), Held *et al.* (1999), Papastergiadis (2000), Faist (2000) and Jordan and Düvell (2002, 2003). In these surveys, a general, somewhat Eurocentric, chronology of migrations is discussed. These migrations include the spread of empires in the middle ages (e.g. the Holy Roman Empire); the spread of the European colonial powers of England, France, Spain, Portugal and the Netherlands around the world in the 15th and 16th centuries; the forced migration of some 10 million African slaves to the Americas from the early 16th century until the mid-19th century; the mass migrations of European peoples such as the Irish, the Italians and the Jews to the Americas and beyond in the 19th and 20th centuries; and the post-Second World War movements of people across borders, classified variously as political refugees, asylum seekers and economic migrants.[1]

One issue that arises in most discussions of migration is the extent to which people today are moving around on an unprecedented scale, far more than has ever been the case in history. For the authors cited above, this notion is false if one considers migration in proportion to the total population of the world. For example, during the 19th and early 20th century migration of Europeans to the Americas and beyond, European countries were losing very large proportions of their considerable population growth to emigration, as much as 40 per cent according to Jordan and Düvell (2003). Sowell (1996) states that 26 million Italians emigrated in the period 1876–1976 and Papastergiadis (2000) offers the figure of 25 million for the number of people who emigrated from Britain from 1815 to 1925. Although these figures are estimations involving some degree of guesswork, they still give us a feel for the magnitude of the great European migrations of the 19th and early 20th centuries. If one compares these proportions with the estimated 100 million migrants in the world at the end of the 20th century (Jordan and Düvell, 2003), the claim about the uniqueness of the times we live in seems somewhat exaggerated. Nevertheless, as I suggest below, there is a case for saying that in the era of globalization, the nature of migration has changed and this means that its impact is greater on receiving societies.

Another issue arising in discussions of migration concerns refugees. According to Jordan and Düvell (2003), of the roughly 100 million refugees in the world in 2000, some 34 million were in sub-Saharan Africa and 51 million were in Asia. Thus it is on the whole the poorer countries of the world that are taking the lion's share of refugees and bearing the brunt of the problems which come with incoming populations which only with great difficulty can be accommodated. Indeed, the very idea that Europe, North America, East Asia and Australasia are being overrun with migrants from all over the world is not only inaccurate; it is laughable, if one takes into account the proportion of migrants worldwide who actually end up in London, New York or Paris, as opposed to cities in the developing world.

Jordan and Düvell's definition of migration cited above clearly lays out the authors' primary interest in a politico-economic angle on the phenomenon, firmly at the crossroads of the globalizing flows and processes outlined above and the geographical and political borders that define the modern nation state. The definition is clarifying in that it excludes from the discussion and analysis of migration holiday travel and short-term business and study travel, all of which could last for days, weeks and even months. Jordan and Düvell also exclude from their discussion and analysis movements inside the borders of nation states, terming such movements 'geographical mobility'.

I see these delimitations of what is and is not migration both positively and negatively. For example, by excluding tourism and short-term business and study travel, the authors have built into their definition the idea that a true migration will involve settling into a routine in a particular locale as opposed to acting as a temporary visitor. Of course, taken literally, this qualification means that Jordan and Düvell cannot account for cases of individuals who continually go back and forth between two or more locations, never spending more than six months in any one of them. As regards the question of intra–nation-state movement, I think Jordan and Düvell do not consider sufficiently the extent to which nation states have traditionally housed very different groups and cultures. Examining some of the larger migrations that have occurred within nation states in the past, one sees that these movements have often led to clashes of cultures no less extreme than those arising in inter–nation-state movements. For example, the early and mid-20th century passage of African Americans from the southern United States to northern cities, such as Chicago, Detroit, Philadelphia and New York, was surely as much a clash of cultures as earlier waves of European immigrants had been. Elsewhere, the mid-20th century migration of people from southern Spain and Italy to the wealthier northern areas of Catalonia and Lombardia, respectively, represented similar intra–nation-state culture clashes.

Elsewhere Papastergiadis (2000), Faist (2000) and Castles and Miller (2003) take a slightly different tack when defining migration. Like Jordan and Düvell, they embed their discussion in the more general context of globalization. And, like these authors, they are interested in the conflicting pushes and pulls at the crossroads of the nation state and globalization flows and processes. However, they provide a more detailed consideration of the alternative theories of migration that have been put forth by migration specialists over the years.

Models of migration

Papastergiadis (2000) frames his discussion of migration as a way out of what he sees as sterile conflicts among sociologists who have traditionally adopted one of two general models of migration. The first model, which Papastergiadis calls the 'voluntarist push–pull model', sees rational choice and individual agency as the driving forces behind migration. According to this model, people move from one place to another in order to improve their economic lot, as Papastergiadis explains:

> According to this model, migration is always caused by twin and counterbalancing forces: people are 'pushed out' of stagnant rural peasant economies, and 'pulled' up towards industrial urban centres. This 'push–pull' model tended to see migration as being caused by the individual calculation of economic opportunity. (Papastergiadis, 2000: 30)

This description makes the model sound extremely simplistic; however, as Papastergiadis notes, most researchers who subscribe to it have considered mediating 'enabling' factors that make migration possible when they apply, and hinder it when they do not. Thus on the push side, economic desperation in isolation cannot cause migration; it must be accompanied by the political right of potential migrants to migrate, transportation to get migrants to their chosen destinations, sufficient money to pay for passage and the skills and intellectual wherewithal to organize a move. An example of the former two factors preventing migration due to their absence is to be found in North Korea. There, many potential migrants have a good economic incentive to migrate to South Korea or elsewhere; however, they lack both the legal right to leave North Korea and readily available transportation. An example of money and skills acting as enabling factors is to be found in the great European migration to the Americas in the 19th and 20th centuries. In this massive migration, poverty was not enough to get one to the Promised Land; rather, one needed the material resources to act on the desire to move. Ultimately, it was the richer members of peasant groups who were able to emigrate (Sowell, 1996; Faist, 2000; Castles and Miller, 2003). Thus in the case of southern Italians who moved in the millions to the United States, Argentina, Brazil and other North and South American countries between 1880 and 1940, it was those who were able to pay (or had family members, already there, able to pay) for transportation and had the skills to organize the Atlantic passage that emigrated. The poorest of the poor were, for the most part, left behind.

On the pull side, one key enabling factor is the relative willingness of receiving states to admit migrants. Historically, nation states built on immigration, such as the United States and Australia, have intermittently opened and closed their doors due to internal political, social and economic factors. Such actions surely have conditioned individual decisions to migrate to these countries or not. Of course, it is worth noting that one of the more interesting aspects of current migration is the growing understanding among both governors and citizens of the richer nation states of the world that they have progressively less and less control over their borders.

Papastergiadis finds much to object to in the voluntarist push–pull model. First, he believes that the model overstates the extent to which poverty leads directly to the decision to migrate. Surely if this were the case, one would expect to see far more migration to the richer nation states of the world than is currently the case. As it is, making a move from one nation state to another involves far more than just hunger; there are serious questions revolving around culture and identity that come into play.

A second problem with the model stems from its inability to account for the fact that migrations follow particular paths that are not always the most logical ones to follow, if one considers factors such as ease of entry and proximity. For example, why do South Asians come in such large numbers to the UK as opposed to Germany, which is nearer geographically? And why do Mexicans and Central Americans often go as far as Chicago or Detroit in the US, thus bypassing several large US cities along the way? The answers to these questions owe more to historical contacts between sending and receiving locations than raw economic issues. Thus there is an ex-colonial situation and a tradition of migration that explains Indians and Pakistanis' preference for the UK. As regards Mexican and Central Americans migrating inside the US, there are Latino communities going back three generations in Chicago and Detroit.

A third problem with the voluntarist push–pull model is that it cannot explain why some people migrate even when their economies are going well. Certainly, a high proportion of the recent migrations inside Europe owe more to lifestyle preferences than the escape of abject poverty. Anyone who has watched British television over the past five years can attest to the rise in the number of programmes about British people abandoning the UK for sunnier and presumably more attractive destinations such as Italy and Spain. While it would be naïve to assume that the individuals who make such moves represent a significant proportion of the total British population, the television programmes themselves are important as a means of putting into general circulation a discourse of lifestyle choice.

An alternative to the voluntarist push–pull model is what Papastergiadis calls the 'structuralist centre–periphery model'. This model is primarily a Marxist model that sees world capitalism as the driving force behind the movement of people from one country to another. Migration serves the function of providing an everlasting supply of cheap and dispensable labour to the developed economies of the world, helping them through the ups and downs of ongoing expansion and contraction. In addition, the flow of migrant workers from the less developed periphery to the wealthier countries serves to strengthen inequality in the world, essentially making the rich richer and the poor poorer. This is because migration means that poorer developing countries lose out doubly. First, they all too often lose the most qualified members of society who are attracted by the prospects of professional fulfilment and/or economic betterment offered in the developed world. Second, the cost of feeding, raising, educating and training people, what Papastergiadis refers to as 'reproduction costs', are all borne by the labour-exporting poorer developing countries and not by the labour-importing wealthier developed countries.

Papastergiadis is no less critical of the structuralist centre–periphery model than he is of the previously cited voluntarist push–pull model. Thus, while acknowledging that its attention to macro-social factors is a useful antidote to the narrow individualism of the push–pull model, he finds fault with the oversimplified constructs that sustain it. For example, migrants are often positioned in research as proletarians who are subject to exploitation by the world economy. However correct such an analysis might be at a macro-economic level, it leads to a blinkering of vision at the micro-social level, rendering the researcher unable to see migrants in other ways, for example as racialized and gendered. Thus a black woman from the Dominican Republic who migrates to Madrid is not just a proletarian moving from the periphery to the centre. She is also a woman and a black person moving to a predominantly white European world and ultimately these social positions might count for more as regards her life conditions in Madrid than the poverty which drove her to migrate in the first place.

Another obvious problem with the structuralist centre–periphery model is the way that agency is totally subordinated to the macro structure of international capitalism. Without falling back into voluntaristic individualism, it is possible to argue for individual agency as a factor in migration. What is needed, however, is a perspective which includes the interaction of structure and agency, one that sees structure as conditioning individual actions while individual actions serve to reshape structures. Thus, in the previously cited example of the black Dominican woman in Madrid, it is preferable to see her race and femininity as conditioning her life while acknowledging how her actions and the activities she engages in serve to constantly reshape what it means to be a black and Dominican woman in Madrid.

For Papastergiadis, then, neither of these traditional approaches to migration really works. Both, it seems, contain the same fundamental weakness, which he explains as follows:

A fundamental weakness that is implicit in both the voluntarist push–pull model and the structuralist political-economy theory is their conceptualization of flow. Both perspectives understand the flow of human migration within a sort of 'water-pump' metaphor. Migration is seen as a system in which the flow is driven by the originating pressures of market needs, the counter-responses of individual migrants, and the regulating valves of state policies. (Papastergiadis, 2000: 93)

What is needed, then, is a model or theory of migration that can take into account the global forces and flows outlined in the previous section. These global forces mean that migration patterns and movements have changed in recent years as they are constantly multiplying, transforming, accelerating and intensifying. As a consequence of these changes in migration, Papastergiadis suggests a shift from the traditional metaphor of the 'water pump' to the more volatile and unstable metaphor of 'turbulence', which he takes from the work of James Rosenau (1990). Papastergiadis draws on the standard definition of turbulence as 'the unsettling effect of an unexpected force that alters your course of movement' (Papastergiadis, 2000: 4). He moves from this prosaic use to consider turbulence as 'a metaphor for the broader levels of interconnection and interdependence between the various forces that are at play in the modern world' (Papastergiadis, 2000: 4). Papastergiadis concludes that '[i]n the absence of structured patterns of global migration, with direct causes and effects, turbulence is the best formulation of the mobile processes of complex self-organization that are now occurring' (Papastergiadis, 2000: 4).

Towards a multi-level migration systems theory

Faist (2000) and Castles and Miller (2003) discuss as an alternative theory of migration what they call the multi-level migration systems theory. According to this theory, migration can be conceptualized as a series of overlapping and interacting systems working at three levels: macro, micro and meso. At the macro level, there is a consideration of the kinds of global forces discussed by the globalization theorists cited above: global politics, global markets, global ideologies, global media and so on. All of these macro-level factors impact on the flow of individuals between and among countries. At the micro level, the human element is introduced in the form of individual values and expectations such as the desire to improve one's standard of living or gain political autonomy. The meso level refers to the various networks that intercede between the macro and micro levels. These networks include social ties (be these family or occupational), symbolic ties (belonging to a particular ethnic, national, political or religious group) and transactional ties (e.g. reciprocity, solidarity, access to resources). Faist understands these networks in terms derived from the work of Pierre Bourdieu (1991), making reference to cultural capital (the educational resources migrants bring with them; the know-how and ability necessary if one is to migrate) and social capital (the safety net of already established relationships among previous migrants, family and organized assistance). In Table 1.3, I present a summary of Faist's three levels of migration.

To show how this model works in practice, it is instructive to consider the previously cited migration of southern Italians to the US in the late 19th and early 20th centuries. This migration was facilitated by macro factors such as overpopulation and a lack of economic opportunity in southern Italy, in combination with a need for manual labour in the US and the greater availability of international transport. At the micro level, many southern Italians wished to improve their economic

Table 1.3   Three levels of migration

Micro (values or desires and expectations)	Meso (collective and social networks)	Macro (macro-level opportunity structures)
Individual values and expectancies • improving and securing survival, wealth, status, comfort, stimulation, autonomy, affiliation and morality	*Social ties* • strong ties: families and households • weak ties: networks of potential movers, brokers and stayers *Symbolic ties* • kin, ethnic, national, political, and religious organizations • symbolic communities *Content of ties/ transactions* • obligations, reciprocity and solidarity • information, control and access to resources of others	*Economics* • income and unemployment differentials *Politics* • regulation of spatial mobility through nation-states and international regimes • political repressions, ethnic, national and religious conflicts *Cultural setting* • dominant norms and discourses *Demography and ecology* • population growth • availability of arable land • level of technology

Source: Adapted from Faist (2000: 31).

position – gaining wealth, status and security – and migration to the US seemed to be the only way to achieve these aspirations. Finally, at the meso level, they very soon developed family and occupational ties among Italians in the US, which facilitated the finding of housing and employment by recent arrivals.

While economic forces have been the key macro-level force behind much migration over the years, so too have political forces, specifically wars and political repression. For example, since the outbreak of war in Sri Lanka in 1983, hundreds of thousands of Tamil speakers have migrated from their home regions, seeking political asylum in locations around the world, in particular India, Canada and Britain. At the meso level, this movement of Tamils has been facilitated by actions of previous refugees who have established themselves in large numbers in cities such as Toronto and London. These previous refugees have set up extensive support networks, which have served to ease the settlement of subsequent arrivals.

According to Faist (2000) and Castles and Miller (2003), the three levels of macro, micro and meso are intertwined and linked to the extent that it is often difficult to keep them separate. Indeed, if one wishes to answer interesting questions about migration, it would not be desirable to keep them separate. Thus for the Italian migrants of the 19th and 20th centuries, the micro-level aspiration for a better life is linked to the relative economic weakness of Italy *vis-à-vis* the US. Meanwhile, migration itself is facilitated by family and occupational links at the meso level. Similarly, for Tamil-speaking refugees cited above, the micro-level need to get away from a violent environment is linked to the macro-level availability of asylum as a migration option. In addition, there are the well-established meso-level family and job networks in refugee-receiving cities. These cases, along with many, many others in the past and present of global migration, point to the need to eschew the mechanistic and deterministic models that had dominated the study of migration for many years, in favour of multi-levelled, more flexible ones.

Settlement options: The rise of transnationalism

Having considered how migration is conditioned and shaped by a multitude of factors at macro, micro and meso levels, I now move to consider how migrants settle into their new surroundings once they are inside the borders of a receiving nation state. In broad terms, settlement has traditionally been conceptualized in terms of straightforward assimilation or multiculturalism. In receiving nation states, whether they are old hands (e.g. the US, Australia) or new (e.g. Spain, Japan), there has been much debate in recent years about whether or not assimilation or multiculturalism should be the policy towards migrants. In general terms, assimilation is a policy that fuses notions of citizenship with identity. In a nation state adopting such a policy, migrants are welcome as long as they conform to mainstream behavioural norms, values and beliefs in the host nation state and they show an exclusive allegiance to that nation state. The goal, then, is to turn immigrants into nationals with little or no sense of affiliation to their country, culture or language of origin. In contrast to the assimilationist model, a multicultural policy means that while migrants are expected to abide by the general rules of coexistence as laid down in the host nation state, they are allowed to self-identify with an ethnic or religious community deemed to be different from the mainstream in that host nation state. The goal here is to grant nationality to, and demand a degree of allegiance and loyalty of immigrants who become not only nationals but members of a minority ethnic group.[2]

These two settlement options are of course not always easy to identify in a discrete manner. For example, in the US they have historically lined up as co-existent and competing discourses of immigration. Indeed, a good proportion of the so called 'culture wars', which have been going on in the US over the past 20 years, centres on whether or not the US is an assimilationist society or a multicultural one. In Britain, a similar kind of debate is going on at the time of writing, with much discussion about the alleged incomplete assimilation of some immigrant groups, in particular, those classified as Muslims, to the rather abstract notion of 'British culture'. Elsewhere, France is currently involved in an often-undeclared national debate over whether or not its traditional assimilationist model is effectively ceding ground to an emergent multiculturalism (see Bleich, 2003, for a comparison of British and French immigration policies over the past 50 years).

For all of the discussions about whether migrants should in effect be forced to be like host country citizens or whether they should be given some leeway in the maintenance of a putative original cultural identity, a new settlement option for migrants is arising independent of any concerted policy on the part of nation-state governments. It owes its development more to the turbulence of globalized migration, as described by Papastergiadis, than to reified cultures in conflict. I refer here to what has come to be known as 'transnational social spaces' (e.g.

Faist, 2000; Jordan and Düvell, 2003) or 'transnational communities' (e.g. Basch, Glick Schiller and Blanc-Szanton, 1994; Portes, Guarnizo and Landolt, 1999; Vertovec, 1999; Castles and Miller, 2003).

Transnationalism

The often invoked concept of 'time-space compression', normally attributed to David Harvey (1989), means, among other things, that both physically and virtually people around the world are in greater proximity to each other, and much faster so, than has ever been the case in the history of the world. In other words, via advanced technology and transportation, people can more easily and quickly be in either physical or virtual contact than has been the case in the past. As Perlmutter (1991) notes, the impact of this time-space compression has meant that that the world is coming to be organized less vertically, along nation-state lines, and more horizontally, according to communities of shared interests and experiences. Thus there are progressively more and more communities which transcend nation-state boundaries and individuals who in much of their lives feel more allegiance and affinity to these communities than they do to the nation sates in which they reside. These communities are based on a long list of shared experiences and orientations, such as tastes in fashion, music, cinema, literature and so on; beliefs and opinions; and lifestyle options.

Given its effect on relatively stable populations, it is not surprising that time-space compression should have a great impact on migration processes. Indeed, once they have settled in a particular nation state, today's migrants are progressively forming part of what are termed transnational social spaces as opposed to traditional immigrant communities. According to authors such as Glick Schiller, Basch and Blanc-Szanton (1992), Basch, Glick Schiller and Blanc-Szanton (1994), Portes, Guarnizo and Landolt (1999), Faist (2000), Foner (2001) and Jordan and Düvell (2003), transnational social spaces emerge at the crossroads of migration-facilitating institutionalized and informal networks: on the one hand, there are international and government agencies and organizations that facilitate the movement of particular groups of migrants back and forth between nation states; on the other hand, there are the migrants themselves, their shared social, cultural and economic capital, which make possible both movement to and fro and settlement. Jordan and Düvell (2003) describe transnational social spaces as sites where groups, defined by ethnicity (Latinos), religion (e.g. Muslim), nationality (e.g. Turkish) or geographical region (e.g. North African), have settled in nation states, but have nevertheless 'retained and developed their cultural and economic links with their homelands, including (in some cases) their political loyalties and commitments' (Jordan and Düvell, 2003: 76). Such groups behave differently from traditional immigrants in that they have not made a firm commitment as regards personal and cultural loyalties to the host society. For Jordan and Düvell, the transnational existence of these groups

> defies notions of assimilation and acculturation to the national 'core', and goes beyond the ethnic pluralism of multicultural membership. It suggests that dual or multiple forms of nationality and citizenship might better reflect and recognize the realities of these socio-economic systems. (Jordan and Düvell, 2003: 76–7)

Elsewhere, Faist (2000) suggests that transnational communities are particular manifestations of transnational spaces; two others are transnational kinship groups and transnational circuits. An example of the former is a family member working as a contract labourer and sending remittances back home to the rest of the family. An example of the latter is trading networks, business ventures set up in two or more nation states. However, transnational communities may be seen to supersede these other two types of transnational space: while kinship systems are too narrow, often involving one extended family, trading networks are too narrowly focused on business and work. Transnational communities are all of this and in addition, sites of any number of transnational connections to ongoing cultural phenomena and processes, such as the world of politics (e.g. participating in electoral processes both in the host country and the home country) and the media (both print and audiovisual). Castles and Miller describe transnational communities as follows:

> The notion of a transnational community puts the emphasis on human agency. In the context of globalization, transnationalism can extend previous face-to-face communities based on kinship, neighbourhoods or workplaces into far-flung virtual communities, which communicate at a distance. (Castles and Miller, 2003: 30)

The agents who make up transnational communities, known as 'transmigrants', act as follows:

> Such migrants do more than stay in touch with family members left behind. They organize daily economic, familial, religious, and social

relations within networks that extend across the borders of two nation-states. Transnational connection takes many forms, all of which go beyond immigrant nostalgia in which a person who is removed from his or her ancestral land tries to recreate on the new land a sense of the old, through foods, music and storytelling. (Fouron and Glick Schiller, 2001: 60)

While transnational communities clearly differ from traditional immigrant communities, they would appear to have something in common with what have historically been known as diaspora communities.

Diaspora communities and transnational communities

According to authors such as Robin Cohen (1997) and Rogers Brubaker (2005), diasporas by definition unify several key features. First, they always imply the dispersal of a people from their original homeland to two or more foreign regions. Second, this dispersal can either be traumatic or forced in nature or voluntary. Third, there will always be a collective memory and idealization of the ancestral homeland – its history, culture and language – and a commitment to its maintenance. Fourth, there will also be a return movement that keeps alive the dream of rejoining one's ancestors. Fifth, every attempt is made to maintain contact with fellow members of the diaspora spread around the world. All of these characteristics contribute to a sixth characteristic, that is a strong sense of ethnic identity separate from that of the host community. This separateness might be tolerated in host environments that have a tradition of pluralism and multiculturalism. However, it can lead to conflict in host societies where the expectation is to assimilate or there is mistrust of difference.

Transnational communities appear to share with diasporas the characteristics outlined by Cohen and Brubaker. They involve the movement outwards of a people from their original homeland to two or more foreign regions. In current times, this dispersal can be traumatic or forced, although it is very often economically motivated or even due to a desire to change one's lifestyle. In transnational communities, there is a collective memory of the history, culture and language of the homeland and often an idealization which accompanies the constant presence of the prospect of 'return'. If nothing else, transnational communities share with diaspora communities the conscious attempt to maintain contact with fellow community members in the home country and, in some cases, around the world, all of which serves to maintain a sense of common identity, separate from that of the host community or communities.

Today all migrants benefit to varying degrees from the advanced technology of the global age such as cheaper, faster and more frequent travel; cheaper and more extensive telecommunications (including global television and radio connections); and cheaper, faster and more polyvalent computer technology. This technology allows migrants to create transnational spaces and communities as defined above. This is the case of wealthy Chinese and Indian business people, who have contacts in two or more continents (e.g. Wong, 1998; Lessinger, 2001, respectively). It is also the case of many Puerto Rican or Haitian migrants in the US who continually go back and forth between cities like New York and Puerto Rico and Haiti (e.g. Conway, Bailey and Ellis, 2001; Fouron and Glick Schiller, 2001, respectively). Thus, owing to the time-space compression of globalization, I think there has been a 'diasporization' (to use a term which Cohen reluctantly coins) of trad-itional migration patterns. In a sense, transnationalism has taken over the conceptual space of much of what has traditionally been called immigra-tion and just about all of what has traditionally been called diaspora.[3]

Conclusion

In this chapter, I have discussed key issues arising in current discussions of globalization, before moving to a more specific focus on migration. After examining models of migration, I have concluded that any model adopted will have to take into account a myriad of global, intermediate and local factors. To this end, I have suggested that because it examines phenomena shaping and conditioning the movement of people at the macro, meso and micro levels, Faist's (2000) multilevel model works best as a tool for understanding migration.

I have also discussed settlement options in this chapter. I have con-cluded that transnationalism, which involves simultaneous, social, political and economic ties with two or more nation states, is becoming a settlement option for many migrants. Indeed, for many researchers it has become a far more useful term than immigration in studies of migrant settlement (e.g. Cordero-Guzmán, Smith and Grosfoguel, 2001).

Nevertheless, as Foner (2001) notes, it is best not to get carried away, using the term 'transnational' too loosely for all migration occurring today. First, one should bear in mind that transnationalism is not entirely a new phenomenon. Earlier immigrants to the US, such as the Italians who entered in great numbers in the period 1880–1930, also maintained contact with their homelands and many did actually fulfil the dream of a return to Italy, often after having lived for decades in the US (Sowell, 1996). In addition, a close examination of the behaviour of today's migrants reveals how not all are living a transnational life. Indeed, many very quickly sever most ties with the homeland and never look back, taking on the mantle of the more classic immigrant.

Another issue to consider, as Foner (2001) and others have done, is whether or not the children of transnationals keep up the transnational customs of their parents. For example, if the second generation of South Asians in London move towards total assimilation, creating a strictly local London space for themselves, then transnationalism will come to look more like a stage in the assimilation process rather than something more enduring.

Notwithstanding Foner's reservations about transnationalism, I still see it as a useful tool for discussing and understanding migration today. This is above all because it captures nicely the ways that migrants today often maintain social, economic and political contacts across geographical and nation-state borders. However, it is also of use because it serves as an interesting reference point between an immigrant subject position, as a permanent settlement option, and expatriate status, as a less permanent option, about which I will have more to say in the next chapter.

2
Multiculturalism and Identities

Introduction

The discussion in the previous chapter was about globalization and the global phenomenon of migration. In this chapter, my aim is to examine ways of qualifying the flesh and blood of people who are migrants. I begin with a consideration of the all-important concepts of culture, multiculturalism and community. From there, I move to a lengthy treatment of identity, considering some of the basic tenets of a post-structuralist approach to identity as well as different types of identity which are relevant to this book: ethnic, racial, national, gendered, social class and above all, language. Finally, I consider specific subject positions that relate to individuals' status as migrants.

What is culture? What is multiculturalism?

In my attempt to define multiculturalism, I need first to take on an even trickier term: 'culture'. According to Raymond Williams, culture is 'one of the two or three most complicated words in the English language' (Williams, 1976: 87). On the one hand, there is the traditional definition of culture as related to civilization, refinement, the high arts and an overall good sense of what is aesthetically correct, what some might call 'culture with a big C'. In the English-speaking world, this view is most famously associated with Matthew Arnold (1882/1971), but to many lay people, it still rings true as what culture is about. More relevant to our discussion here, however, is the development of anthropological definitions of culture, which are meant to be more descriptive and analytical than prescriptive and evaluative. As Tony Bennett (1998) suggests, perhaps the first such definition of culture is found in the work of Edward Tylor (1874). Tylor wrote that 'Culture or Civilization, taken in its wide ethnographic sense, is that complex whole which includes knowledge, belief, art, morals, law, custom, and any other capabilities and habits acquired by man as a member of society' (Tylor, 1874: 1, cited in Bennett, 1998: 93). Whatever criticisms one might formulate, as regards the overall work of Tylor (and Bennett formulates a few), this definition is significant because it has beliefs, behaviour and cultural artefacts at its centre, a tendency that has continued to this day. For example, in his in-depth discussion of multiculturalism, Bhikhu Parekh offers the following definition of culture:

> Culture is a historically created system of meaning and significance, or, what comes to the same thing, a system of beliefs and practices in terms of which a group of human beings understand, regulate and structure their individual and collective lives. (Parekh, 2000: 143)

This is a fairly standard definition of culture and it is one that would be acceptable to many anthropologists and sociologists. However, not all social scientists would agree that culture can or should be defined only in this way, in terms of systems, structure and regulation. (Indeed, Parekh elsewhere in his writing seems to reject this seemingly static view.) In his incisive treatment of multiculturalism, Gerd Baumann (1999) outlines what he believes to be the two general views of culture dominant in current thought: the 'essentialist' and the 'processual'. In the former case, 'essentialist' refers to the assumption or belief that cultures exist in pure, homogenous and unified forms. Baumann explains this view as follows:

> The collective heritage of a group, that is a catalog of ideas and practices that shape both the collective and the individual lives and thoughts of all members. Culture thus appears as a mold that shapes lives or, to put it somewhat polemically, as a giant photocopy machine that keeps turning out identical copies. (Baumann, 1999: 25)

In contrast to this relatively static view of culture, the 'processual' view frames culture as dynamic and emergent, that is, it takes into account how culture arises from the social practices of individuals on a moment-to-moment basis. Baumann explains matters as follows:

> Culture ... is not so much a photocopy machine as a concert, or indeed a historically improvized jam session. It only exists in the act of

being performed, and it can never stand still or repeat itself without changing its meaning. (Baumann, 1999: 26)

Baumann's views of culture parallel structuralist and poststructuralist approaches to the study of social phenomena. Definitions of structuralism vary, but they all converge around certain key ideas (see Lévi-Strauss, 1963, for a classic exposition of structuralism in anthropology). The foundation of structuralism is the belief that all social phenomena are determined by social and material structures in the world. As a result, structuralism involves the search for fixed universal principles and laws that determine, govern and structure the activities of human beings in the world. Papastergiadis's 'voluntarist push–pull' and 'structuralist centre–periphery' models of migration, discussed in Chapter 1, are structuralist in that they frame migration as a phenomenon governed by fixed universal principles and laws and determined by social and material structures in the world.

Poststructuralism grew out of the belief of social theorists and researchers that structuralism presented an over-simplified, one-dimensional view of the world. A poststructuralist view of social phenomena allows for both individual agency and social structures; however, it sees the two as inextricably linked and intertwined, and as less stable and fixed over time. Giddens's (1984) 'structuration theory' is a good example of a poststructuralist social theory. According to this theory, social structures facilitate and constrain the activities of individuals, which in turn reproduce and change these same social structures. Thus, in the multilevel model of migration discussed in Chapter 1, the activity of individual migrants impacts on and alters the meso-level kinship and occupational groups, which in turn condition the actions of individual migrants who belong to them. Similarly, individual migrants are influenced by the economic disequilibria existent between sending and receiving states. However, the very act of migration serves to alter such disequilibria, and the cumulative actions of many migrants can cause realignments of economic orders at the macro level.

Baumann's definitions of culture also resonate with Seyla Benhabib's (2002) and Nederveen Pieterse's (2004) respective discussions of two opposing views of multiculturalism. Benhabib contrasts the viewpoints of what she calls 'deliberative democratic' and 'multiculturalism' theorists. The former are social constructivists who take the view that cultures are formed through contested deliberative practices. In this view, human actions and relations may be accounted for in different ways by different participants and observers and these accounts may be evaluated in very different ways as 'good/bad', 'right/wrong' and so on, by the same participants and observers. Multiculturalists, by contrast, tend to reify cultures, that is they treat 'the products of human activity [e.g. concepts such as culture] *as if* they were something other than human products – such as facts of nature, results of cosmic laws, or manifestations of divine will' (Berger and Luckman, 1966: 107; italics in the original). Multiculturalists adopt what Benhabib calls 'mosaic multiculturalism', that is 'the view that human groups and culture are clearly delineated and identifiable entities that coexist, while maintaining firm boundaries, as would pieces of a mosaic' (Benhabib, 2002: 8).

Nederveen Pieterse (2004) similarly contrasts two views of multiculturalism, although he does so in slightly different terms. The first view he discusses is similar to Benhabib's social constructivist 'deliberative democratic' model, in that it sees multiculturalism as dynamic and emergent in the social and discursive practices of people. According to this view, multiculturalism is 'intercultural interplay and mingling, a terrain of crisscrossing cultural flows, in the process generating new combinations and options...in relation to political interests, lifestyle choices, and economic opportunities' (Nederveen Pieterse, 2004: 36). Nederveen Pieterse's second view of multiculturalism, which he terms 'static', is much like Benhabib's reified 'multiculturalism'. According to this view, multiculturalism is 'an archipelago of separate communities, a mosaic of fixed pieces, like a series of ghettos, or apartheid multiplied' (Nederveen Pieterse, 2004: 36).

In this book, I adopt a view of culture and multiculturalism which might variably be qualified as poststructuralist, processual (Baumann, 1999), deliberative democratic (Benhabib, 2002) and dynamic (Nederveen Pieterse, 2004).

What is community?

Most discussions of culture and multiculturalism at some point or another evolve into a discussion of another key concept: 'community'. Although much has been written about community, from a variety of anthropological, political and sociological perspectives (see Delanty, 2003, for a thorough examination), here I will use this term with two general meanings. The first is shorthand for any kind of recognizable collective identity. In a sense, as soon as there is a critical mass of people of a certain national origin, racial phenotype or religious affiliation in a particular nation state, then one will begin to hear talk of the 'X community'. This definition of community begins as something statistical: How many of them are there? What percentage of the total population do they represent? However, it generally evolves in a social and socio-political direction. First, the group of people defined as the 'X community' is considered by others to be bound together by a common and shared set of beliefs values, practices, language and artefacts. Second, the group is seen to have legal rights, to vote as a block, to have marketing potential (it can be marketed and marketed to) and so on.

All of this can lead to an essentialist view of community, similar to the essentialist models of culture and multiculturalism outlined above. In this case, there is kind of sclerosis that sets in as culture and community move from descriptivism to prescriptivism. This move means that there is a self-conscious adoption of membership in a distinct community with a distinct culture by those who self-identify with that community and an overt recognition of the community's existence and its differentiated culture (but crucially not necessarily the right to exist) by those who do not self-identify with it. However, as Gayatri Spivak (1990) notes, members of a particular group may, in some cases, decide that it is in their interests to adopt such an essentialized view of community as a means of political resistance to dominant and hegemonic discourses of citizenship and ethnicity. Thus, researchers such as Eades (1989, 2000) and Jacobs (1996) note how many Bangladeshis in London have accepted (and indeed, actively sought) being essentialized as a community as a way to gain control over or at least have a say in local urban regeneration schemes.

There is also a second definition of community, one discussed by social theorists such as Zygmunt Bauman (2001) and Alain Touraine (1997). Bauman views community as more a feeling than a demographic, the metaphorical space in which people feel a sense of belonging to a collective and trust in their acceptance by that collective. For Bauman, community can be a refuge from the alienating times of contemporary life. These are times which Touraine (1997) frames as *demodernization*, that is the breaking down of traditional cornerstones of modernity such as the nation state, institutions, political parties, employment security and so on. Although Bauman and Touraine are sceptical about the rise of 'community' as a substitute or alternative to 'society', they nonetheless recognize a certain inevitability in its coming to the fore as key concept in current debates in the social sciences. For both authors, community means a return to the sense of essential being in the face of feelings of emptiness and isolation in the late modern age. And this concern with being is related to a broader concern with identity and one's sense of self, to which I now turn.

What is identity?

> identities are about questions of using the resources of history, language and culture in the process of becoming rather than being: not 'who we are' or 'where we came form', so much as what we might become, how we have been represented and how that bears on how we might represent ourselves. (Hall, 1996: 4)

> I define identity . . . as the ongoing sense the self has of who it is, as conditioned through its ongoing interactions with others. Identity is how the self conceives of itself, and labels itself. (Mathews, 2000: 16–17)

These are two examples of how many sociologists and anthropologists today frame identity (and identities) as a construct in their work. First and foremost, identity is seen not as something fixed for life, but as fragmented and contested in nature. In particular, people who have migrated from one geographical location to another find that their sense of self is destabilized and that they enter a period of struggle to reach a balance. Identity thus becomes contested in nature as the new and varied input provided to the individual serves to upset taken-for-granted points of reference. However, the outcome of such a struggle towards balance is not generally neat and tidy; rather it is ambivalent. Ambivalence is the uncertainty of feeling a part and feeling apart. It is the mutually conflicting feelings of love and hate. And it is the simultaneous affirmation and negation of such feelings. For Bauman, it is a 'language specific disorder' (albeit a natural one), '. . . the main symptom of . . . [which] is the acute discomfort we feel when we are unable to read the situation properly and choose between alternative actions' (Bauman, 1991: 1). Papastergiadis (2000) relates ambivalence to the notions of 'nearness' and 'farness' put forward by Simmel (1950) in his discussion of the 'stranger', that is the state of being intimate with one's surroundings while remaining, metaphorically, outside them.

Ambivalence, it would seem, is the natural state of human beings who are forced by their individual life trajectories to make choices where choices are not easy to make. However, it is not a simple half-and-half proposition whereby the individual becomes half of what he/she was and half of what he/she has been exposed to. Rather the result is emergent in that it arises in an unpredictable way and it cannot be reduced to the constituent parts which make it up. It occupies what Bhabha (1994) and Hall (1996) have termed a 'third place', where there is what Papastergiadis (2000) calls a 'negotiation of difference'. During this negotiation of difference, the past and the present are said to 'encounter and transform each other' (Papastergiadis, 2000: 170).

This mention of negotiation of difference raises the issue of the extent to which identity is, at least to some extent, a self-conscious, reflexive project of individual agency, created, maintained and furthered by individual subjects. Stephen May (2001) argues that much of the current work in the social sciences on hybridity and third places is 'overstatement' and '[i]f taken to an extreme, for example, all choices become possible; a position represented by the methodological individualism of rational choice theory' (May, 2001: 39). In making his criticism, May is defending the notion that social constructs such as ethnic affiliation, while not fixed for life, do nevertheless provide grounding for much of an individual's day-to-day activity. May accepts some degree of instability in such constructs, in the form of ongoing negotiation (as argued by Papastergiadis), but he does not want to throw away all notions of structure which condition people's lives. Nor does he wish to make the extreme suggestion that all individuals in a particular community or society have the same range and quality of choices before them as their lives unfold, something which authors such as Giddens (1991) and Mathews (2000) come dangerously close to doing. May explains his position as follows:

> Negotiation is a key element here to the ongoing construction of ethnicity, but there are limits to it. Individual and collective choices are circumscribed by the ethnic categories available at any given time and place. These categories are, in turn, socially and politically defined and have varying degrees of advantage or stigma attached to them (Nagel 1994). Moreover, the range of choices available to particular individuals and groups varies widely. (May, 2001: 40)

I agree with May that it is wrong-headed to take concepts such as hybridity, third places and choice to the extreme of arguing that social phenomena such as ethnic affiliation cease to have any meaning. Indeed, I see parallels to his views in current discussion and debates about gender (e.g. Alsop, Fitzsimons and Lennon, 2002; Eckert and McConnell-Ginet, 2003), where there is disagreement about whether or not postmodernism, associated with arguments against fixed and 'essentialized' notions of femininity and masculinity, offers a way forward, or simply serves to drain debate of any foundation from which to argue. As I observed above, there may be strategic reasons for engaging in essentialized community politics. However, such strategic activity takes place at the surface level of people's day-to-day activities and while essentializing might work at this level as a tool to get things done, it does not seem a good strategy to adopt when working as a researcher, trying to construct understandings and explanations of observed phenomena. Working as researcher, I think that hybridity and third places work far better than essentialized notions of identity when it comes to making sense of the cases of individuals who have moved between and among qualitatively different sociocultural contexts. Indeed, all of the individuals discussed in Chapters 5–8 have had experiences that would qualify to varying degrees as hybrid or third place in nature. In their life-story interviews, they construct identities which are neither the sum of the new and the old, nor half of what they were and half of what they are; rather their stories seem more the result of the negotiation of difference cited above, as their past and present interact and transform each other.

One way to take on board May's concerns about identity as an individual project is to adopt a 'communities of practice' framework (Lave and Wenger, 1991; Wenger, 1998). Such a framework starts with the assumption that learning is situated 'in the context of our lived experience of participation in the world... [and] is a fundamentally social phenomenon, reflecting our own deeply social nature as human beings capable of knowing...' (Wenger, 1998: 3). Lave and Wenger also believe that the relationship between social participation and communities of practice is crucial. Social participation refers 'not just to local events of engagement in certain activities with certain people, but to a more encompassing process of being active participants in the *practices* of social communities and constructing *identities* in relationship to these communities' (Wenger, 1998: 3). Communities of practice correspond to the different subject positions people adopt on a moment-to-moment and day-to-day basis, and indeed throughout their lifetimes, depending on who they are with (examples cited by Wenger include the family, colleagues at work, social groups at schools).

Reference to communities of practice and individual participation reminds us that identity is a process that takes place at the crossroads of structure and agency. This means that while identity is conditioned by social interaction and social structure, it at the same time conditions social interaction and social structure. It is, in short, constitutive of and constituted by the social environment. This is the two-way action of 'structuration theory', as outlined by Giddens (1984). As I observed above, Giddens rejects the structuralist approach to social phenomena whereby the actions of individuals are determined by structures; however, at the same time, he does not want to account for human activity by solely depending on agency. Thus, for Giddens individuals do not develop their sense of self working exclusively from the inside out or from the outside in; rather, their environments provide conditions and impose constraints whilst they act on that same environment, continuously altering and recreating it.

Structuration theory and other poststructuralist models of identity share the view of identity as process as opposed to essentialized fixed product. One consequence of this view is that the very term 'identity' might well be seen as too static in its nominal form. Thus, some authors (e.g. Gilroy, 1993; Hall, 1995) prefer to use 'identification' in an attempt to capture this processual angle. Elsewhere, Weedon (1997) does not even mention 'identity' in her discussion of poststructuralist constructions of the self. Weedon rejects '[h]umanist discourses [that] presuppose an essence at the heart of the individual which is unique, fixed and coherent'. Instead, she refers to 'subjectivities', which she defines as the 'the conscious and unconscious thoughts and emotions of the individual, her sense of herself and her ways of understanding her relation in the world' (Weedon, 1997: 32). Finally, for authors such as Rom Harré, identity is about the constant and ongoing positioning of individuals in interactions with others. The key concept of 'positioning' is defined as 'the discursive process whereby people are located in conversations as observably and subjectively coherent participants in jointly produced storylines' (Davies and Harré, 1999: 37). In this book, the term 'identity' will be used as a cover for identifications, subjectivities and positions. In some cases, however, the term 'subject positions' will be used as an alternative referent to identity.

Ethnicity, race and nationality

An issue related to identity which is relevant to this book is the way that it is often discussed in terms of particular cultures and communities (see my discussion of these terms above). And following the distinction between static structuralist and processual poststructuralist views of cultures and communities, it becomes easy to see traditionally demographic categories such as ethnicity, nationality and race not as biologically and/or socially determined, but as socially constructed, unstable and fluid dimensions of identity. Thus, while ethnic, national and racial identities are often ascribed and attributed to migrants in an inexorable once-and-for-all manner, it is often difficult to decide which category to emphasize and in any case, what each category actually means. This is especially the case when attempts are made to label members of migrant groups that progressively take on the characteristics of transnational communities.

A good example of how difficult it can be to fix identity drawing on traditional social sciences categories is to be found in 2001 national census for the UK. This census aimed to improve on methods used in previous censuses to capture the ethnic diversity and multiculturalism of present-day Britain. This was to be achieved in part by expanding the number of choices provided in answer to the question: 'What is your ethnic group?' Respondents were given five general categories with corresponding sub-choices as follows:

(a) White
     (i) British ☐   (ii) Irish ☐   (iii) Any other White background ☐

(b) Mixed
     (i) White and Black Caribbean ☐   (ii) White and Black African ☐
     (iii) White and Asian ☐   (iv) Any other Mixed background ☐

(c) Asian or Asian British
     (i) Indian ☐   (ii) Pakistani ☐   (iii) Bangladeshi ☐   (iv) Any other Asian background ☐

(d) Black or Black British
     (i) Caribbean ☐   (ii) African ☐   (iii) Any other Black background ☐

(e) Chinese or other ethnic group
     (i) Chinese ☐   (ii) Other ethnic group ☐

One initial problem with this question is related to exactly what one means by ethnicity. As May (2001), notes, most social scientists who use the term do not bother to define it. This situation generally leaves one to wonder if it is being used to mean something akin to culture, or if it is a polite way to talk about race. In the former case, ethnicity may be seen to be more about 'common descent and ... a cultural heritage shared because of common descent' (Joseph, 2004: 162). Or as Puri (2004) explains in more detail:

> Ethnicity is ... a form of collective identity based on shared cultural beliefs and practices, such as language, history, descent, and religion. Even though ethnicities often allude to enduring kin-based and blood ties, it is widely recognized that they are cultural, not biological, ties. (Puri, 2004: 174)

Above, I examined some of the pitfalls of trying to encapsulate people and their beliefs, dispositions and behaviours inside 'culture'. In a culturist interpretation of ethnicity, Jews would no doubt be considered an ethnic group. However, in responding to the census form item above, should a man who is phenotypically white, carries a British passport and self-identities as Jewish, tick the box for 'White British'? Should he tick the box for 'Any other White background'? Should he tick the category for 'Jewish' elsewhere in the form, where religion is asked about. Or, should he tick all three options? Surely, those who write such questions do so with firmer and more exclusive categorizations in mind.

Similar problems arise when ethnicity is understood in terms of race, although many authors would argue that these two terms should be kept separate:

> Race and ethnicity both involve drawing boundaries between people. A conceptual distinction can, however, be made between race and ethnicity. While racial boundaries are drawn on the basis of physical markers, ethnic boundaries are drawn on the basis of cultural markers. (Pilkington, 2003: 27)

However, perhaps in recognition of the inherent instability of social constructs and the kind of conceptual bleeding and slippage that commonly goes on in the world (both lay and academic), Pilkington goes on to acknowledge that 'the two may empirically overlap, with people defined as a race becoming over time an ethnic group' (Pilkington, 2003: 27).

Elsewhere, MacMaster (2001) expresses a view held by many who have focused on race (e.g. Gilroy, 2000, 2004; Solomos, 2003), stating that '[r]acial categories cannot be explained through a scientific system of classification based on biological/genetic methods, but are ideological constructs, forms of boundary definition between groups that have evolved within specific historical and social contexts' (MacMaster, 2001: 1). Obviously, the authors of the census questions were not particularly bothered about such nuances and they opted for an essentialist biological version of race as synonymous with ethnicity. Not surprisingly, this kind of conflation is not unproblematic, as illustrated by a close examination of the category of 'Mixed' with the subcategory options: 'White and Black Caribbean', 'White and Black African', 'White and Asian' and 'Any other Mixed background'.

The inclusion of mixed race as a possible response was intended to make the question about ethnicity more accurate and discriminating than it had been in previous censuses. The thinking was that it would elicit a more accurate estimation of the number of individuals who consider themselves to be of mixed race. With some 226,111 people choosing this response (ONS, 2001), there would appear to have been some degree of success in this regard. However, solving one problem all too often leads to others. For example, is 'mixed race' a category easily separable from White or Black? Examining the variety of stories told in the accounts provided by children and parents in mixed race contexts (e.g. Tizard and Phoenix, 1993; Alibhai-Brown, 2001; Parker and Song, 2001; Ali, 2004), it is easy to see that mixed race does not tell the whole story of how individuals self-position, nor how they are positioned by others. There might be a question of how phenotypically mixed race one is. For example, is one talking about the actor Thandie Newton, the daughter of a White English father and a Black Zairian mother? Or is one talking about the singer Melanie Brown (aka 'Scary Spice'), the daughter of a Black British man and a White British mother? What about Afro-Caribbeans who are themselves mixed race when they arrive in Britain and then have children with people classified as White English? Is the category 'Any other Mixed background' enough for such cases?

Equally problematic is the way this ethnicity question incorporates nation-state affiliations, such as Irish, Indian, Pakistani and Bangladeshi. As a broad range of authors writing on the topic of national identity (e.g. Gellner, 1983; Hobsbawm, 1990; Anderson, 1991; Billig, 1995, Reicher and Hopkins, 2001; Puri, 2004) suggest, national identity is a tricky category even in the most ideal of circumstances. In a poststructuralist framework, national identity is no longer seen as fixed at birth and tied to one's birthplace; rather, it is an ongoing project, recreated daily via actions such as flag-waving and the invocation of historical events to explain present-day phenomena (Billig, 1995).[1] Thus even in the cases of individuals who are born, raised and educated in a particular locality of a particular nation state, their sense of national identity is an ongoing project that must be nurtured by any number of symbols and activities. In this context, brandishing a list of nation-state identities is always going to be problematic. It is even more so in the census question above because, as Dhooleka S. Raj (2003) observes, the categories offered under the general heading 'Asian or British Asian' conflate nationality and ethnicity and ignore differences that are perhaps more salient among Londoners of South Asian heritage, namely religion:

While the 'Asian community' is fractured into 'communities' of religious difference and calling for recognition of such distinctions, the nation-state readily identitifies other differences by emphasising ethnicity. The specific forms of this emphasis highlight an alternative national identity (Indian, Pakistani, Bangladeshi) and thereby keep Asians distinct as a perpetual 'other' in which ethnicity is first judged by phenotypic racial category. (Raj, 2003: 193)

Thus, the census is probably looking in the wrong direction when it conflates ethnicity and national identity under the general rubric of Asian communities. In a sense, it is ignoring a more grassroots manifestation of ethnicity: religion. In this book, religion will not be focused on in any detail, while subject positions related to ethnicity, race and nationality will be explored. This decision is primarily because the research reported on did not pursue this particular angle on participant identity. However, this in no way negates religion as a chief marker of identity in London.

Gender

Apart from identity framed in terms of ethnicity, race and nationality, I will also be concerned in this book with gendered identities, especially as these relate to language. In recent years, there has been a great deal published on gender. According to authors such as Deborah Cameron (1995, 1996, 2004), from a feminist linguistics perspective, there have been four approaches to language and gender over the past 30 years, each of which frames gendered identities in very different ways. In one approach, known as the *deficit* model, women are framed as disadvantaged speakers and communicators, particularly in professional settings. This disadvantage is said to arise from their upbringing and socialization as females (Lakoff, 1975) and the way forward for women is to align their speech to male-dominant norms. A second approach, the *cultural difference* model, is also about different socialization patterns, namely that men and women belong to separate but equal cultures (Tannen, 1990). Unlike the deficit model, the *cultural difference model* does not see difference in a negative light; rather, it adopts the socially liberal position that men and women are different but equal: women's speech and communication styles are not inferior to men's; rather, the relationship between the two is problematic at least in part due to the clashing of cultures.

A third approach to language and gender is the *dominance* model. In this model women are seen to perform their femininities in patriarchal societies, in which they negotiate, as best they can, their position of relative powerlessness *vis-à-vis* men (West, 1984; Fishman, 1990). This approach is far more politically radical than the previous two as it does not accept the status quo. Instead, it calls for the restructuring of society away from traditional capitalism and towards socialism. Still, the *dominance* model shares with the other two approaches a modern/structuralist approach to social phenomena where, among other things, notions of clear boundaries, social stability and determinism are manifest. In this sense, like the *deficit* and *cultural difference* models, this model is not powerful enough to adequately represent and explain the increasing complexity of language and gender in late modernity (Giddens, 1991). What is needed and has emerged in recent years is a less essentialized poststructuralist approach to gender.

Such a poststructuralist approach to language and gender has been derived from the work of feminist theorists such as Judith Butler (1990, 1993) and Chris Weedon (1997) and is captured well by the many contributors to Holmes and Meyerhoff's (2003) *Handbook of Language and Gender*. Notwithstanding their differences, most language and gender specialists share several key views. First, there is a consensus that gender is about doing as opposed to having or being. Second, gender is the outcome of engagement in social practices mediated by language as opposed to the predecessor and causant of such engagement. Third, gender is imminently unstable across different contexts. Fourth and finally, gender work is done by all human beings, not just those classified as female. Adopting a poststructuralist approach also means that language and gender cannot be studied in isolation from other angles on identity, such as the aforementioned ethnicity, race and nationality, as well as social class, to which I now turn.

Social class

Social class has traditionally served as label in the social sciences for any one, some or all of the following variables: wealth, occupation, education and symbolic behaviour (e.g. language, clothing, pastimes). However, a perusal of recent books on topics such as globalization, migration and sociolinguistics reveals how class as an angle on identity has all but disappeared. Given its association with Marxism, in its extreme form a structuralist, deterministic and exclusively economic take on human activity, this shift away from studying identity in terms of social class is perhaps not surprising. As I argued in Chapter 1, while the Marxism-inspired 'structuralist centre–periphery model' is strong on identifying macro-level phenomena such as economic inequalities across nation-state borders, it is inadequate in the way that it positions migrants as pawns of international capitalism.

Social class has also come to be seen by some as a kind of screen which prevents researchers from seeing other more important elements that are factors in human interaction. The rise of dimensions such as ethnicity and gender in poststructuralist approaches is due in part to the inability of social class to account for a good number of phenomena. Thus, as was observed in Chapter 1, a Black Dominican woman who migrates to Madrid can be positioned as an exploited member of the new economic underclass; however, this classification will only get us so far. Equally important for the life chances of this migrant are her racial phenotype, her language identity as a Caribbean Spanish speaker and the fact that she is a woman.

Nevertheless, social class understood as the composite of wealth, occupation, education and symbolic behaviour is useful if one wishes to develop a complete understanding of identity. To be sure, these sub-categories are in need of updating, because occupations are not what they used to be in today's postindustrial world (Reich, 1991) and therefore the identification of the individual with a job takes on new meanings. Similarly, education might be understood as ultimate attainment of academic credentials; however, it might more usefully be understood in terms of Bourdieu's (1991) cultural capital, that is the possession of socially optimal and valued knowledge, taste and know-how. Finally, with the emergence of multimodality as a powerful analytic framework (see Kress and van Leeuwen, 2001), different forms of symbolic behaviour have become the key focus. Thus an examination of working-class youth would have to include a focus on the phonology, syntax, morphology and lexis employed in speech, the physical movements made, different aspects of dress and so on. This reference to aspects of linguistic and non-linguistic forms of semiotic behaviour brings us to another angle on identity which is the most important in the different stories told in this book: language identity.

Language identity

Language identity will be understood here as the assumed and/or attributed relationship between one's sense of self and a means of communication which might be known as a language (e.g. English) a dialect

(Geordie) or a sociolect (e.g. football-speak). A language identity is generally about three types of relationship with such means of communication, what Leung, Harris and Rampton (1997) call *language expertise, language affiliation* and *language inheritance*. Expertise is about how proficient a person is in a language, dialect or sociolect, that is if he/she can talk a particular talk in such a way that he/she is accepted by other users of the language, dialect or sociolect in question. Affiliation is about the individual's attitudes towards and affective connection to a language, dialect or sociolect. In effect, it is the extent to which a person identifies with and feels attached to a particular form of communication. Finally, inheritance is a matter of being born into a family or community setting which is associated with a particular language or dialect. Importantly, this birthright says nothing about one's expertise in the putative language or dialect. Nor does it guarantee any degree of positive affiliation. One can inherit a language or dialect, but feel no affiliation towards it nor have expertise in it. As is the case with other types of identity, language identities can shift dramatically during one's lifetime. Thus, one can be born into one language community – a question of inheritance and possibly expertise – but later in life develop a strong affiliation to and expertise in another language community. However, the development of new language affiliations and expertises later in life is contingent on access to, engagement with, and membership in communities of practice in which the new language mediates communication. This is the case of some of the migrants discussed in this book, although by no means all of them.

In addition, language identity is understood in terms of what Le Page and Tabouret-Keller (1985) call 'acts of identity'. For these researchers, all utterances can be interpreted as an index of the speaker's identity. In addition, this process of indexing is not just two-dimensional, as was the case for early sociolinguistic work which focused on associations such as accent–social class (e.g. Labov, 1966); rather it is multidimensional. This multidimensionality means that emerging from all human utterances, framed as acts of identity, is the enactment of all of the previously discussed dimensions of identity: ethnicity, nationality, gender and social class. In addition, this multidimensionality occurs simultaneously, that is utterances index ethnicity, nationality, social class, gender and other dimensions of identity at the same time. In this book, 'acts of identity' will primarily appear as reported by individuals when they talk about their associations with and uses of language. However, in the case of Carlos in Chapter 7, there is some scrutiny of actual utterances as acts of identity.

Table 2.1 Individual/collective identity types

Ascription/affiliation	Based on
Ethnic	shared history, descent, belief systems, practices, language and religion, all associated with a cultural group
Racial	biological/genetic make up, i.e. racial phenotype
National	shared history, descent, belief systems, practices, language and religion associated with a nation state
Gendered	nature of conformity to socially constructed notions of femininities and masculinities
Social class	income level, occupation, education and symbolic behaviour
Language	relationship between one's sense of self and different means of communication: language, dialect or sociolect

Identities in this book

In Table 2.1, I summarize the different angles on identity discussed thus far. This table, I believe, requires several qualifications and clarifications. First, all of the identities listed and glossed in the table are about positionings by others and self-positionings, about ascriptions from without and affiliations from within. The different identity types are, therefore, co-constructed and furthermore, simultaneously individual and collective in nature. Second, although I list and gloss these different identity types separately, I in no way wish to suggest that they stand independent of one another in the larger general identity of a person. As I point out above, when discussing race, ethnicity, nationality, gender, social class and language, it is indeed difficult to discuss one type of identity without mentioning others. Thus, masculinities and femininities must be understood in terms of language positionings (Eckert and McConnell-Ginet, 2003; Holmes and Meyerhoff, 2003); race and ethnicity are interrelated in many people's minds (Pilkington, 2003; Ali, 2004); language and social class have always been seen as interrelated by sociolinguists (e.g. Labov, 1966, 2001; Eckert, 2000); and so on. Third and finally, there obviously are other angles on identity not listed or glossed. Those that are listed and glossed here are those deemed most salient in the stories told in Chapters 5–8.

Migrant subject positions

A final angle on identity is connected to the discussion of migration in Chapter 1, namely the kind of subject position the migrant adopts *vis-à-vis* the host environment. On the one hand, migrants might take on the subject position of classical immigrant. As I observed above, immigration is about settling into a new life in a new country. Immigrants might or might not have the intention to return to their country of origin. If they do, they often find that as years and decades go by, this prospect becomes less likely and even less attractive as the host country becomes home. Because they remain in their new homes for a long period of time, immigrants either assimilate to local culture or come to change it via their day-to-day activities. Inside most immigrants, there is a tug of war going on, between cultural maintenance and fitting into the new environment.

A very different subject position available to migrants is that of expatriate. Expatriates are individuals who have chosen to live abroad for an extended period of time, but who know that whenever they want, they can return home. The period of time they live abroad may vary from months to years and this time period may be divided up into shorter sojourns or it may be one long extended stay. In many cases, such individuals would appear to be exercising what Ong (1999) has a termed 'flexible citizenship'. Flexible citizenship refers to how progressively more individuals with the requisite social, cultural and economic capital are making choices about where in the world to situate their various work and leisure activities. The flexible citizen might choose to live between New York and Paris, benefiting from what each city offers while avoiding the entanglements of traditional citizenship responsibilities. However, in many cases, flexible citizens will, in effect, live a quasi tourist existence, which prevents them from acquiring local social and cultural capital and the cosmopolitanism necessary to be qualified as a transnational.

In order for expatriates to become transnationals, they need to have acquired in their lifetimes a certain intercultural competence known as cosmopolitanism. Held (2002) defines what he calls 'cultural cosmopolitanism' as follows:

> Cultural cosmopolitanism should be understood as the capacity to mediate between national cultures, communities of fate [*sic*] and alternative styles of life. It encompasses the possibility of dialogue with traditions and discourses of others with the aim of expanding horizons of one's own framework of meaning and prejudice. (Held, 2002: 57–8)

In a similar vein, Hannerz (1996) writes the following about cosmopolitans:

> Cosmopolitans tend to immerse themselves in other cultures, or in any case be free to do so. They want to be participants, or at least

do not want to be too readily identifiable within a crowd of participants, that is, of locals. They want to be able to sneak backstage rather than being confined to the frontstage areas. (Hannerz, 1996: 105)

In these two definitions, there are both sides of the cosmopolitan transmigrant coin. Held emphasizes the idea that the cosmopolitan maintains the home culture while negotiating subject positions beyond this culture and the newly encountered culture. Hannerz, on the other hand, emphasizes the extent to which cosmopolitans are good at fitting into their new environment. In both cases, the message is that expatriates cannot be true cosmopolitans unless they move towards immersing themselves in local ways and practices. If they do make this move, they cease to be expatriates in the purest sense of the word (e.g. as a German living abroad as a German), and they begin to carve out third-place identities. In a sense, cosmopolitanism is what makes expatriates transnationals and even immigrants; simply living in a new home for years will not, on its own, do it.

Conclusion

In recent years, there has been much discussion and debate in the social sciences about two general views of the social world, and specifically about social phenomena such as culture and identity. On the one hand, there is an in-general static, essentialized structuralist perspective, which frames social phenomena as relatively fixed and stable. On the other hand, there is a processual, de-essentialized poststructuralist perspective, which sees the social world as inherently variable and unpredictable. In this chapter, I have argued for the usefulness of taking the latter perspective, viewing community, multiculturalism, community and identity through a poststructuralist lens. Regarding identity, I have introduced a further qualification, which is that identity is about a range of subject positions that form part of an individual's general sense of self. Relevant to the stories in Chapters 5–8 are subject positions related to ethnicity, race, nationality, social class and language. However, it is not a question of studying such subject positions in isolation; rather, they are inter-linked, such that a gendered subject position might overlap with a language subject position or ethnicity is difficult to understand without also considering race and nationality. Finally, I concluded my discussion of identity by returning to the concept of transnationalism introduced in Chapter 1. Whereas in Chapter 1,

I discussed transnationalism in terms of migrant group settlement options, here I considered the transnational as a migrant subject position, along with the expatriate and the immigrant. I concluded that cosmopolitanism, understood as fitting into one's new environment whilst maintaining contact with 'home', is a key element in classifying migrants as expatriates, transnationals or immigrants.

3
The Global City and the History of Migration and Multilingualism in Britain and London

Introduction

In this chapter, my aim is to situate the reader as regards the precise sociohistorical and geographical context of the stories told in Chapters 5–8. I do this by expanding on the two main themes discussed in Chapter 1, that is globalization and migration. With the discussion of globalization as a backdrop, I begin with an examination of the phenomenon of global cities, arguing that when all is said and done, there are perhaps just three cities in the world that merit this qualification: London, New York and Paris. With the general discussion of migration as a backdrop, I examine the history of migration to Britain as a whole, and London, in particular. I also examine two alternative ways of charting migration, by country of origin and languages spoken. I end this chapter by making the case that while there has been fairly extensive coverage of some of the larger and more established immigrant groups in London and their language practices, what is lacking is a consideration of more recent arrivals to London.

The global city

In Chapter 1, I observed how over the past three decades there has been a boom in the number of publications about globalization, examining the phenomenon from different angles. One such angle, not discussed in Chapter 1, is to explore how globalizing forces coalesce in particular geographical locations, specifically large cities. In the past 20 years, there have been a good number of publications in which authors have discussed in detail what are variably known as 'world' or 'global' cities (e.g. Friedmann and Wolff, 1982; Friedmann, 1986; King, 1990;

Sassen, 1991, 2001; Hannerz, 1996; Cohen, 1997).[1] An early discussion of 'world cities', provided by Friedmann and Wolff, looks as follows:

> [World cities are] the principal urban regions...in which most of the world's active capital comes to be concentrated, regions which play a vital part in the great capitalist undertaking to organize the world for the efficient extraction of surplus...the world economy is defined by a linked set of markets and production units, organized and controlled by transnational capital; world cities are the material manifestations of this control, occurring exclusively in core and semi-peripheral regions where they serve as banking and financial centers, administrative headquarters, centers of ideological control and so forth. (Friedmann and Wolff, 1982, cited in King, 1990): 12–13)

However, as I suggest in a moment, this definition is far too narrow, concentrating solely on economic dimensions. There is far more to a global city than banking, finance, administration and control of ideology.

One issue that often arises in publications about global cities is when they first appeared on the scene. Another issue concerns how one decides that one city is a global city and another is not. In her detailed analysis of global financial flows and global cities, Saskia Sassen (2001) argues that while there have been large trade-oriented cities with international projections and connections for centuries in many parts of the world, it is only in the period since 1973, with the advent of post-industrial economies, that a select few cities have attained the status of global city. As Sassen puts it, 'the more globalized the economy becomes, the higher the agglomeration of central functions in a relatively few sites, that is in global cities' (Sassen, 2001: 5). For Sassen, in order to qualify as truly global, a city must have the following characteristics:

- It must be an essential command centre in the world economy.
- It must be the location of high-powered service industries and centres of international finance, where formerly it would have been a centre of manufacturing.
- It must be the site of development and innovation in the services and finance sectors.
- It must be a market for these developments and innovations.

According to Sassen, only three cities – New York, London and Tokyo – embody these characteristics sufficiently to merit being called global cities.

While extremely rigorous and detailed, Sassen's discussion of the concept of the global city is nonetheless limited almost exclusively to financial factors and in this sense it resembles earlier attempts to characterize global cities, such as Friedmann and Wolff (1982), as well as Friedmann (1986) and King (1990). However, other authors have moved beyond a narrow economic framework, defining the global city in terms of a broader range of parameters. For example, Ulf Hannerz (1996) defines what he calls 'world cities' as cities which are centres not only for services and financial markets, but also sites which are 'fairly durable sources of new culture' (Hannerz, 1996: 128). What Hannerz means by this criterion is that in order for a city to be classified as a 'world city', it is not enough for it to be the headquarters for international corporations, the recipient of immigration from around the world and wired up with the rest of the world. Indeed, there are perhaps 50 cities in the world that meet these criteria. For Hannerz, the truly world city must also be an active producer of the symbols and ideas that move the world today. World cities, thus, are not only national cities that happen to have connections to the rest of the world; they are cities that bring together sufficient cultural, financial and human capital to be major players on the world scene. In a sense, they are cities that simultaneously bring together Appadurai's (1990) *ethnoscapes, technoscapes, financescapes, mediascapes* and *ideoscapes*, discussed in Chapter 1. In Hannerz's view, the only cities that clearly qualify as world cities are London, Los Angeles, New York and Paris.

Elsewhere, Robin Cohen (1997) goes over some of the economic and financial criteria covered by Sassen and others. However, given his interest in migration, he goes on to add criteria related specifically to global cities as sites of migration. First, due to their economic and cultural vitality, global cities attract a disproportionately large number of migrants, compared to other cities. These migrants come not only from the hinterlands of their nation states, but also from all over the world. They may be seen to be of four general types: (1) long-term tourist types (e.g. international celebrities who maintain 'homes' in New York, London and Paris); (2) what Robert Reich (1991) terms 'symbols analysts', that is the movers and shakers of the new world economic order who come to these cities to provide expertise; (3) more modest professionals, such as budding actors, artists and writers, who come to the global city to 'make it', as well as students and educators; and (4) low-paid labourers who come from the poorer corners of the world seeking a better life.

Because of the scale and consistency of the migration they receive, global cities are the sites of international and cosmopolitan cultures.

In addition, the different lifestyles realized inside them are drawn more from outside than inside the national culture. This is due above all to the increasing number of migrants in global cities who carry out their lives as transnationals as opposed to immigrants. The result is that in cities like London, New York and Paris, there is probably a greater offer of food, entertainment, religions, cultural ways and artefacts from around the world than there is from Britain, the US or France, respectively. It is for this reason that Cohen adds another characteristic of global cities: their positioning as 'different' by most citizens of the nation states where they are located. Thus, London is not *really* England (or Britain), New York is not *really* America and Paris is not *really* France.

For all the reasons I have just discussed, an additional characteristic of global cities, and one which is directly relevant to this book, global cities are often described as 'pluralist', 'multicultural', 'multiethnic' and 'multilingual'. In other words, the global city is the site of multiple forms of identity, as discussed in Chapter 2.

Finally, I would add population size to the previously cited criteria. Global cities are not just big cities which are world economic players, culture brokers and home to people from all over the world: they are all of these things hugely so. A final criterion, therefore, is that global cities will have a dependent population of 10,000,000 or more. This figure includes not only the population of the incorporated city, but also the metropolitan area, and in addition, the millions more living outside the metropolitan area for whom the city is a focal and/or reference point for activities of various kinds: social, economic and political. Thus while Greater London's population is estimated to be between 7 and 8 million, socially, economically and politically it is the centre of a huge section of the Southeast of England, with a population of over 20 million. And this is to say nothing of the incalculable number of people around the world who are connected to and possibly even dependent on London for some aspect of their lives.

Drawing on the different criteria laid out by Sassen, Hannerz and Cohen, as well as earlier work on the topic (e.g. King, 1990), it seems that three cities are always at the top of the list of global cities: London, New York and Paris. All three cities share the characteristics outlined in Table 3.1. Although these global city criteria form a backdrop to the four London stories told in this book, I will be concerned primarily with London as a multicultural and multilingual city, to a degree rivalled only perhaps by New York and Paris, and as the site of multiple and massive migrations of people from all over the world. It is to these

Table 3.1   Criteria for global cities

---

1. They are essential command centres in the world economy.
2. They are the locations of high-powered service industries and centres of international finance.
3. They are the sites of development and innovation in the service industries and international finance.
4. They are markets for these developments and innovations in the service industries and international finance.
5. They are the sites of culture industries and innovations in these industries.
6. They are the sites of multiple and massive migrations of people from all over the world.
7. They are diverse in every sense of the word: ethnically, racially, religiously, culinary, culturally, and so on.
8. They are mega-cities, the centres of metropolitan areas exceeding 10 million inhabitants.
9. They have reached a point in their development that they are de-nationalised as regards lifestyle and points of reference (London is not *really* England [or Britain], New York is not *really* America and Paris is not *really* France).

---

migrations and the making of London as multicultural and multilingual city that I now turn.

Early immigration to Britain

Where does one begin a short history of immigration to Britain, when historically this part of the world has always been at the crossroads of people on the move, acting as host country for migrants from around the world? One could go back as far as Robert Winder (2004), who documents the movement of people in and out of the British Isles from the end of the Ice Age, some 25,000 years ago. Or one could begin, as Paul Johnson (1992) does, with the Mesolithic era (approximately 4000 BC). However, going back so far in time does not tell us much of relevance today, especially if, as Johnson (1992) suggests, the population of Britain in the Mesolithic era was estimated to be about 3000 people. Perhaps then, one should begin with the Romans, who ruled London from AD 43 to AD 410. Or perhaps it is better to focus on the Angles, Saxons and Jutes, invaders from roughly AD 400 to AD 600, or even the Danes and Norwegians, who subsequently invaded from the late 8th century to the 11th century. Finally, there is the Norman Conquest, which began in 1066. However, all of these influxes of newcomers were invasions, certainly a peculiar type of migration and not what most people have in mind when they consider the topic. Thus, if one wishes to examine migrations similar to those of today, one must start with the arrival of the Jews who came after the Normans took over in 1066 (Holmes, 1988; Winder, 2004). It was at this time that William the Conqueror first invited Jewish moneylenders to London. However, some two centuries later, in 1290, the migration was halted when the Jews were expelled by Edward I. At this time, Italian moneylenders were brought in as replacement for the Jews. However, they too were eventually to fall victim to the same xenophobia that had driven the Jews out, in the form of anti-Italian uprisings, which took place in 1456 and 1453. Meanwhile, during the 14th, 15th and 16th centuries northern Europeans from what are now Germany, Belgium and the Netherlands migrated into and out of Britain as trans-European trade developed (Holmes, 1988; Winder, 2004).

Nevertheless, the first substantial and concentrated migration to Britain was that of the French Huguenots, who began to arrive in the latter part of the 17th century (Holmes, 1988; Merriman, 1993a; Kershen, 1997; Winder, 2004). The Huguenots emigrated because of the revocation of the *Édit de Nantes* in 1685, which had meant limited freedom of worship and physical protection for Protestants in France. Between 40,000 and 50,000 Huguenots made their way to Britain and perhaps as many as half settled in Spitalfields, in East London. As Kershen (1997) notes, this is not an insignificant number, given that the estimated population of London at the time was about 600,000. Calvinist and entrepreneurial, the Huguenots very quickly assimilated in an atmosphere of nascent capitalism and they are recognized as having dynamized the British economy. As Winder explains:

> The Huguenots possessed exactly what the country needed: the know-how necessary to transform an agricultural economy into an industrial one. They became spinners in Bideford, tapestry weavers in Exeter and Mortlake, wood carvers in Taunton, and calico workers in Bromley. (Winder, 2004: 63)

Later the Dutch, Germans and the Mediterranean Sephardic and Northeast European Ashkenazi Jews were to arrive (Holmes, 1988; Palmer, 2000; Winder, 2004), the former two groups were able to fit in, much like the Huguenots. For the Jews however, conditions were worse. Traditional suspicions, historically common to the whole of Europe, meant that heavy restrictions were placed on Jewish migration and the activities that Jews could engage in. At the same time, this migration continued and some Jews prospered, becoming pillars of British society in the clothing and banking trades. By the mid-19th century, the Jewish population in London was estimated to be about 20,000.

Another group of migrants often forgotten in the chronicles of Britain's ethnic history are the African slaves and 'servants' who were brought to Britain during the 17th, 18th and 19th centuries and the African sailors who during this period sailed the world on British merchant ships (Fryer, 1984; Holmes, 1988; Ramdin, 1999; Winder, 2004). As Winder (2004) notes, estimates of how many Africans might have lived in Britain circa 1750 vary considerably, from the inflated figure of 50,000 to the lower figure of 10,000, preferred by authors such as Colin Holmes (1988) and Ron Ramdin (1999). About half of these 10,000 people would have been living in London. In addition, the actual fate of the descendents of these first Black Britons is hard to trace. Were they expelled to the colonies? Did they die childless? Or did they stay, contributing to the gene pool in local populations? Winder seems to suggest that while there is surely more African blood flowing in the veins of White Britons than many imagine, it would be wrong to exaggerate the presence of Africans in Britain and London during this period. He calls the findings of African ancestral ties by White Britons 'rare but eloquent reminders of the connection between modern Britain and a time we have since tried hard to forget' (Winder, 2004: 111).

The beginning of larger migrations: The Irish and the Jews in the 19th century

All of the migrations I have mentioned thus far were significant at the time that they occurred. However, apart from the Huguenots, none of them appear to have exceeded 20,000 and most would have been under 10,000, judging by the figures offered by migration historians such as Holmes (1988), Johnson (1992) and Winder (2004). It is not until the 19th century, then, that the first migrations in excess of 100,000 occurred. As Fishman (1997) notes, it is at this time that, first the Irish, and then the Eastern European Jews, came in high numbers.

The Irish had been migrating to Britain for centuries, starting with the beginnings of English attempts to control the island in the 12th century. From the beginning of this migration, the Irish were looked on with suspicion by the host populations. To make this point, Fishman (1997) cites restrictive laws and anti-Irish riots taking place during the 16th, 17th and 18th centuries. However, as regards absolute numbers, it is not until the 19th century and above all the potato famines of the 1840s that Irish immigration was to take off. Already in 1841, the national census showed almost 300,000 Irish-born people in Britain (Winder, 2004) and this figure had more than doubled by 1851, when Castles and Miller (2003) estimate that there were over 700,000 Irish in Britain. Interestingly, a century and half later, the 2001 census showed the Irish population to be almost exactly the same (691,000), even if it had, by this time, fallen to just 1.2 per cent of the total population (ONS, 2001). Although cities such as Glasgow, Liverpool and Manchester have traditionally taken the lion's share of Irish migrants, London has in recent years been the largest single recipient. The 1991 and 2001 censuses showed 214,083 and 220,488 self-identified Irish people in London, respectively, putting the Irish in the top ten of non-British nationalities resident in the city.

As I stated above, the Jews have been present in Britain for as long as the Irish. However, unlike the Irish, it was not until the late 19th century that they migrated in significantly large numbers to alter the demographic landscape of London. From the 1870s until the beginning of the First World War, some 100,000–120,000 Russian and Polish Jews were estimated to have made their way to London's East End, settling above all in the Spitalfields area (Holmes, 1988; Kershen, 1993; Fishman, 1997). While the Jewish incomers were considered far more industrious than the Irish, they were viewed with suspicion. The Alien Act of 1905 and the Alien restriction Act of 1914 were passed by parliament in an attempt to stem the tide of the immigration of Eastern European Jews and other unwelcome foreigners. However, official restrictions were just part of the opposition which these immigrants faced. There was also the long-standing British tradition of xenophobia, most sinisterly perpetrated in the 1930s by the followers of Oswald Mosley and his British Union of Fascists.

Post-Second World War immigration

Europeans

The major immigrations of the 19th and early 20th centuries – the Irish, the Jews and in lesser numbers, the Italians and the Germans – did much to alter the ethnic landscape of Britain. However, ultimately their status as Europeans meant that these groups were at least partially and perhaps even fully assimilated into British society. The same applies to other European groups who have migrated to Britain in the post-Second World War era. On the one hand, significant numbers of Eastern Europeans came to Britain during the late 1940s and the early 1950s.

By far the largest group was the Poles, who came in one sudden burst at the end of the Second World War. Some 160,000 arrived on British shores, most of whom are estimated to have stayed in Britain after the war ended (Holmes, 1988; Sword, 1993; Winder, 2004). On the other hand, Southern Europeans came in even larger numbers, the most significant source being Cyprus (primarily Greek Cypriots, but some Turkish Cypriots as well). The Greek Cypriot population is estimated at over 160,000 for London alone (Kyriacou and Theodorou, 1993), and is probably well over 200,000 for Britain as a whole.[2] Meanwhile, during the period 1946–71, some 80,000 Italians and 50,000 Spaniards made their way to Britain (Holmes, 1988). While all of these migrant groups have maintained their heritage cultures and languages to some degree, they have also assimilated to dominant White British culture to a significant degree. For example, Greek Cypriots in London have made great efforts to maintain the Greek language via an extensive system of support schools. In addition, the Greek Orthodox Church has maintained a strong presence in the lives of second and third generations. However, despite the conservation of what Kyriacou and Theodorou (1993) describe as a Greek Cypriot 'colony' or 'outpost' in London, Greek Cypriots have become an accepted part of the London landscape and by now have joined the general category of 'Other White' in the national census.

In recent years, there have been two distinct large migrations to Britain from other European countries. On the one hand, Eastern Europeans, from countries such as Poland and Slovakia, have come in the tens of thousands in search of work. These migrants will have benefited from their recent change in status, from Non-European Union citizens to European Union citizens, as of the January 2004 enlargement. The other type of European migration comes from long-standing EU member states, such as France, Germany and the Netherlands. Since the Maastricht agreement of 1993, which allows for free movement across EU member-state borders, there has been a small-scale invasion of what might be called 'young Europeans', that is citizens of EU member states who are between 18 and 30 years of age. These migrants come for a variety of reasons, ranging from study to work to leisure. As I will suggest in Chapter 6, the French population in London alone has swelled in recent years to well over 100,000.

According to the 2001 census, the White British, Other White and Irish populations together make up 92.1 per cent of the total British population (ONS, 2001). This figure is down from the 1991 census figure, which was 94.4 per cent (Peach, 1996), although in absolute numbers the overall White population increased from 51,810,555 in 1991 to

54,153,898 in 2001. The more than 2 per cent drop in the share of the population classified as White can be explained by the larger proportional increase in the non-White population. The latter group has increased from an estimated 3 million in 1991 to well over 4.5 million in 2001. This part of the population comes, above all, from the former Commonwealth countries of the Caribbean and from South America, such as Jamaica, Barbados, Trinidad and Guyana, and those of South Asia, such as India, Pakistan and Bangladesh. However, there are also significant numbers coming from East Asia and other parts of the Pacific. I now turn to a brief discussion of each of these non-White migrant groups, beginning with Caribbeans.

Caribbeans

The arrival of the passenger vessel Windrush in London in 1948 marked the beginning of significant immigration from the former Commonwealth countries of the Caribbean – above all, Barbados, Jamaica and Trinidad and Tobago – and Guyana (Phillips and Phillips, 1998). Invited to Britain to make up labour shortages in the public sector, most of all in public transport and the health service, these migrants were officially welcomed initially; however, unofficial treatment by the local white populace was, loyal to tradition, not so hospitable. According to Winder (2004), by 1958, some 115,000 people from a long list of countries in the Caribbean and Guyana had migrated to Britain, and most of them would have settled in different parts of London. As Winder explains:

> Trinidadians and Barbadians drifted to Notting Hill and Paddington; Guyanans congregated in Tottenham and Wood Green; Montserratians plumped for Stoke Newington and Finsbury Park. (Winder, 2004: 268)

Surely, the people described by Winder would today be classified as Afro-Caribbean. However, it is worth bearing in mind that prior to 1991, this category did not exist in the census, the preference being for a question about birthplace. While many readers of census data would assume that Caribbean and Guyanan referred to Black people, Ceri Peach (1996) makes the interesting point that not all migrants from the Caribbean and Guyana have been Black. He estimates that some 15 per cent were not, with Whites making up 7 per cent of the total and people of South Asian origin, 2 per cent (Peach does not account for the other 6 per cent). Nevertheless, the remaining 85 per cent of Caribbean and Guyana immigrants were classified as 'Black' and this has led to general conflation of the category 'Caribbean' with 'Black'.

Between the 1951 and 1961 censuses, the population of this group increased from a rather modest 28,000 to a far more significant 209,000. This sudden rise in the Caribbean population, in combination with an on-the-whole racist press eager to play on public fears of the outsider, led to the view among many White Britons that the Black population was increasing too fast. This feeling, which in far too many cases evolved into hysteria, was a key factor in the rise of violence against Blacks in Britain, perhaps best exemplified by the riots of 1958 which took place in Notting Hill in London and the northern city of Nottingham. In a still hostile, if less violent, manner it also led to the national debate about immigration at the beginning of the 1960s, culminating in the passing of The Commonwealth Immigrant Act in parliament in July 1962. This Act was meant to stem the tide of Caribbean immigrations, although it does not seem to have had that effect until many years later. I say this because of the marked increase in the 'Caribbean born' population registered during the 1960s, from 173,659 in 1961 to 304,070 in 1971, and the increase in the total 'Caribbean' population from 209,000 in 1961 to 548,000 in 1971.

However, by the late 1960s immigration from the Caribbean was slowing and in the period 1973–82 net migration was down, totalling just 1800. One factor in this very low figure for net migration was the increasing tendency during this period for the original settlers to return 'home' after retirement. As Nanton (1997), Phillips and Phillips (1998), Phillips (2001) and Winder (2004) suggest, the conditions of racism and poverty endured by many of these migrants for decades meant that ultimately they did not really feel that Britain was their home. In such a situation, it was easy for many Caribbean immigrants to leave behind their adopted home, even after 30 years. Still, despite the return 'home' of many of the early Caribbean migrants, the natural population growth of those who have stayed behind has meant that the population of this community has stabilized at over half a million, the 1991 figure being 499,964 and the 2001 figure showing an increase to 561,246 in Britain, with 343,567 living in Greater London [alone].

Africans

African migration to Britain dates back centuries: first, as observed above, via the slave trade, but progressively during the 19th century, via international shipping. Still the actual number of Africans living in Britain permanently at this time could not have exceeded a few thousand and Patricia Daley (1996) estimates that before the 1950s, the total population, including students, would have been under 10,000. From the 1950s onwards, however, the number of students from the former colonies in West Africa increased markedly.

Census figures from 1971 to 1991 show that the total African-born population went from 164,205 in 1971 to 378,238 in 1981 to 331,134 in 1991. However, as Daley (1996) points out, a high proportion of migrants from South Africa were White, most of the migrants from East Africa were South Asian and it was only the West African migrants who were, in their vast majority, Black. The census figures provided by Daley show that the Nigerian population increased from over 28,000 in 1971 to about 47,000 in 1991 and the Ghanan population increased from around 11,000 to 32,000. By the time of the 2001 census, with its more explicit question about ethnicity, Black Africans ranked as Britain's sixth largest ethnic minority at 475,938, of whom 378,933 lived in Greater London. These census figures show Nigerians numbering about 70,000, Kenyans, over 66,000; South Africans over 45,000 and Zimbabweans, about 17,000. Elsewhere figures for Somalis (70,000) and Ethiopians (20,000) are provided (United Colours of London, 2004). These latter figures are based on unofficial estimations, which might or might not be more accurate than official census figures. What does seem more certain, however, is that the Black African population of Britain is increasing and that several African communities now exceed 50,000 in Greater London alone.

South Asians

According to Rozina Visram (2002), the presence of South Asians in Britain goes back some four centuries. However, in most accounts of the history of migration to Britain (e.g. Holmes, 1988; Winder, 2004), authors begin to discuss a South Asian presence in Britain in the 19th century, when seamen hailing from countries as diverse as India, Burma and Malaysia, called *lascars*,[3] began to be a common sight in port cities such as Cardiff, Liverpool and London. Many of these *lascars* eventually moved ashore taking jobs in the local economy and settling down. Nevertheless, the permanent South Asian presence in Britain by the time of the Second World War would not have numbered much more than 10,000 (Winder, 2004). After the Second World War, South Asians began to come to Britain in greater numbers, though not on the same scale as the Caribbeans. Thus while the latter numbered well over 100,000 by the end of the 1950s, the figure for South Asians was still only about 55,000 (Winder, 2004). However, from the 1960s onwards, South Asian migration increased gradually and by the early 1970s those listed in the census as Indians and Pakistanis had overtaken Caribbeans as the largest ethnic minority group in Britain.

This gradual increase has gone hand in hand with legislation, which, although designed to stop migration, has served on occasion to accelerate it. For example, the increase in migration from Commonwealth countries in the 1950s led to calls for the government to do something to stop it. The result was the above-cited Commonwealth Immigrant Act in 1962, designed to control immigration through the imposition of quotas. However, as Winder reports, in anticipation of the passing of this act in parliament, some 210,000 migrants entered Britain in the 18-month period January 1961–July 1962, with a high proportion of these immigrants coming from South Asia. From 1962, it was theoretically more difficult for citizens of the Commonwealth countries to enter Britain. However, Winder cites immigration figures that suggest otherwise: 70,000 per year as the average over the decade.

Two critical events in Africa, however, led to sudden increases in the number of South Asian immigrants. Kenyan independence in 1963 led to calls for Africanization, which, among other things, meant divesting South Asians of their control over a large part of the Kenyan economy (Brah, 1996; Anwar, 1998). In the early 1960s, Kenya had a South Asian population of about 140,000 and although most members of this community could trace their Kenyan roots back at least one generation, only 61,000 actually had Kenyan citizenship (Holmes, 1988). In 1967, Jomo Kenyatta 'invited' the Kenyan Asians to leave the country and over the next several years, tens of thousands 'accepted' this offer, many going to Britain. In 1971, the Ugandan dictator Idi Amin adopted a more aggressive policy than Kenyatta when he tried to force all of the country's 74,000 South Asians to emigrate. As had been the case in Kenya, many of the Ugandan South Asians had lived in the country for generations. In the end, some 28,000 Ugandan Asians came to Britain (Robinson, 1995; Anwar, 1998). Unlike the majority of immigrants, the East African Asians were middle class and often wealthy in their home countries, and although they had lost much of their wealth in the process of being expelled, they had the cultural capital and business acumen to reinvent themselves and recover fairly quickly. The arrival of the East African Asians in British cities was dramatic as wherever they went, they revitalized sinking economies and added a cultural dimension that had hitherto been lacking. The northern city of Leicester, with the largest concentration of Indians in Britain (72,033, or well over a quarter of the city's population), is perhaps the best example of the transformation brought by the sudden influx of East African Asians.

The Indian population has gradually grown to the point that self-identified Indians are by far the largest ethnic minority group in Britain. This is illustrated in Table 3.2, which shows census figures for the top five non-White groups in Britain over the 50-year period 1951–2001. Of the 1,028,000 Indians in Britain as a whole, 436,993, or 43 per cent, live in Greater London. Thus, Indian immigration has been more like Irish immigration than Jewish or Afro-Caribbean immigration in that the majority of migrants have settled outside of Greater London.

Pakistani immigration, the second largest originating from South Asia, has occurred in parallel to Indian immigration, taking off in the 1960s and continuing to this day. And as has been the case with Indian immigration, it has from the start had strong ties with cities north of London. Indeed, the 2001 census shows a Pakistani population of 706,539, with just 142,749, or 20 per cent, living in Greater London. Cities such as Bradford (70,000) and Birmingham (104,000) have far larger Pakistani populations proportionately than London.

In Greater London, both Indians and Pakistanis have settled more in outer London than inner London. Thus, of the nearly 450,000 Indians living in London, 350,00 live in outer London. Of the over 140,000

Table 3.2 Comparative figures 1951–2001 for five major immigrant groups in Britain

Group	1951	1961	1971	1981	1991	2001
Indians (Robinson, 1996: 98; ONS, 2001)	30,800	81,400	375,000	676,000	840,255	1,053,411
Pakistanis (Ballard, 1996: 124; ONS, 2001)	N/A	24,900	127,565	285,558	476,555	747,285
Caribbeans (Peach, 1996: 26; ONS, 2001)	28,000	209,000	548,000	546,000	499,964	565,876
Africans* (Daley, 1996: 47; ONS, 2001)	N/A	N/A	164,205	378,238	331,134	485,277
Bangladeshis (Eade, Vamplew and Peach, 1996: 150; ONS, 2001)	N/A	6,000	22,000	64,561	162,835	283,063

* A good proportion of the estimated totals for 1971, 1981 and 1991 include North Africans, East African Asians and White South Africans. According to Daley (1996), the 1991 figures include 44,615 North Africans (from Algeria, Egypt, Libya, Morocco and Tunisia), 61,000 White South Africans and a large number of East African Asians. The 2001 figure, by contrast, is only those who self-identify as 'Black African'.
N/A = Not available.

Pakistanis in London, about 100,000 live in outer London, although it is the inner London borough of Newham, which has the largest concentration, at 20,644. This tendency to live in outer London is shared by the fourth largest Asian group, those classified as 'Other Asians', a substantial proportion of whom are Sikhs. Just over half of the 237,810 other Asians in Britain, that is 133,058, live in London. And of this group, just under 100,000 live in outer London. By contrast, Bangladeshis, the third largest South Asian immigrant group in Britain, show a different settlement pattern. Of the 275,394 Bangladeshis in the 2001 census, 153,893, or 56 per cent, live in London, with very high concentrations in Tower Hamlets, where over 65,000 live (one-third of the total population of the borough), and Newham, where about 22,000 live. The Bangladeshis are therefore more concentrated in Greater London than other Asian groups.

The Chinese and/or other ethnic group

According to census figures, the ninth and tenth largest ethnic groups in Britain – after White British, Other White, Indian, Pakistani, Irish, Caribbean, Black African and Bangladeshi – are the Chinese and the bizarrely named 'Chinese or other Ethnic group: Other Ethnic Group'. The Chinese are seen as a recent, post-Second World War immigrant community; however, for migration specialists such as Holmes (1988), there is a longer history, dating back to the 19th century, when there were small Chinese settlements in cites like London and Liverpool. Holmes estimates the Chinese population in Britain as a whole to have numbered in the thousands at this time.

According to Yuan Cheng (1996), the Chinese community was not properly counted in censuses prior to 1991. Until this census, local councils provided estimates of the Chinese population, a method that Cheng deems suspect and lacking in rigour. According to the 1991 census, the Chinese community in Britain numbered 156,938. Just over one-third of this number is accounted for by migration from Hong Kong, but over 28 per cent of the Chinese in the census are listed as having been born in Britain. The rest of the population was born in Malaysia, Singapore, China, Taiwan and Vietnam. In the latter case some 20,000 Vietnamese Chinese entered Britain in a short time span after the fall of Saigon in 1975. In the wave of immigration from the 1960s onwards, the tendency was for migrants to set up small businesses in particular in the catering sector. By the time of the 2001 census, the Chinese population in Britain had increased to 247,403, a third of whom (80,201) live in Greater London. Much like the Indian population, the second generation Chinese community includes a large proportion of university-educated professionals, upwardly mobile and prosperous, relative to most other ethnic groups.

The grab bag 'Chinese or other Ethnic group: Other Ethnic Group' of the 2001 census and the no less fuzzy 'Other Asians' of the 1991 census seem to refer to various East Asian, Indian Ocean and Pacific populations.

Table 3.3   Largest ethnic groups in Britain

Census category	Population	% of total
White (includes the categories White British, Other White and Irish)	54,153,898	92.1
Indian	1,053,411	1.8
Pakistani	747,285	1.3
Mixed	677,373	1.2
Black Caribbean	565,876	1.0
Black African	485,277	0.8
Bangladeshi	283,063	0.5
Other Asian	247,664	0.4
Chinese	247,403	0.4
Other Ethnic Group	230,615	0.4
Black Other	97,585	0.2
Total: All people	58,789,194	100

Source: ONS, http://www.statistics.gov.uk; accessed 1 November 2004.

Table 3.4   Largest ethnic groups in London

Census category	Population
White: British	4,287,861
White: Other White	594,854
Asian or Asian British: Indian	436,993
Black or Black British: African	378,933
Black or Black British: Caribbean	343,567
Mixed (all mixed)	226,111
White: Irish	220,488
Asian or Asian British: Bangladeshi	153,893
Asian or Asian British: Pakistani	142,749
Asian or Asian British: Other Asian	133,058
Chinese or Other Ethnic Group: Other Ethnic Group	113,034
Chinese or Other Ethnic Group: Chinese	80,201
Black or Black British: Other Black	60,349
Total: All people	7,172,091

Source: ONS, http://www.statistics.gov.uk, Table KS006, accessed 1 November 2004.

In 1991, this group numbered just under 200,000 and included groups such as Sri Lankans (about 30,000), Japanese (about 25,000), Filipinos (about 18,000) and Mauritians (about 11,000), just to name the four largest groups. In the 2001, the 'Chinese or other Ethnic group: Other Ethnic Group' figure was slightly higher, at 230,615, and again it appears to refer to a very long list of countries and nationalities. In Table 3.3, I list the largest ethnic groups in Britain, according to the 2001 census.

In Table 3.4, I list the top ten ethnic groups in London, according to the 2001 census.

Examining census data from another angle: Birthplace

One can examine the 2001 census to see how people define themselves in response to the question about 'ethnicity' (see my discussion of this question in Chapter 2). However, another way to approach the issue of migrants in London is to examine nationality and birthplace. Drawing on census data collected in the period just after the 2001 census (March 2000–February 2001), Lorna Spence (2003) divides up London residents into two general categories: those who have British or other EU member-state nationalities and those who have non-EU nationalities, termed 'third country nationals' or '3C nationals'. According to Spence's calculations, of the 7,271,000 people this updated census shows as living in London, 27 per cent, or over 2 million were born in countries outside of Britain. This number is of course less than the sum of categories 2–10 in Table 3.4 in the previous section, as many of the claimants of these ethnic categories would have been born in London.

Of the 2 million born outside of Britain, some 1.6 million, or 22 per cent of the population of London, were born outside of the EU, which means that some 400,000 non-British EU nationals are estimated to be resident in London. And of the 1.6 million 3C nationals, over half, 872,000 do not have British nationality. These 3C nationals come from both high-income countries, such as the US, Australia and Japan – some 17 per cent – and from developing countries such as India, Ghana or the Philippines – some 83 per cent. Figure 3.1 provides a breakdown of 3C nationals living in London.

Those who fall into the category of high-income countries tend to be classified as 'White' (some 78.2 per cent), and those falling into the category of developing countries tend to be classified as 'Black and minority ethnic' (76.2 per cent). A breakdown of all 3C nationals shows

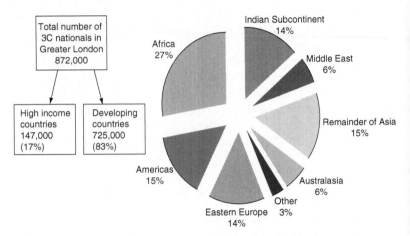

Figure 3.1   3C nationals living in Greater London by region of nationality, 2000/2001 (based on Spence, 2003: 8)

that 33 per cent (or approximately 530,000) are classified as 'White', 28 per cent (approximately 450,000) as 'Black' and 16 per cent (approximately 250,000) as Indian, Pakistani or Bangladeshi. Table 3.5 shows a breakdown of the population by country of birth.

Table 3.5   Population by country of birth, Greater London 2000/2001

Group	Population	% of total
UK	5,352,000	73.5
Irish Republic	153,000	2.1
Other EU15	200,000	2.7
Other Western Europe	61,000	0.8
Eastern Europe	146,000	2.0
America	222,000	3.1
Africa	442,000	6.1
Indian Sub continent	329,000	4.5
Middle East	86,000	1.2
Remainder of Asia	195,000	2.7
Australasia	59,000	0.8
Other	33,000	0.5
Total	7,277,000	100
3C (non-EU15) countries	*1,573,000*	*21.6*

Source: Adapted from Spence (2003: 17).

Spence's statistics make clear several tendencies in London's demographic development worthy of comment in the context of this book. First of all, they point towards a future when the majority of those classified as Black Britons will be from Africa and not the Caribbean, as has been the case until now. Second, the numbers confirm that there is continued migration from South Asia (here referred to as the 'Indian Subcontinent'). Third, they show a general rise in the number of Europeans, be they in the EU15 group (the European Union until January 2004) or the EU25 group, which came into existence after Spence's calculations were made. Finally, they confirm a smaller but significant tendency for more people from East Asia, the South Pacific and the Middle East to come to London.

In general, Spence's statistics point to the continued diversification of London's population, in short, an increase in multiculturalism. What they do not tell us, however, is anything about the different languages spoken in London, a primary concern of this book. Indeed, until now national census and national census style surveys have rather pointedly avoided questions about what languages other than English are spoken in British households. Fortunately, there have been over the past 30 years several major studies which have focused explicitly on this angle on multicultural Britain. I now turn to this body of research.

The languages of London

In the past 30 years, there has been a slow but steady flow of publications about the languages spoken by migrants in Britain. Kiran Campbell-Platt (1976) and June Derrick (1977) were two early attempts in this direction, as both authors compiled lists of the most-spoken languages in London besides English.[4] However, given that these publications relied primarily on census data from 1971, figures provided for numbers of speakers tended to be sketchy and on the conservative side, and many languages were left out of the picture. For example, widely spoken European languages such as Italian and Greek do not appear. In addition, as Harold Rosen and Tony Burgess (1980) note, lists and figures tell us nothing about the ethnolinguistic vitality (Giles, Bourhis and Taylor, 1977) of these languages. Ethnolinguistic vitality refers to factors such as whether or not a language has sociohistorical and socio-economic status in the host community, whether or not there are enough speakers of it and whether or not there is sufficient institutional support for it (e.g. via schools and the media).

In an attempt to remedy this situation, Rosen and Burgess, assisted by Jane Miller and John Snodgrass, set up the Languages and Dialects of London School Children Project in the late 1970s. Their aim was to explore, in more depth than had previously been done, the state of play of languages in schools located in several London boroughs: the inner-London boroughs of Camden, City, Greenwich, Hackney, Hammersmith, Islington, Kensington and Chelsea, Lambeth, Lewisham, Tower Hamlets, Wandsworth and Westminster, and the outer-London borough of Haringey. These researchers used detailed questionnaires and interviews, which allowed them to make fairly reliable estimates of the numbers of speakers of different languages as well as the vitality of these languages. In their report, Rosen and Burgess (1980) provide a great deal of information about the English of West Indian immigrants as well as languages such as Gujarati, Punjabi and Greek. As a snapshot of the times, the study is remarkably informative and has been foundational to subsequent surveys of the languages of London, such as the Linguistic Minorities Project (1985), Alladina and Edwards's (1991a,b) *Multilingualism in the British Isles* and Baker and Eversley's (2000) *Multilingual Capital*.

The Linguistic Minorities Project was carried out by Xavier Couillard, Marylyn Martin-Jones, Anna Morawska, Euan Reid, Verity Saifullah Khan and Greg Smith. The full report, which includes an excellent historical overview of migration to Britain and a theoretical discussion of bilingualism and society, is based on three questionnaires – the Adult Language Use Survey (ALUS), the Schools Language Survey (SLS) and the Secondary Pupils Survey (SPS) – and interviews. The research was carried out in Bradford, Coventry, the London boroughs of Haringey and Waltham Forest and Peterborough (Cambridgeshire) between 1980 and 1983. The main focus was on South Asian Languages – Bengali, Gujarati and Punjabi; European languages – Greek, Italian, Polish, Portuguese and Ukrainian; Chinese and Turkish. Several conclusions can be drawn from the massive amount of data collected as part of this project, but I will mention just two. First, the survey confirmed the existence of a vibrant and growing multilingualism in British cities. Second, the survey confirmed that where ethnolinguistic vitality existed it was due primarily to individual and community-level efforts towards language maintenance; institutional support for 'other' languages was founded be lacking.

A few years later, Safder Alladina and Viv Edwards's ambitious two-volume set, *Multilingualism in the British Isles* (Alladina and Edwards, 1991a,b), presented detailed coverage of more languages and language varieties than had previously been surveyed, over 30 in total. The categories covered were: British languages, Eastern European languages, Mediterranean languages, African and the Caribbean languages, South Asian languages, East Asian languages and Middle Eastern languages. Some of the categorizations look odd in retrospect (e.g. putting Moroccan Arabic, Turkish, Greek, Italian, Portuguese and Spanish together as 'Mediterranean languages'). In addition, some of the coverage seems scant, considering the importance of the language in question (e.g. Arabic is only covered as Moroccan Arabic, and even this variant merits under six full pages of discussion). Finally, as regards demographic information, there is an over-reliance on the same database used by the Linguistic Minorities Project, and in this regard, the collection does not move matters on. Nevertheless, despite these shortcomings, Alladina and Edwards was at the time a landmark in that is was the first time that discussions of a good number of the different languages of Britain had been brought together under one title.

Published nine years after Alladina and Edwards, Baker and Eversley's (2000) *Multilingual Capital* is based on the work carried out by the Languages of London Project. It is an edited collection of reports, constituting a general survey of the languages spoken by London schoolchildren. The chief aims of the Languages of London Project were to bring together reliable data on the number of speakers of languages other than English in London's schools and to suggest how multilingualism might be seen as an educational advantage. In the collection, Baker and Mohielden (2000) stands out as an exhaustive cataloguing of all of the languages spoken in London's schools (down to one Basque speaker living in Barnet!), running over 55 pages. Storkey (2000) is a much shorter piece, which contains estimates for the total number of speakers of different languages, based on data gathered from schools. Storkey is careful to point out the tentativeness of her data, some of which I produce in Table 3.6.

Some of these estimates might initially seem to be on the low side if one considers what is known about the populations of different groups in London. However, in the cases of the larger, more-established immigrant groups, they seem fairly accurate. For example, Indians, Pakistanis and Bangladeshis, together numbering more than 850,000 in the 2001 census, do not always claim to speak any of the languages associated with their nationalities, such as Panjabi, Gujarati, Urdu and Sylheti. Such language loss would account for the difference of over 250,000 observed between the national census figures for ethnicity and the under 600,000 people listed in Table 3.6 as speakers of these languages. However, with reference to migrant groups with lower populations, the

Table 3.6   Languages spoken in London by number of speakers

Rank	Language	No. of speakers*
1	Panjabi	155,700
2	Gujarati	149,600
3	Hindi/Urdu	136,500
4	Bengali + Sylheti	136,300
5	Turkish	73,900
6	Arabic	53,900
7	English Creoles	50,700
8	Cantonese	47,900
9	Yoruba	47,600
10	Greek	31,100
11	Portuguese	29,400
12	French	27,600
13	Akan (Twi + Fante)	27,500
14	Spanish	26,700
15	Somali	22,343
16	Tamil	19,200
17	Vietnamese	16,800
18	Farsi	16,200
19	Italian	12,300
20	Tagalog	9,300

Source: Based on Storkey (2000: 65).
*Estimated total number of speakers of languages other than English in London (rounded to the nearest 100th).

numbers for some languages are notably conservative and seem to be well below other estimates I have seen. Focusing exclusively on the main languages of the three groups discussed in Chapters 5–7, I see that Storkey fixes the numbers of Japanese, French and Spanish speakers at 4000–4300, 25,300–27,600 and 24,500–26,700, respectively. The Japanese figure seems ludicrously low when one considers that in 1991 there were probably about 30,000 Japanese people living in Greater London (Sakai, 2004 [2000]), almost all of whom would have been proficient speakers of Japanese.[5]

As regards French, matters are far more complicated. As I will show in Chapter 6, the number of French nationals registered with the French consulate as London residents stood at just over 37,000 in 2003. Storkey's figures for 1999 stand at about two-third of this total. However, as I mentioned above and will explain in more detail in Chapter 6, the number of unregistered French nationals living in London has increased dramatically since the Maastricht treaty of 1993 and this means that more accurate figures would be two or three times higher than those cited by the consulate.

Finally, I come to the figures for Spanish speakers. As I will show in Chapter 7, Dempsey and Lema (1998) put the estimated population of Colombian nationals in the mid-1990s at 30,000–50,000, a conservative estimate, as I will explain. Assuming that most of these Colombians speak Spanish, they already account for more than the roughly 25,000 Spanish speakers cited by Storkey. Taking into account that there will still be some Spanish speakers among the possibly 40,000 Spaniards who have lived in London from the 1970s onwards (Estebanez, 1991), to say nothing about the Ecuadorians, Peruvians, Bolivians, Argentineans, Chileans and other Spanish speakers who have come to live in London in recent years, Storkey's figures look to be well below the probable real total.

Conclusion

Writing some 30 years ago, Kiran Campbell-Platt noted that 'it is impossible to construct from published sources, an accurate linguistic map of minorities in Britain' (Campbell-Platt, 1976: 15). It is my view that as regards 'bigger' and more established minority languages, this situation has improved markedly, thanks most of all to the pioneering work of individuals like Campbell-Platt herself, Derrick, Rosen and Burgess. Nevertheless, as regards the migrants examined in Chapters 5–8 of this book, this statement still stands as far as I can see. Indeed, one of the main points of this book is that there is a need to study a greater variety of the different ethnolinguistic groups that inhabit multilingual and multicultural London. On the one hand, this means examining wealthier migrants, such as the Japanese students discussed in Chapter 5 and the French teachers discussed in Chapter 6. It also means examining new and fast-growing immigrant groups, such as the Spanish-speaking Latinos discussed in Chapter 7 as well as the diversity of subject positions adopted by the children of migrants from South Asian 3C countries, explored by Siân Preece in Chapter 8.

4
Researching London Stories

Introduction

In Chapters 1–3, I discussed key conceptual frameworks and issues such as globalization, migration, multiculturalism and identity, as well as London as a global city and its history as the home of migrant groups from all over the world. These chapters set the scene for Chapters 5–8, in which the stories told by individuals representing four migrant groups in London are examined in detail. These migrant groups are: Japanese graduate students, French teachers, Spanish-speaking Latinos and British Asian university students. Before moving to the details of these stories, however, I would like to discuss in this chapter several issues relevant to the research behind them. First, I return to the research questions outlined in the Preface, before considering how each question is to be answered. The latter discussion dovetails into a discussion of interviews as the primary means of data collection. However, I also examine additional data sources, such as previous publications on migration, Internet documents and research participants' recordings and field notes. Finally, ethical considerations are briefly discussed.

Research questions

The stories of Japanese students, French teachers, Spanish-speaking Latinos and university students told in Chapters 5–8 vary somewhat in format. However, in general terms they are organised as responses to the first two questions outlined in the Preface. These questions are

1. What is the history of this migrant group in London?
2. Who are these people and how do they 'doing being' in London?

In addition, Chapters 5–8 set up Chapter 9, in which I will take stock, attempting to answer the following question:

3. What do the stories tell us about migration as a global phenomenon; multiculturalism and multilingualism; migrant identities in the early 21st century; and London as a global city?

Answering each of these three questions requires different knowledge bases. Answering question 1 requires the consultation of existing academic literature, websites, government statistics and other documents. Answering question 2 requires some form of data collection. Finally, question 3 requires thought about how to link the answers to questions 1 and 2 with the concepts and the theoretical frameworks introduced in Chapters 1–3. As the last question does not require or involve doing research, *per se*, I will say no more about it for now. However, the first two questions and how they are answered, I think, do require some explanation.

Answering question 1: Reading documents and secondary sources

Answering general question 1 has meant the consultation of as many publications and websites with information about migration to Britain and London as I have been able to locate or access. Published academic literature often ignores the very information or focus that the researcher is seeking. This has certainly been the case regarding the different migrant groups discussed in Chapters 5–7, as quite simply, not very much research has been done about these groups. As regards websites, there is always the suspicion that the information is not reliable. This is above all the case with websites such as the 'United Colours of London', which provides no information about the data collection procedures behind the demographic information displayed. Still, as a supplementary data source, such websites can be helpful as they provide population estimates that often fall between officially sanctioned ones and more anecdotal ones. Finally, there are census statistics. In this book, I take the view that the National Census is a reliable data source in that it is an example of rigorously controlled data collection. However, as I will argue in Chapters 5–7, the census tends to err on the side of a caution as regards the estimated populations of different migrant groups in London.

Answering question 2: Interviews

In contrast to question 1, question 2 requires the collection of data directly from members of the groups being researched. The main form of data collection used in this book has been interviews, specifically life-story interviews. Following Atkinson (1998), I understand a life-story interview to be 'the story a person chooses to tell about the life he or she has lived, told as completely and honestly as possible, what is remembered of it, and what the teller wants others to know of it, usually as result of a guided interview...' (Atkinson, 1998: 3). Such interviews have become popular in the social sciences in recent years, with marked increases both in the number of published studies based on this form of data collection and in the number of publications about biographical research in general (e.g. Atkinson, 1998; Seidman, 1998; Mishler, 1999; Chamberlayne, Bornat and Wengraf, 2000; Wengraf, 2001; Roberts, 2002; Kearney, 2003).

Some authors argue that life-story interviews must follow a particular format. For example, Seidman (1998) argues that the researcher will need to carry out three interviews, spaced days apart, and not just one. Each interview should last no longer than 90 minutes and should have a clear focus that differentiates it from the other two. The purpose of the first interview, called the 'focused life history', is to elicit as much biographical information as possible via questions about 'what happened' and 'how'. Seidman emphasises that at this stage, there should be no 'why' questions that might lead the interviewee to evaluate his/her past experiences. The second interview seeks 'the details of experience', that is concrete details about the interviewee's current activities and experiences. Again, there is an attempt to avoid eliciting opinions from the interviewee: descriptions and reconstructions of events are sought instead. The third and final interview in Seidman's method is concerned with 'reflection on the meaning'. This interview is based on the past and present events and activities produced by the interviewee in the first two interviews. In contrast to these first two interviews, however, the interviewer at this stage openly seeks opinions and evaluations from the interviewee, specifically his/her views on what has happened in the past and what is going on in the present.

Elsewhere, Wengraf (2001) proposes an approach that involves what he calls sub-sessions, three in total, which take place on two separate days. In the first sub-session, the interviewer works at a general level, asking the interviewee to take his/her time in relating as much detail as possible about past events and experiences. The interviewer is advised to take notes as this interview unfolds, writing down the main topics and issues covered. This note-taking is meant to prepare the interviewer for the second interview, which Wengraf says should occur on the same day as the first session, preferable after a fifteen-minute break. In the second interview, the interviewer goes back through the topics and issues noted down, attempting to elicit more detailed information than was provided in the first interview. Wengraf's third interview should take place on another day, and like Seidman, he sees it as an opportunity for the researcher to seek more detail about topics and stories that arose during the first two interviews.

In this book, the elicitation of life stories has varied across the different studies reported on in this book. The Japanese graduate students and the Spanish-speaking Latinos, discussed in Chapters 5 and 7, respectively, all produced life stories in interviews lasting between one and two hours. The interviews followed a format that conflated the three stages of Seidman's and Wengraf's models. Thus, the interviewer attempted to elicit from interviewees accounts of their past and present experiences, provided in as much detail as possible, as well as opinions and evaluations of these past and present experiences.

In her contacts with four British Asian students, Siân Preece also elicited life stories. However, the process she followed was quite different from the one described above. In effect, the life stories were produced as her informants talked about their language practices, in particular their relative expertises in and affiliations to home languages and academic English. Preece found that in talking about their literacy practices these students ended up telling her their life stories.

Another way of eliciting life stories is to move beyond one or even two interviews and maintain longer-term contact with an individual, in other words, conduct periodic interviews over an extended period of time. In this case, the interviewer and interviewee construct the interview around general questions, such as 'how are things going?' and references back to what has been discussed in previous interviews. In such interviews, there is also an element of what Rubin and Rubin (1995) call 'hanging loose', that is allowing the interview to go where the interviewee wishes to take it. This generally more relaxed approach to constructing life stories was used with one of the Japanese students, Yukiko (see Chapter 5) and one of the Spanish-speaking Latino participants, Carlos (see Chapter 7). Over a period of six months, I conducted three interviews with Yukiko and over a period of 12 months, I conducted four interviews with Carlos. The first interview with both was a language biography, as described above. The remaining interviews, however, had two purposes: to allow me to pursue in more detail themes and issues arising in the first and subsequent interviews and to allow Yukiko and Carlos to introduce new themes and issues of their own choosing. Yukiko very effectively achieved the latter on two occasions: first, she came to one interview with eight pages of fieldnotes about her work-based conversations; second, she came to another interview ready to talk about how she had interviewed two co-workers about their British Japanese identities. As regards Carlos, he made some 20 separate recordings of his talk at work and at home (in Spanish and English) over a five-month period (roughly, November 2003–March 2004). These recordings were integral to three of our interviews, providing a springboard for in-depth discussions about the different subject positions he adopted at work and at home.

The stories told by the French teachers in Chapter 6 are an even better example of prolonged contact. In this case, I carried out 10 interviews with each participant over a 40-month period of time. These interviews were at first theme based, that is they revolved principally around the teachers' adaptations to British education while attending a PGCE (Post Graduate Certificate of Education) course in the academic year 1999–2000 (see Block, 2001, for an account). In this first stage, the teachers were interviewed in groups, with Laure and Nancy forming part of one group and Lise and Chantalle forming part of another. However, from the autumn of 2000 to the autumn of 2002, I carried out six interviews on an individual basis. These interviews continually revisited themes that had come up in earlier interviews while allowing for the introduction of new themes that arose as we conversed. Some of these interviews were structured around academic literature about French and British education (see Block, 2005) and one entire interview, carried out in Spring 2002, was essentially a life-story interview. While these life-story interviews will be foundational to the discussion in Chapter 6, I will also draw on the other interviews conducted over the 40-month period.

On the nature of interviews

The purpose of interviews in this book has been to engage individuals in conversations about their experiences as members of particular migrant groups, talking both directly and indirectly about their ethnic, national, gendered, social class, and language identities, as well as their relative transnational status. These interviews may be qualified as 'in-depth' (Johnson, 2001), in that they were attempts to gain deep understandings of interviewees' experiences as well as the way they position themselves *vis-à-vis* these experiences. However, it would be naive to think that just because a researcher is able to record a lot of in-depth talk about interviewees' lives, he/she has managed to get inside their heads and arrive at the entirety of who they are. In other words, the interviewer can never reasonably assume that interviews are clean and easy information transfers providing interviewers with windows on the minds of interviewees (Block, 1995, 2000).

As authors such as Linde (1993) note, one problem is that all accounts of life experiences are told in the present and therefore perhaps tell us more about how interviewees wish to position themselves now than what really happened in the past. The extent to which this state of affairs is a problem is proportional to the extent to which the researcher is concerned with obtaining a veridical account of past events or a story that offers insights into how interviewees self present. In the research described in this book, how interviewees define themselves in the present, via the stories they tell, is the priority. In principle, the research is not concerned with whether or not these individuals are telling the truth about what has happened to them. Nor is it about what they have done or whether or not what they have said about any number of topics is *really* what they think. Instead, there is a view of interview talk as the enactment of what Chris Weedon (following the work of Foucault, 1981, 1986, 1988) calls *discursive fields*.

Weedon defines discursive fields as 'competing ways of giving meaning to the world and of organizing social institutions and processes' (Weedon, 1997: 34). She cites the example of legal discourses in Britain where there are conflicting voices over what constitutes proper trial practice as regards procedure, sentencing and modes of punishment. Following Weedon, any conversational interaction produced by a speaker is the expression of a subject position which is linked to a particular *discursive field*. What is actually said and how it is said may be classified as plausible or reasonable within that particular *discursive field*. It is, therefore, a particular voice which a particular speaker has adopted momentarily with a view to projecting a particular subjectivity. And the sum total of subjectivities embodied by an individual at a given time constitute her/his individual identity.

It is worth noting that the reference to plausibility in the previous paragraph is not idle and indeed, it is essential to my understanding of what people do when they participate in interviews. Plausibility moves us away from the 'anything goes' and 'nothing is real' traps of extreme relativism to the idea that the things that people say during interviews are the kinds of things that people in a particular sociohistorical context say when talking about a particular topic. It points to the fact that people could not live as discursively constructed beings if in every moment the discourses associated with them, and those around them, arbitrarily and unpredictably changed. There is always some centre that must hold. This is not to say that at any one time, that centre is the entirety of who a person is; however, it is to say that people have neither the time nor the energy, neither the cognitive skills nor the sufficient wherewithal, to be making up a new life story every split second.

One matter related to an informant's sense of self in interviews has to do with the language employed. In the case of Siân Preece's study, English was the most natural language to use in interviews because two of her informants were born in Britain and the third came at the age of 8. Crucially, they had all been educated primarily or totally in English. In my contacts with the French teachers, all but a few exchanges were in English, and in the case of the Japanese students, all contacts were in English. In neither case, however, was the use of English an impediment to smooth communication. All of these informants were comfortable speaking English and more importantly, they all projected a strong self-identification with English as the language through which they constructed themselves as individuals living in London.

A different tack was adopted as regards the Spanish-speaking Latinos. In this case, the default language was Spanish and not English. This occurred above all because in most of my contacts with Spanish-speaking Latinos, my interlocutors expressed a preference for speaking in Spanish. Given that I am generally positioned as a worthy interlocutor in Spanish, the natural choice of language in this study tended to be Spanish. Nevertheless, some Speaking-speaking Latinos in London have a stronger self-identification with English than others. This is the case of Luis in Chapter 7, who chose to speak to me in English when I interviewed him.

To aid readability, all interview excerpts in this book are presented with standardized spelling and punctuation. Suspension points (i.e., . . .) mean either a pause or that a part of the reproduced excerpt has been removed to aid readability. Comments about paralanguage or other relevant additional information appear in brackets as follows: (laughing). Words inserted by the author to add coherence are in brackets as follows: [in the]. Capital letters are used to indicate that the person has raised his/her voice suddenly.

Additional data sources

Interviews carried out by the researchers provide the entire empirical database for Chapter 6 and most of the database for Chapters 5, 7 and 8. In the latter three cases, there were additional sources of data. As I explained above, Yukiko took fieldnotes about her telephone conversations at work and she interviewed two of her colleagues, recording the latter with the interviewee's permission. In Chapter 5, I quote the fieldnotes on several occasions. As regards the interviews that she recorded, I do not reproduce any excerpts; however, I do reproduce some of Yukiko's talk about her colleagues which is based, in part, on the content of the interviews.

As I mentioned above, Carlos gathered for me over 20 instances of his talk at work and at home, in Spanish and English. He recorded conversations with clients, work colleagues and family members. In most cases, this participant-generated data collection was done with permission of all concerned and therefore the data could, ethically, be used by the researcher. However, in some cases, permission was not secured because the recorded exchange occurred so quickly as not to allow time for Carlos to stop the individual recorded to explain the research being carried out. In these cases, data were discarded for direct use in the study. In Chapter 7, I reproduce three of Carlos's recorded conversations for analysis and discussion.

Finally, in Siân Preece's research, there is also an additional source of data. This was a group discussion task that her students carried out one day in class. Preece had put students in groups of three or four and asked them to respond to questions about the languages in their lives and their attitudes towards academic literacy practices. All groups were audio recorded and the recorded discussions were later transcribed. In Chapter 8, Preece reproduces five excerpts from these recordings for analysis and discussion.

The following conventions, based on those used by Jennifer Coates (2003), have been followed in the reproduction of Carlos's conversations and student discussions:

- X means an unidentified speaker.
- / – A slash shows the end of a chunk of talk.
- - – A hyphen illustrates an incomplete word or utterance.

- ? – A question mark indicates question intonation.
- (.) – Pauses of less than one second are shown with a full stop inside brackets.
- (3) – Pauses of one second and longer are timed to the nearest second and the number of seconds is put in brackets.
- [...[... – Square brackets on top of each other indicates the point where speakers overlap.
- = – An equals sign at the end of one utterance and the start of the next speaker's utterance shows that there was no audible gap between speakers.
- ((...)) – Double brackets around a word or phrase shows that there is doubt about the transcription.
- ((xxx)) – Double brackets around x's shows that the speaker's utterance is inaudible or cannot be made out.
- <...> – Phrases or words in angled brackets is an additional comment by the transcriber on what is happening at the time or the way in which something is said.
- CAPITAL, CAPital – Words or syllables in Capital letters are spoken with extra emphasis.
- %...% – Words or phrases enclosed by percentage symbols are spoken very quietly, almost like an aside.
- : – A colon means an elongated vowel (e.g. no:o).

Ethics and the researched

In the previous section, I briefly discussed ethical issues with reference to data collected by two informants. Here I would like to say something about ethical issues as they relate to the informants whose stories are told in this book. All informants were informed of the purpose of the research as well as the procedures that would be followed. Anonymity was both explained and guaranteed and in the presentation of stories, pseudonyms have been used. All informants were adults who gave their consent, not only for their interviews to be recorded, but also for the researchers to reproduce portions of interview transcriptions in publications like this one.

However, informant permission granted at the beginning of data collection is just one part of the story. There is also the responsibility of the researcher to use this permission granted in an ethical manner. I refer here above all to the way in which researchers portray informants via the selective production of interview data and how they tell the story of what was said. In Chapters 5–8, Siân Preece (Chapter 8) and I are confident that we have not produced anything that the informants would find objectionable. Indeed, where possible (i.e. informants could be found), we have asked informants to read chapters to see if they found anything objectionable. The informants who have read their chapters have recommended no significant changes.

5
Japanese Graduate Students in London

> Japan is a very closed society and there are so many tacit agreements, what to do, what I should not do and the criteria is very different from London. So now basically I haven't got that criteria so I have no idea what I should do.
>
> – Mie, 26/1/2004

> I took a lift in a tall building in Tokyo and that went so fast and I said 'whooo' (laughing) and my friend stopped me and 'shhht, don't say anything' 'Why, it's exciting?' and I was so happy to say 'it's erm Japan!' but I couldn't say anything. I wasn't allowed to say anything.
>
> – Mie, 26/1/2004

In these two quotes, Mie explains her feelings about going back to Japan after spending two and half years in London. In the first quote, she explains how she has lost the ability to function competently in Japan, which she presents as a closed society of tacit agreements. In doing so, she produces what some authors (e.g. Sugimoto, 1997; Kubota, 1999) would qualify as unacceptable generalizations about Japan and its people and customs as exotic and unique. These generalizations can be found both in Euro-centric accounts of Japanese culture (e.g. de Mente, 1994) and homegrown works on *nihonjinron*, that is the discourse on Japaneseness (see Mouer and Sugimoto, 1990; Yoshino, 1992, for critical discussions of this viewpoint). However, in Mie's case, the route to such a generalization has not been the reading of Euro-centric accounts of Japan or the *nihonjinron* literature; rather it has been her life in London. In the second quote, Mie exemplifies the theory expressed in the first quote. She describes a situation in which she wished to express her happiness and excitement at being in a fast lift in Tokyo. However, her friend, who was presumably applying the rules described in the first quote, is attempting to silence her. Thus, with the linguistic act of identity of uttering 'whooo', she has positioned herself as someone who does not know the etiquette of taking a lift, effectively as someone outside Japanese sociolinguistic and sociocultural norms.

Mie is a member of a growing, but under-researched migration group in London: Japanese graduate students. My aim in this chapter is to explore, via life-story interviews, the backgrounds and present lives of Mie and four other female graduate students. I conclude by linking the stories told by these graduate students to some of the frameworks and issues discussed in Chapters 1–3. However, as will be the case in subsequent chapters, I begin with a macro-level discussion of the history and sociology of Japanese migration to London, with the aim of setting the scene for the reader.

The Japanese in the UK and London

Until the post-Second World War period, Japanese migration to the UK and London was all but non-existent. When the Japanese did emigrate en masse in search of opportunities in other countries, primarily in the period 1868–1935, they went to countries of the 'new world' such as Brazil (where the largest community outside of Japan exists to this day), the US or Peru (Sowell, 1996). However, in the post-Second World War period, Japan's rapid economic growth made it one of the more powerful players on the world economic scene and marked the beginning of Japanese business migration to all parts of the world (Pang, 2000). According to Junko Sakai (2004 [2000]), from 1952 onwards, Japanese banks began to operate in The City in London and by the end of the economic boom of the 1980s they were the source of a quarter of the total assets and were the largest providers of capital. These movements of capital required personnel to monitor activities and provide services and those taking these responsibilities account for a major proportion of the rapid increase in the Japanese population in the UK and London, in particular since the mid-1980s. In addition, from the late 1970s onwards, the government-led policy of *kokusaika* (internationalization) meant, among other things, greater cultural exchange with the industrialized countries of North America and Western Europe (Pang, 2000; Borg, 2005). However, in this chapter it is not the relatively early arrival of the Japanese business community in London that will concern us; rather, it is the increase in the number of Japanese nationals, in particular women aged 18–35, who have come to London in the last 20 years to spend a year or more as students. As Kelsky (2001) notes, study abroad has become particularly attractive to Japanese women wishing to improve their professional career prospects or simply to escape from what they perceive to be a male-dominant, oppressive society (more on this below).

An examination of current patterns and figures shows that there are four key reasons for Japanese migration to the UK and London. By far the most common reason is related to professional and career development: an employee is transferred to the UK by a Japanese company, bank or government agency. This is almost always the male head of household who moves with his family, generally consisting of a wife and one or two children. Such overseas assignments tend to last for one to ten years, although three to five years is generally the norm (Yamada-Yamamoto, 1998). After this period abroad, the employee and his family usually go back to Japan. The return to Japan can be permanent or it might be for several years or more before there is another assignment abroad. According to Sakai (2004 [2000]), for the Japanese companies with international operations, sending employees abroad serves two main purposes. First, it is a way for Japanese companies to maintain Japanese control over their operations abroad. Second, transfers are seen as learning experiences: major financial centres like London are seen as centres of innovation both as regards production development and business practices.

For Japanese nationals working for companies with overseas operations, transfers are seen as positive and indeed, as both Yamada-Yamamoto (1998) and Sakai (2004 [2000]) note, a way to improve one's standard of living: on the one hand, these Japanese families live in luxury; on the other hand, they are able to live more or less Japanese lives in their host countries. Sakai describes a typical scenario in London as follows:

> Inside this Japanese community in London the delegates and their families enjoy luxurious lives... The families of Japanese company men are provided with comfortable houses by their company welfare systems. Their children either go to the Japanese school in London or to the local school, though some families send their children to boarding schools or Oxbridge to give their children the 'best' education in Britain. Their wives send their children to school by car, and enjoy flower arranging with other Japanese wives living nearby, and they shop together... These people have close relations with each other.

They express the opinion that their lives are better than they were in Japan, as companies pay double salaries to those working abroad, and houses are provided by the companies. (Sakai, 2004 [2000]: 59–60)

The second reason for Japanese migration to the UK is related to Japan's historic interest in 'western' culture and education, and more recently, the drive towards internationalization cited above. Given the strong association of 'western' and 'international' with the US and/or the English language (Kubota, 2002), most Japanese students abroad are concentrated in English-speaking countries such as the US and the UK, although China is the second most popular destination overall, after the US. According to the Central Education Council, an advisory council attached to the Japanese Ministry of Education, there were 46,872 Japanese nationals studying at universities in the US in 1999, 12,784 in China in 1999, and 5686 in the UK in 1998.[1] However, as we shall see in a moment, the Central Education Council figures proved for the UK are substantially lower than those provided by the Japanese Embassy in London.

The most common scenario in the UK is a student on a postgraduate course on a one- or two-year student visa. A high proportion of these graduate students are women, at least 70 per cent, according to Japanese Embassy statistics (see Table 5.1). However, as Masami Yoshida (work in progress) notes, the type of study programme followed by Japanese students in Britain has begun to change in recent years. The shift has been away from the postgraduate-level courses to one-year undergraduate exchange programmes organized by universities in Japan or short stays in Britain, ranging from one month to one year, to attend English courses in universities or language schools.

The third reason for Japanese migration to the UK arises from the presence in the country of family units and students. These family units and students require a long list of services and this leads to a growing population of Japanese nationals who live in the UK in order to operate businesses which either cater exclusively to Japanese nationals (e.g. hairdressers, supermarkets, estate agents) or offer everyone living in Britain a taste of Japan (establishments selling Japanese products and Japanese restaurants). In such cases, settlement may be permanent, as individuals come to resemble immigrants far more than expatriates.

The Japanese Embassy provides, upon request, information about Japanese-oriented facilities in London. Data collected in 2002 and 2003 show that there are some 40 Anglo-Japanese organizations in Britain and over 20 education faculties catering for the education of Japanese nationals. In addition, there are some 25 shops selling Japanese goods, seven weekly or monthly publications in Japanese, six art galleries exhibiting Japanese art, five Japanese bookshops and four Japanese temples of worship. Elsewhere, Baker and Kim (2003), focusing exclusively on London, corroborate the numbers provided by the Japanese Embassy, adding to them a long list of additional categories such as agencies devoted to accommodation for Japanese nationals in London (over 20), Japanese hairdressers in London (over 25) and Japanese restaurants in London (well over 100). Together, all of these facilities, and many I have not mentioned (see Baker and Kim, 2003, for more), point to a well-developed network of Japanese services in Britain as a whole, and London specifically, which are staffed in their majority by Japanese nationals.

A fourth reason for migrating from Japan is the desire to live new experiences, in a sense to 'hang out' somewhere different from home. As I suggested above, it is becoming increasingly common for Japanese students in London to extend their stays after they have finished their studies. This might have a negative motivation: it is a way of putting off the inevitable return to a predictable existence back home. Or, it might be more about simply wanting to live somewhere that just happens not to be Japan. Certainly, many Japanese young people are drawn to London's multiculturalism and vibrant, albeit chaotic, lifestyle.

The 2001 census listed the UK Japanese population at 19,185, down considerably from the 1991 census, which according to Owen (1996) showed 24,482 Japanese nationals. In absence of any detailed breakdown, it is difficult to know if either figure includes Japanese residents belonging to all four of the categories listed above. What does seem clear, however, is that the 2001 figure is far lower than estimates made by the Japanese Embassy's consular office in London. Japanese Embassy figures for 2003, which are broken down according to motive for migration to London, are listed in Table 5.1.

According to this information, the total number of Japanese nationals in the UK, as of October 2003, is just over 50,000. Of these, 22,950 are estimated to live in London and 31,473, in what the Embassy refers to as 'Greater London' (a larger area than what is normally meant by 'Greater London', including London, Surrey, Kent, Essex, Hertfordshire and Middlesex). In London, the greatest concentrations of Japanese nationals are in the western and northern boroughs of Ealing and Barnet. Perhaps the most notable aspect of these numbers is the male/female imbalance: over 60 per cent of Japanese nationals are female. This imbalance is most pronounced in the category for students and researchers

Table 5.1 Japanese people in the UK in October 2003

	Employed		Family		Total
	Male	Female	Male	Female	
Private company staff	7,719	2,951	2,095	5,548	18,313
Journalists	143	77	38	99	357
Self employed	291	377	77	208	953
Students/researchers/ministers	5,704	11,185	464	1,121	18,474
Working for government	379	202	68	182	831
Other	230	1,053	355	329	1,967
Subtotal	Male = 17,563;		Female = 23,032		40,895
Residents in UK	Male = 2,428;		Female = 7,208		9,636
Grand total	Male = 19,991;		Female = 30,549		50,531

Source: Japanese Embassy in Britain, August 2004.

('ministers' seems an odd inclusion here), with 70 per cent of the total, that is 12,316 out of 18,474, listed as female. The imbalance also holds for the categories 'Other' and 'Residents', where almost 75 per cent of the totals are female. I suspect that a large proportion of the 'Other' and 'Resident' categories are individuals who have finished or abandoned their studies but decided to continue living in the UK. As most students are women, it stands to reason that most of those extending their stays are women.

Apart from the male/female imbalance, I find these statistics somewhat puzzling when I compare them with an almost identical breakdown reproduced by Sakai (2004 [2000]) for October 1992. These Embassy figures are in Table 5.2.

A close comparison of Tables 5.1 and 5.2 reveals some changes that are worthy of comment. First, there is the slight decrease in the total number of Japanese nationals living in the UK, from 54,415 in 1992 to 50,531 in 2001. The hardest hit category is private company staff, down to 18.313 in 2001 from 32,428 in 1992. Such a drop no doubt reflects the enduring economic crisis in Japan that began in the early 1990s (Gao, 2001; Maswood, 2002). Offsetting to a great extent the loss of population in the private company staff category are increases in other categories. Most notably, the population linked to education (students, researchers, teachers) has gone up, from 15,629 to 18,474, and the residents category has leapt from 3361 to 9636. There have also been less dramatic increases in the categories 'Self employed' and 'Other'. Though these figures do not show an overwhelming influx of Japanese

Table 5.2   Japanese people in the UK in October 1992

	Employed		Family		Total
	Male	Female	Male	Female	
Private company staff	12,024	566	5,646	14,192	32,428
Journalists	151	23	88	215	477
Self employed	153	49	45	140	387
Students/researchers/teachers	5,770	5,552	1,218	3,089	15,629
Working for government	246	47	129	289	711
Other	481	485	152	304	1,422
Subtotal	Male = 26,103;		Female = 24,951		51,054
Residents in UK	Male = 700;		Female = 2,661		3,361
Grand total	Male = 26,803;		Female = 27,612		54,415

Source: Japanese Embassy in Britain, cited in Sakai, 2004 [2000]: 58.

nationals to the UK, they do point towards the maintenance of the UK as a preferred destination for Japanese students and researchers. Perhaps more importantly, emerging from these figures is the suggestion that more Japanese nationals are settling in the UK in order to run their own businesses (e.g. restaurants, shops) or simply to have what they consider to be a more interesting life than they would have in Japan.

If I take into account all of the information discussed above, what kind of estimate for the Japanese population in Britain and London can I make? As I explained above, I am more inclined to believe the numbers provided by the Japanese Embassy than those provided by the National Census, that is that there are roughly 50,000 Japanese nationals in Britain as a whole and about 30,000 in Greater London. These figures are cited by King (1990), Yamada-Yamamoto (1998) and Sakai (2004 [2000]), and the general consensus seems to be that Japanese population has remained relatively stable at these figures since the late 1980s.[2]

In my view, there are two forces pulling in opposite directions which are affecting the Japanese population in London. On the one hand, the economic situation in Japan has no doubt reduced the number of Japanese nationals coming to London for business purposes. However, at the same time, the number of students has increased and more importantly, there are progressively more Japanese people choosing to live in London for lifestyle reasons. In some cases, these are entrepreneurial types who are setting up businesses which cater to Japanese tastes and those with a taste for Japanese services and products. In other cases, they are students extending their visas and staying on for a few years and perhaps even forever. It is this latter migration pattern that is perhaps beginning to fall outside the control of the Embassy, given that it is not 'official'.

The stories in this chapter

In the remainder of this chapter, I examine the life stories of five Japanese graduate students. I have chosen to focus on this particular subgroup among Japanese migrants in London for two reasons. First, there is a convenience question: my professional activities mean that I have contact year after a year with a good number of Japanese graduate students. Second, in very interesting ways, these informants' experiences cut across the different migrant options discussed in Chapter 2. Thus, in their stories, there are elements of the expatriate (living in London as a Japanese national), the flexible citizen (choosing London to situate work and study, while retaining strong ties to Japan), transnational (opening up a new life in London, whilst maintaining contact with Japan and Japanese culture) and the immigrant (settling definitively in London, leaving Japan and Japanese culture behind).

My intention here is to offer the reader a glimpse of how these students position themselves as Londoners, focusing on the varying degrees of cosmopolitan baggage they all bring with them and how they 'do being' a Japanese national in London. All five informants, who have been assigned pseudonyms, were students on an MA TESOL programme at a London university at the time of their contacts with me. However, they did not all stay in London for the same length of time. Two informants, Motoko and Naomi, lived in London for one academic year, the time it took them to finish their MAs. While Motoko was a 28-year-old single woman who had come to London on her own, Naomi was with her husband, an engineer on a one-year posting, and her 14-year-old daughter. A third informant, Akira, a divorced 47-year old, would eventually spend almost two years living in London. She arrived six months before her intended one year of study and stayed an additional six months when she did not finish on time. The other two informants, Mie and Yukiko, came to London in 2000 and 2002, respectively, and at the time of writing, were still living in London. Both initially came to London on one-year student visas and then subsequently extended their stays due to work and further study options that they had taken up.

In the case of the four informants – Motoko, Naomi, Akira, and Mie – my exclusive source of data is one single life-story interview, lasting between one and two hours. However, for Yukiko, the database consists of three interviews, multiple informal contacts and some data collected in the informant's work context. In common, all five informants are women, highly proficient in English. However, there is a distinction to be made among them, in particular how the three with the most cosmopolitan baggage, prior to their arrival in London, frame and live their lives in very different ways from the two women with less cosmopolitan baggage. It is to the three women with *kikokushijo* experience that I turn first.

Having *kikokushijo* experience

Kikokushijo are the sons and daughters of Japanese families who have lived abroad for a period of time usually ranging from two to five years, although periods abroad can be as short as one year and as long as 15 years.[3] They are the children of the private company staff, journalists, government employees and students in the population statistics cited above. The word is composed of two parts, meaning 'sons and daughters' (*shijo*) and 'return to one's home country' (*kikoku*). Given the by now well-established global spread of Japanese nationals, there are an estimated 50,000 *kikokushijo* living outside Japan, at different stages of their foreign experience (Yashiro, 1995; Richards and Yamada-Yamamoto, 1998; Yamada-Yamamoto and Richards, 1998; Pang, 2000; Kanno, 2003). Of the English-language publications, it is those of Pang (2000) and Kanno (2003) that provide the richest accounts of what it is like to be a *kikokushijo*.[4]

Pang (2000) is an ambitious anthropological study of Japanese returnees, drawing on three databases. Over a period of six years (1990–96), Pang spent a great deal of time in contact with three generations of a Japanese family living in Brussels – two grandmothers, the husband and wife and two daughters, recording informal conversations, collecting correspondence and taking field notes. She also carried out interviews and administered questionnaires to some 60 other returnees studying at an English-medium international school in Brussels and completed her study by interviewing 20 *kikokushijo* who, upon returning to Japan, had enrolled in international schools operating primarily for *kikokushijo*.

In her study, which extended over about three years (1992–95), Kanno conducted interviews, kept fieldnotes and maintained correspondence with four *kikokushijo* with whom she had contact as a teacher at a Japanese *hoshuko* (Saturday School) in Toronto. In her book, she explores how these four individuals constructed and made sense of their bilingual and bicultural identities during the period of time spanning their final months in Toronto and their first three years back in Japan.

Among the many interesting dimensions of *kikokushijo* lives discussed by Pang and Kanno, I see three as directly relevant to the *kikokushijo* status of three of the participants in my study. The first dimension is the relative determination of *kikokushijo* to maintain their Japanese-ness in anticipation of the their eventual return to Japan. In a sense, there was a kind of virtual Japanese society set up around these students, in Brussels, via a small but very compact Japanese enclave in one particular part of the city, and in Toronto, via an active *hoshuko*, where Kanno was working at the time. However, while all four of Kanno's informants opted for the maintenance of a strong Japanese identity, Pang's considerably larger sample showed greater diversity, from strongly embracing all things Japanese to outright rejection of the home culture.

The second dimension of note in both Pang and Kanno is the degree to which students participated in and felt a part of their secondary school's activities. In Kanno's study, all four individuals lived their lives in Canada as outsiders, a status which resulted in equal part from self-positioning and other positioning by their schoolmates. Thus, while some insider subject positions were available to the four students, such as good student or good at sports, others that clearly marked them as different from the mainstream, such as ESL students and visible minority (racially different), were imposed on them. Meanwhile, Pang's survey once again showed a greater diversity of responses, although the general view was that Japanese students were relatively marginalized in the international school that they attended.

The third dimension of interest of the *kikokushijo* experience here is related to what happens to *kikokushijo* upon their return to Japan. Kanno charts in great detail her informants' negotiations and struggles with the ambivalent feelings that arose at the crossroads of the need to hold on to a sense of being different and a desire to fit in. She shows how three out of four of the *kikokushijo*, in essence, re-adapted and carried on with their lives in Japan, while one eventually moved back to Canada. Similarly, Pang found that of her many informants, 'very few perceive themselves as non-Japanese, living at the edge of society with no hope of reinclusion into mainstream Japanese society' (Pang, 2000: 287). Indeed, of the 20 *kikokushijo* interviewed after their return to Japan, all but two seemed on the way to full assimilation. Pang categorized her informants as follows:

- 'Ordinary Japanese' – Six who did not feel that their overseas experience made them different from other Japanese students at all.
- 'International Japanese' – Six who saw their overseas experience as an asset in their future lives in Japan.
- 'New type of Japanese' – Five who saw themselves as different from other Japanese, retaining strong emotional links with the countries they had lived in.
- 'Others' – Two who actually positioned themselves as 'non-Japanese'.

These three aspects of the life of the *kikokushijo* – maintaining Japanese culture while abroad, outsider status while abroad and the tricky negotiation of re-entry into Japanese life – all figure in the biographies of three of my informants: Motoko, Akira and Naomi. However, they do so in extremely different ways as all three women present a distinctive profile. Before examining exactly what I mean by this statement, it is helpful to consider the amount of time each of these women actually spent outside of Japan from birth to the age of 20. This information is provided in Table 5.3.

Table 5.3 Kikokushijo experience

Age	Motoko	Akira	Naomi
3			
4	Chicago (Age 3–5)		
5		San Francisco (Age 4–6)	
6			
7		New York (Age 6–8)	London (Age 6–9)
8			
9			
10			Sudan (Age 9–12)
11			
12			
13	New York (Age 12–15)		
14			
15			
16			New York (Age 15–20)
17			
18			
19			
20			

Childhood *kikokushijo* experience

Born in 1976 in Yokohama, Motoko spent a part of her early childhood in the US, two and a half years between the ages of 3 and 5. Her family had followed her father to Chicago, where he was sent by his company to complete an MBA. Regarding this early experience, Motoko remembers very little, although her mother later told her that by the time she returned to Japan she only spoke English. Still, Motoko is sure that by the time she started formal schooling, she was speaking Japanese just like all of the other children. During her primary school days, her mother taught her English, in an attempt to maintain the linguistic capital acquired in the US. However, Motoko does not think that she gained much from this extra tuition. Indeed, she recalls that when, at the age of 12, she moved with her family to New York, she had to start learning English again.

Akira's experience as an early *kikokushijo* was different from Motoko's in two senses. First, it lasted longer and took Akira well into her first two years of formal schooling. Second, by her accounts, it had a great impact on her sense of self, in particular her affiliation to the English language. Akira was born in 1955 in Tokyo into a family where Catholicism combined with a familiarity with American culture. She went to a Catholic nursery school as a small child and at the age of four, she moved to San Francisco with her family, when her banker father was transferred there in 1959. Upon her arrival in the US, Akira was put directly into an English-medium pre-school. From this episode, she does not remember anything at all and her parents never mentioned any adaptation problems. Indeed, they have told her that by the time she was five, she was using English far more than Japanese.

After two years in San Francisco, the family moved to New York for an additional two years. Again, Akira does not recall anything traumatic about this change. Indeed, it was not until her family returned to Japan, when she was eight, that she recalls having adaptation problems. Akira remembers that she felt 'terrified' at the time, not least because, although she was in the third grade, she could not read a first grader's textbook in Japanese. She also remembers that her parents were very worried and that her mother made an extra effort to teach her how to read in Japanese.

When her family went back to Japan, she was put in a Japanese Catholic school. However, due to her poor Japanese language skills, she was put back a year, a common practice with *kikokushijo* at the time, as Kanno (2003) notes. This must have been a shock to a child that had been until that time an A student in the US. In this sense, Akira's return experience was far more traumatic than Motoko's. As I explained above, Motoko was still only 5 when she returned and therefore had not yet begun formal schooling. Akira, by contrast, had to catch up quickly with children who had been doing academic work for over two years. As both Pang (2000) and Kanno (2003) note, until the 1980s, *kikokushijo* were generally considered to have few, if any, redeeming qualities. Indeed, such students 'were considered a societal and educational liability...deemed deficient in Japanese language proficiency...[and] behind in other subject matters' (Kanno, 2003: 17–18). Had Akira's return taken place 15 or 20 years later, she would surely have received more assistance in a Japanese-medium school or she would have found a place in one of the many international schools that exit today. Unfortunately for her, in the early 1960s such alternatives for *kikokushijo* did not really exist.

Naomi's childhood *kikokushijo* experiences contrast markedly with those of Motoko and Akira. First, she did not leave Japan until she was six. Second, because her father was a career diplomat, she spent all but three of her years of formal education (including two years of university) in English-speaking environments. When at the age of six her family moved to London, Naomi was immersed in an English-speaking environment for the first time. She remembers her first three months as a period dominated by 'a feeling of uneasiness' and that she had cried every day. However, she also remembers efforts being made by teachers and school staff to make her feel comfortable in her new environment. Naomi recalls that after six months in London, she was a fully functioning English-speaking student and she remembers that at some time during her first year in London she began to speak English with her brother and then later with her parents as well. However, her parents insisted on maintaining Japanese as a family language, aware that that sooner or later her father would be transferred back to Japan and that a lack of fluency and literacy skills in Japanese would be a problem. When her father was transferred again three years later, however, it was not to Japan, but to Sudan. There, Naomi continued to study in English-medium schools, this time as part of the predominantly European elite in that country.

Adolescent *kikokushijo* experience

For the rest of her schooling, Akira had no further *kikokushijo* experience. After her return to Japan, she eventually caught up with students in her age group, and due to a lack of contact with English speakers, her

English assumed its natural position, a distant second place after Japanese. Still, when I suggest to Akira that she perhaps had by this time become Japanese again, she makes the point that to this day she finds that she still monitors her behaviour to make sure it is appropriate in Japanese contexts, asking herself: 'Will this be accepted by them or not?' This feeling of distance towards Japanese behaviour is no doubt attributable to the fact that she lived in the US for five years when she was in her 20s (more on this in a moment). However, it also must be related to the fact that she attended Catholic schools for all of her formal education in Japan, from the age of 8 to the age of 22. At the time of the interview, Akira said that she did not consider herself a religious person; however, she did recognize the influence of the Catholic Church in her life and she attributed to her Catholic education a strong affiliation to western culture and her feelings about being different from other Japanese people. She explains the role of the Catholic Church in her education as follows:

> I think that's possibly true because...well, yeah, because it does, in a way, I think the religion itself is quite westernized. I mean you go into the religion of the dogma and everything, it's about the individualism and personality...I'm not quite sure whether that concept has actually took root in Japan...In my school there was, at least, a lot of foreign nuns, I mean Irish, American, so there was always an element of sort of western culture in the school as well. (Akira, 11/6/2002)

In contrast to Akira, Motoko and Naomi did have *kikokushijo* experience as adolescents. As I noted above, by the time Motoko moved with her family to New York at the age of 12, she had lost most of the English she had acquired when she was in Chicago as a pre-schooler. In contrast to her first stay in the US, this one, taking place in the middle of adolescence, is remembered vividly. And, these memories are not on the whole positive:

> To be honest I hated living there because my parents didn't give me a choice. They just put me into a local school. (Motoko, 26/1/2004)

The local school was in a wealthy New York suburb, where a substantial number of Japanese families, most only temporarily in the US, lived. However, a visible Japanese presence in her school proved to be a negative element for Motoko, as regards any attempts to have contact with 'American' kids. She explains:

> [It was a] nice area where loads of Japanese live so that's why at our school there was a big ESL class and also in each class there were many Japanese students and we wouldn't speak in English and I think even American kids they're young still and they know we were living a few years they didn't really want to get close to us. And it was difficult times. Now I can understand but at that time, I just hated them, for not bullying. but ignoring or making fun of us. (Motoko, 26/1/2004)

Motoko's account resonates with some of the experiences of Pang's (2000) and Kanno's (2003) informants, who talked of feeling excluded from mainstream school life in Brussels and Toronto, respectively. This exclusion applied not only to a tendency for dominant groups of students to segregate themselves from anyone who did not conform to the mainstream discourses of school life,[5] but also, as Kanno (2003) reports in her study, to abuse Japanese students verbally on occasion, using 'ESL student' as a derisive term, as if not speaking English was handicap. In addition, in a predominantly European American context, being Japanese meant being seen as a darker skinned ethnic minority. Thus while Motoko managed to adapt to the educational system during the three years she was in New York, even acquiring a great deal of expertise in English and becoming a top student, she maintained her foreigner/outsider status in just about all non-academic aspects of her life. She recalls that she spoke Japanese as much as possible and that she associated almost exclusively with Japanese and other East Asian minority students (e.g. Koreans and Chinese). She thus acquired expertise in English without little or no concomitant sense of affiliation.

It is little wonder, then, that when she was told that she was returning to Japan, she was 'so happy'. Looking back at this experience, almost 15 years later, Motoko still feels bitter about how she was treated as an outsider while in the US; however, she also says that she now feels 'grateful' for the opportunity to have learned English. The former emotion, according to Kelsky (2001), is not uncommon among *kikokushijo* who, several years and even decades after their experiences abroad, cannot forget episodes involving racism and exclusion, which they encountered. As regards the latter feeling, Motoko gives voice to one of the findings of Kanno's study, namely that *kikokushijo* may eventually reconcile their ambivalent feelings about who they are by moving from 'an *either-or* orientation to bilingualism and biculturalism toward a more balance *both-and* approach' (Kanno, 2003: 128).

In many ways, Naomi's adolescent experiences are the exact opposite of Motoko's. By the age of 12, she was six years into formal education, all of which had been in English: she studied for three years in London and for three years at an English-medium international school in Sudan. This means that by the time she left Sudan to return to Japan at the age of 12, Naomi was far more proficient in English than Japanese. In addition, she recalls that she could remember very little about Japan, as she had not been back there since the age of six. Thus, the culture shock she experienced at age 12 was that of a cosmopolitan English speaker going to Japan as if for the first time. She explains matters as follows:

> Actually, that was a big shock. I mean ... at school they did things very differently and ... of course I had to catch up with my Japanese because when I went back to Japan I could hardly read or write, so I had to start from grade 1. I mean I was in the 7th grade, but I had to do all the stuff that was covered from grade 1. (Naomi, 11/6/2002)

Unlike Akira, Naomi does not harbour bad memories of her return to Japan. In particular, she does not recall being forced to become Japanese immediately upon arrival. As I noted above, the treatment of *kikokushijo*, as regards allowances for their atypical education backgrounds, did not improve until well into the 1980s. However, Naomi recalls that she was not the only *kikokushijo* in the school and that as a group, the *kikokushijo* were isolated from 'normal' students, while they caught up with the other students. She recalls catching up, but she also recalls that the *kikokushijo* maintained an identity distinct from the rest of the student body through their continued use of English. She therefore was able to maintain her considerable expertise in English as well as the positive affiliation to western culture. After two years, Naomi was back in mainstream classes; however, she remembers that at the age of 14, she was intent on remaining 'different'. Making reference to one of Kanno's (e.g. 2000) publications, which Naomi had read as part of her MA studies, she explains:

> I think I tried to maintain the difference. ... It's very strange. Kanno, you know, has written something about this in her article ... Once you're back in Japan and if you have no control over the language, you kind of feel a so-called elite and you're more flexible in the things that

you want to do...I think I did try to maintain that difference. (Naomi, 11/6/2002)

Fortunately for Naomi, fostering an identity that was never completely Japanese was not detrimental to her development as an adolescent. Indeed, she was able to convert her expertise in English and her affiliation to western culture into substantial social and cultural capital. For example, she recalls that was always able to translate Beatles songs for her friends, which gained her popularity. It also meant that when the time came for another move, this time to New York when she was 15, she was, in a sense, ready.

Ultimately, the New York experience was to cement an English-speaking identity that Naomi maintains to this day. The family moved into a suburb of New York and she was enrolled in a private all-girls school. She recalls some of her schoolmates making fun of her British accent, acquired during earlier sojourns, but on the whole, she remembers her period of adaptation as being relatively easy. She was soon speaking with an American accent and she became part of a group of high achieving students.

Unlike her previous experiences abroad, this experience afforded Naomi greater contact with other Japanese nationals of her age. There were a few *kikokushijo* in her school, but more importantly on Saturdays, she went to a *hoshuko*, where she was meant to maintain contact with Japanese culture. Naomi recalls that there were two groups in this school:

When you look at that Saturday Japanese school, it was interesting because there were distinctly two groups. One group would be more geared toward the Japanese stuff, like, you know, they would always be talking about the presenters on Japanese TV. The other group would be more oriented toward the American stuff. And they would even...be talking in English, as a matter of fact. And the group geared toward the Japanese culture, they would be talking in Japanese and they dressed differently too.... The kids that identified themselves with, more with the American culture, they would be in jeans and you know, just like your average American kid. In the Japanese group, they'd be wearing things that their friends or their grandparents had sent them over from Japan. (Naomi, 11/6/2002)

Of the two groups, Naomi tended to identify with the American-oriented group. She thus maintained in this supposed Japanese capsule, a multimodal American identity based on her use of English, her dress and her cultural consumption (e.g. what television programmes she watched). Still, she found associating with other Japanese adolescents like herself comforting in many ways, and thus accepted, to some extent, what Kanno calls the 'sanctuary' role of the *hoshuko* (Kanno, 2003: 112).

Naomi finished high school in New York and then went to Columbia University to study biology. However, after her second year, her father was once again called back to Japan. Naomi wanted to stay in New York, but ultimately ceded to her father's wish that she should stay with the family. She returned to Japan reluctantly and continued her studies at a Japanese university with ties to an American university. This change meant that while she could continue her studies in English-medium classes, she could not major in biology as she had originally planned (it was not offered as part of the programme). She majored in liberal arts and communications instead. It also meant that notwithstanding her predominantly 'western' education, her considerable English-medium social and cultural capital (linked to her English language expertise and affiliation), she was finally to 'return' to Japan to engage in a long and sustained process of Japanization. However, this process was never completely to purge her of the worldview, values and tastes she had acquired during her many years away from Japan. To this day, Naomi speaks excellent English with great confidence and manifests, via her words and actions, a great affinity for western culture.

What does *kikokushijo* experience mean?

Motoko, Akira and Naomi's respective *kikokushijo* experiences affected them in very different ways. For Motoko, being an early *kikokushijo*, living in the US as a small child, was a fleeting experience that presumably would have faded away completely with time. However, there was a second half to her American experience. While she is very emphatic that she did not enjoy spending her early adolescence in suburban New York, she acknowledges that the experience gave her a high level of expertise in English language for life. Thirteen years after her return to Japan, she could still speak English, confidently, with a near-perfect American accent. Motoko is thus much like Pang's (2000) 'international Japanese' described above, in that she values the linguistic skills she gained from her experiences abroad.

For her part, Akira had only one experience abroad during her formal education. However, that experience, coupled perhaps with her Catholic education, left her with positive childhood memories, a positive disposition towards difference and the dream that she might, as an adult, be able to live abroad once again. At the age of 22, her dream came true as she married a man who was soon after transferred to San Francisco. The San Francisco experience was to alter Akira's life in very profound ways. For five years, she lived an up-market suburban house-wife lifestyle. During this time, she developed a great deal of expertise in English via her membership in the community of practice comprised of her female neighbours. So thorough was her integration that one of her neighbours wondered how she would ever be able to live in Japan again after becoming so 'California-ized'. Above all, during these five years, Akira led a life almost completely independent of her husband. She ran the family home and did more or less whatever she wanted to do. After moving back to Japan, Akira felt that the power differential had shifted back in her husband's favour and that she could no longer live as she had in the US. Not content with her condition, she filed for divorce.

Because of her explicit self-positioning as not completely Japanese, Akira would qualify as an early version of what Pang (2000) calls the 'new type of Japanese'. Many years after her most significant overseas experience, in California, she retains a great deal of expertise in English and a strong feeling of affiliation to the English-speaking world.

In contrast to Motoko and Akira, Naomi had both extensive childhood and extensive adolescent *kikokushijo* experience: by the time she was 20, she had only spent three years of her formal education in Japan. In add-ition, when she did return to Japan, finished her studies in an English-medium programme. Like Akira, she also spent time in San Francisco as a young adult: she followed her engineer husband who was sent there for almost five years. However for Naomi, this experience was not defining; rather she was already defined years earlier as someone not totally Japanese in her self perceptions, with high levels of expertise in and affiliation to English. Thus, like Akira, Naomi can be categorized as one of Pang's (2000) 'new type of Japanese', although, like Akira, she was a 'new type' well before the time of Pang's informants. The following comment about reconciling her Japanese and western lives makes this point well:

> I think I had to...I couldn't be constantly trying to find my place and going...I think at one point I gave up the image of trying to, I don't know, mingle into one culture. I think I kind of made my own culture. (Naomi, 11/6/2002)

Importantly, being a *kikokushijo* has led to Motoko, Akira and Naomi positioning themselves as different from other Japanese women as regards their gendered selves. For example, when reflecting on her five-year sojourn in California mentioned above, Akira spoke of different ways of doing femininity in Japanese and English:

> I think I do present a bit of a different personality when I'm speaking in English and when I am speaking in Japanese... when I'm speaking in Japanese, I really have to think about all the things, you know, what's the proper style and... sort of kind of try to adjust myself to the identities, what the other person is projecting on me.... I mean, how are they looking at me? And how am I supposed to match that idea?... Whereas in English, I mean I don't really feel that much.... If they say something like, 'Oh, I thought you were a kind of typical Japanese woman', I could say, 'Not really'. Or if they say 'Oh, I thought Japanese women were always polite, bla, bla, bla', I can say , 'Well, most of them are, but maybe I'm not'. And I don't feel uncomfortable being that way. So in a way, it's a lot easier that way. (Akira, 11/6/2002)

In her interview, Motoko described such language-related gendered positionings as follows:

> I feel western woman are very strong (laughing) quite scary sometimes but I think Japanese women are too submissive sometimes. So I think I'm considered to be rather erhm assertive in Japanese terms and I don't really care. (Motoko, 26/1/2004)

In these two comments, there is an interesting discourse of difference between Japanese and English. On the one hand, Japanese language is said to impose strict rules of usage on women, whilst preventing them from saying what they think or feel. English, by contrast, is positioned as a language in which women feel no such pressures or constraints. This view of Japanese and English is fairly generalized among many Japanese women today if one is to judge by research that has explored the inter-relationships between Japanese women and Japanese language and culture. For example, in the autobiographical *Polite Lies: On Being a Woman Caught Between Two Cultures*, Kyoko Mori (1997) discusses her experiences as a woman who, at the age of 20, migrated to the US and stayed. Describing herself as living between two languages and cultures, Mori laments that in Japanese, she lacks 'a voice for speaking...[her] mind' (Mori, 1997: 16). Elsewhere, in her study of the interrelationships between English language and feminist ideologies, Cheiron McMahill (2001) found that the EFL learners enrolled in a 'grass-roots feminist English class' conflated their study of English with feminism and saw a link between English and their sense of independence as women. Elsewhere, in more anthropological works, Buckley (1997) and Kelsky (2001) have noted similar associations between the English language and independence and internationalism.

How do the *kikokushijo* live London?

Given their *kikokushijo* experiences, all three of these women spoke fluent English with great confidence and manifested, both semiotically (e.g. language, dress, movement) and via their behaviour, a great deal of what might be termed western social and cultural capital. Still, none of them ever seriously entertained the notion of staying for longer than it took them to finish their studies. Motoko and Naomi both left London after one year, as soon as they finished their MA courses. In Naomi's case, her return was linked to that of her husband and daughter. As I explained above, the family were on a one-year sojourn in London and all three had their respective occupations to go back to in Japan. Motoko, by contrast, had no such limitations on her movements, as she was on her own and had quit her job before going to London to do the MA course. In addition, it was not as if London was not an attractive city to live in, as the following comment, comparing London with American cities, suggests:

> I've felt that I don't need to lose my Japanese identity here because even on the tube you can hear different languages, I really think it's international...they don't look at me [here] if I'm speaking Japanese because everybody else is speaking different languages. But in America, if I'm speaking Japanese, people will stare at me like: 'oh, you're speaking Japanese...This is America, why don't you speak English?' or something like that. (Motoko, 26/1/2004)

However, ultimately, she could not see the point of staying in London, to take a job she did not want, living in a city she finds too expensive:

> We [overseas MA students] talk about this...because it seems that many many people want to stay in London. We are talking, you know: 'How can you get a job?' And they say: 'You can teach Japanese'. But I don't know how to teach Japanese. And they say: 'Oh, maybe you can work in a Japanese school teaching English'. And I feel, then what is the meaning of me staying here where things are expensive? (Motoko, 26/1/2004)

For her part, Akira would eventually spend almost two years living in London: she came six months before her intended one year of study and stayed an additional six months when she did not finish on time. However, she too went back to Japan to work and further her career. When asked if she would ever consider staying more permanently in London, she said she would not, explaining her response as follows:

> I think, you know, because I know I won't be able to keep the standard of living, the status I have in Japan, even if I bring all the money and all the assets and everything, I probably will be lowering my... So I think that's one thing that is kind of holding me back. And on the other hand, I think probably, just getting to this age of thinking, well, I won't be able to really assimilate to any of these countries now.... I won't be able to be an English person. And I'm not comfortable in Japan, so I probably will have to kind of – but, at least in Japan, I'm – you know, well, I can find a job and I can live... even though I feel a bit awkward... (Akira, 11/6/2002)

Thus, despite their obvious cosmopolitan credentials, gained via their *kikokushijo* experiences, Motoko, Naomi and Akira live their lives in London more as expatriates than transnationals, with one foot firmly planted in Japan whilst the toes of the other foot are dipped in the waters of London. One obvious reason alluded to by all three women is related to job stability and socio-economic status: staying in London would lead inevitably to a lowering of their standard of living. However, there is also an aspect of the *kikokushijo* experience that might go far in explaining why none of these three women has been tempted to stay in London. As both Pang (2000) and Kanno (2003) note, *kikokushijo* live abroad always knowing they will have to go 'back' sooner or later. As a result, they learn to live their experiences outside Japan as a kind of controlled cosmopolitanism. Indeed, while they know-how to move among their temporary hosts (above all, because they have the language expertise to do so), they nonetheless do so at no cost to their sense of Japanese-ness, whether this national affiliation is more or less strong (as it perhaps is in Motoko's case) or not (as is the case for Akira and Naomi). Somewhat paradoxically, then, the most internationalized informants in my study are the ones least impressed by London. Let us now move to the stories of Mie and Yukiko, two women who did not have *kikokushijo* experience, and for whom cosmopolitanism has been, in its entirety, an experience of young adulthood.

Adult cosmopolitans

In contrast to Motoko, Akira and Naomi, Mie and Yukiko did not live away from Japan for any extended period of time until they were 21 and 19, respectively: Mie went to London to study English for a month, while Yukiko went on a holiday to London and Paris for two weeks. Still, in both cases, there was an element of foreignness in their upbringings. Mie's parents were English teachers and she recalls being surrounded by books written in English. Meanwhile, Yukiko explains how her mother, perhaps influenced by her father who spoke German fluently, inculcated a somewhat eccentric sense of foreignness in her children by dressing them in Scottish kilts and leather shoes.

Mie and Yukiko both found their first lengthy stays outside of Japan fulfilling. Mie described her month in London as follows:

> I came here to study English for one month but it was a big change or it had a big impact on me because it was my first time to leave Japan and see many different things and meet different people.... I was so excited, what I remember is I phoned my mother and said: (raising her voice) 'IT'S ME, IT'S ME, IT'S ME, I'M IN LONDON. I'M IN LONDON!' Everything three times, I was so excited. (Mie, 26/1/2004)

Meanwhile, Yukiko responded as follows, when asked how she felt when she made her first trip to London:

> Very comfortable. Even though I don't remember when I first arrived at Heathrow Airport, I felt very comfortable. I don't know why. Maybe it was my dream country. (Yukiko, 12/2/2004)

Given these positive first experiences, both subsequently found ways to repeat the experience. Smitten after her first visit to London, Mie became a serial visitor, coming back for short stays on six occasions between the ages of 23 and 32. Meanwhile, Yukiko made three trips to Australia with students as a part of her job as an English teacher at a private school between the ages of 22 and 28. As I noted above, Mie and Yukiko differ markedly from Motoko, Akira and Naomi in that they did not have cosmopolitan experiences until they were young adults. However, discovering other worlds late in life has come to mean a serious consideration of the ultimate cosmopolitan experience: staying in London for good.

Life in London

This chapter opened with two quotes, both taken from an interview with Mie. In these quotes, she expressed the idea that Japan is a closed society and that she has lost sociolinguistic expertise in Japanese, the latter occurring as her affiliation to the English language increased. Such losses and gains proved to be the driving force behind most of what was discussed in my interview with Mie, as well as my contacts with Yukiko. They also are a well-documented phenomenon in the literature on Japanese women living outside of Japan, usually in western contexts (e.g. Buckley, 1997; Kelsky, 2001).

Originally, Mie came to London with the sole intention of completing an MA course in one year. However, at some time during that year, she decided to stay. When asked what it was that 'turned her', she responds as follows:

> I think its multicultural atmosphere and erhm in London we can find very contemporary things and traditional things mixed together and that attracted me. Basically I feel more comfortable in London more free...I've got many friends now here and I've got my life here. (Mie, 26/1/2004)

Meanwhile, Yukiko describes this atmosphere as 'free':

> I feel comfortable because nobody cares [about] me. It means there are many many varieties of people [and] they don't care: Japanese walking, Chinese walking...And in Tokyo maybe if you are American...you might have people stare at you. Even in Tokyo. So it means here is more free. (Yukiko, 12/2/2004)

In addition, in common with Motoko, Akira and Naomi, Yukiko and Mie both give voice to the view of English as a language of liberation, in which they can develop new femininities, for example saying what they think and feeling more independent. Yukiko describes her mother's reaction to the way she spoke Japanese after over a year in Britain:

> Actually, my mum said to me one day when I went back to Japan last March and she said your Japanese has become more aggressive than before I think because...I tend to say conclusions fast I mean 'I think bla bla bla'. I didn't do that before. (Yukiko, 12/2/2004)

Meanwhile, Mie explains the difference between communicating in Japanese and communicating in English as follows:

> The main difference in Japan is that you're not supposed to say everything and especially for women I don't think it's a good thing to say everything to erm show your emotion but when I speak English or when I am in London I can say everything. And I think I should so I'm getting used to it but it isn't in Japan. When I went back to Japan this summer [2003] and some somebody asked to my friends: 'where is she from?' and 'Is she Japanese? or is she from somewhere else'? And I thought: 'right, I don't look like Japanese now'. (Mie, 26/1/2004)

Later in the interview, Mie recounted a somewhat bizarre encounter that took place during the afore-mentioned visit to Japan in 2003. It shows how distant she now feels from Japanese norms of communication, and more importantly, how she does not even wish to make the effort to re-engage with these norms.

> There was a misunderstanding between my friends and me because I didn't understand when of course we wanted to meet and we wanted to arrange the date and time and I suggested some certain time and she said 'Oh, yeah' So I thought meant 'yes' but on that day she didn't phone me and I thought: 'but she said yes'. That meant she was listening and I forgot about it 'yes' can mean 'no' 'mm', so 'mm' means yes for me. So I thought we were meeting up and I was waiting for her call and she didn't call me. And that happened twice or three times and I did not get that 'yes' and finally I thought 'I don't like this'. (Mie, 26/1/2004)

The big test for Mie's developing and increasing loyalty to London was to be her trip to Japan in the summer of 2003. This was the first time she had been there for two years. She explains her feelings as follows:

> T: If I hadn't gone back to Japan last summer I wouldn't have thought of this affection of London. But I did it and I felt very different.
> D: You found yourself missing London?
> T: Oh, yes.

D: How long were you in Japan?

T: Just one month.

D: One month

T: And it was after one month I thought: 'That's enough, I have to go back to London' always. (Mie, 26/1/2004)

As for the specifics of why she did not like being in Japan, she explains:

> When I was walking down the streets in Tokyo, I felt so lonely and I was not wear[ing] what I was supposed to wear and didn't know where to go and I felt so different. And here I don't face [that]. Nobody cares anyway (laughing). (Mie, 26/1/2004)

It was during this visit that the lift episode described at the beginning of this chapter occurred, an episode that symbolized her difficulty in reconciling her London self with her Japanese self.

When I interviewed Mie in January 2004, she was studying for a PhD at a London university and working part time serving drinks in a University of London bar. At the time of writing, she continues with her studies, although her job situation has changed: in early March 2005, she informed me that she was about to take up a post as an English teacher in a Japanese school in London. Overall, she seems to be immersing herself more and more into London life. She has hobbies such as singing in a choir and she has a circle of friends from different parts of the world. She estimates that at least 80 per cent of her daily communication is in English, a believable figure when one considers that she does not really spend very much time with Japanese speakers. Indeed, were it not for the fact that her mother was living in London at the time of the interview, this figure might have been higher. Certainly one important component in Mie's desire to stay in London is the proliferation of communities of practice in which she can claim membership: at work, at university, in her leisure activities. In the sense that people's identities are linked to the activities they engage in (Lave and Wenger, 1991; Wenger, 1998), Mie is doing all of her identity work in London.

Meanwhile, Yukiko is also working and studying in London. However, unlike Mie, Yukiko claims to have few friends in London. She says that most of her contact with people has been via her studies and her place of work. In her studies and indeed in her social life, she uses English almost exclusively. However, in her place of work, a Japanese owned and operated hair salon in central London, she uses both Japanese and English in equal quantities. This is because the client base is split roughly between Japanese nationals and English speakers, with the latter being further sub-divided by Yukiko into what she calls 'British' (i.e. White British) and British Chinese. I now turn to an examination of how she does her language identity work in the hair salon.

In the hair salon

The hair salon where Yukiko works is owned and operated by a friend of her family in Japan, a woman who is about ten years older than Yukiko. All of the employees are Japanese and this means that there is a distinctly Japanese way of doing business in the salon. This is especially the case when Japanese customers are involved. In response to questions asked about her job during our first interview in February 2004, Yukiko began to write field notes about her language-related practices at work. In a subsequent interview, about a month later, we discussed these notes, which contained a detailed breakdown of the clientele and her relationships with them. As regards Japanese customers, she wrote the following:

> Commonly, conversations in Japanese tend to take less time than in English and these two languages demonstrate different manners. In Japanese, I use quite formal expressions; honorific words, even though some customers are obviously younger than me...Overall, the Japanese customers speak respectful Japanese to receptionists without any significant differences, because of their age or gender. As a result, automatically, my responses would be more polite to them in order to show respect to them as a [member of] staff of a salon. It would help to understand this stance, between customers and staff through a basic concept for business in Japan: 'The customers is God'. I am also expected to behave and dress or wear make up commensurate with my age, even though I am a full-time student in the UK. Surely, I have been in a small Japanese society, even in London. (Yukiko, field notes, February 2004)

Here Yukiko describes how her workplace is in part a fairly insular Japanese oasis in central London. In a sense, it is a transnational place of the kind described in some of the contributions to Cordero-Guzmán *et al.* (2001) and Farr (2004), about different ethnolinguistic groups living in New York and Chicago, respectively. Everything she discusses in this excerpt is about enacting Japanese subject positions, according to age, gender and profession. And it all happens in a highly indexical culture, where one must be attentive to what is taken for granted. This explains Yukiko's claim that 'conversations in Japanese tend to take less time than in English'.

If there is little margin for error in her Japanese conversations, Yukiko's English conversations often include communication breakdowns. However, Yukiko notes that these are generally resolved in friendly manner. Indeed, on the whole, English conversations are related to 'relaxed atmospheres' and as regards content, more 'private things' than is the case with Japanese conversations, which are generally about what she calls 'safe topics'. They are also about work, as Yukiko explains:

> when I speak ... in Japanese, Actually I'm WORKING ... I don't really get involved into their privacy things not I [that I] don't care, but I'm not interested in or I shouldn't be interested in their private ... but if customers are western or European foreign people for me I would talk to them. I would ask them based on my interest because I wonder what are they doing. Of course they also wonder what I'm doing. (Yukiko, 8/3/2004)

A third large clientele in the hair salon is made up of what she terms 'Chinese', a fairly broad group that includes both British-born Chinese and more recent arrivals. If the Japanese are familiarly ritualistic and the so called 'British' customers are easy going and friendly, the 'Chinese' are qualified as 'difficult'. The big problem it seems is English language skills, as she explains in the following excerpt:

> For both some Chinese people and me, English is not the first language. Therefore, some customers' English are really hard to understand for me in terms of pronunciation, grammatical mistakes and their names. It goes without saying that my English is also not understandable for them. (Yukiko, field notes, February 2004)

Apart from difficulties with pronunciation and names, Yukiko also claims that Chinese customers are too demanding and less polite than others. Still, as she says in the above excerpt, part of the problem might be her own English.

In her descriptions of dealings with customers, Yukiko situates herself at the crossroads of the three different customer groups, all using language in different ways. As regards the Chinese customers, Yukiko's attitude ranges from indifferent to hostile. She shows no interest in the contacts she has with these customers and on occasion, she sees them as creating extra work for her, tying her up on the telephone, for example. The Chinese, therefore, are English speakers towards whom she feels no affiliation.

As regards the Japanese customers, Yukiko sees them as an integral part of the hair salon, the base clientele. She does not find it difficult to conform to the gendered and age norms of this 'small Japanese society', as her expertise in Japanese remains intact. However, she claims to find the atmosphere stifling, both as regards the rules of engagement laid down by her boss and the use of Japanese language. It seems, then, that Yukiko tolerates, more than she embraces, the world of the hair salon. Indeed, rather than seeing her contacts with Japanese customers and her co-workers as a means of maintaining contact with Japanese culture, she seems to consider them more as a price she has to pay for an easy and steady job.

Far more rewarding for Yukiko are her contacts with the English-speaking Britons and other 'western' customers, about whom she only has good things to say. Surely one part of this preference is the sense of accomplishment she feels when using English, observing her progress as she communicates in what for her is a foreign language. However, she also sees them as representatives of the cosmopolitan London she has chosen to inhabit to which she affiliates. Indeed, while she professes to embrace the London where 'nobody cares' and people from all over the world can be seen walking the streets, the most authentic Londoner is European and speaks English.

Apart from customers, Yukiko also deals with her co-workers, all of whom are Japanese. In particular, she has spoken at length about Mae and Keiko, two 20-year-old university students, both born in Japan but both raised and educated in London. Yukiko's comments about these two young women are interesting for what they tell us about how they and she are engaging with Japanese-language and English-language subject positions. The two students, not surprisingly, are fully proficient in English and to a certain extent, both seem to take for granted a certain Britishness that comes with growing up in London. However, they both profess to Yukiko that they are not British, but Japanese. Yukiko casts doubt on this claim at several levels. First, she talks about their lack of expertise in Japanese, noting that 'they can't read some difficult Chinese characters' and how they make 'some...grammatical mistakes...like prepositions' (Yukiko, 17/5/2004).

Yukiko concedes that Mae and Keiko know a lot about Japan and contemporary Japanese literature. However, she attributes this knowledge to guidance they would have received from their parents. Perhaps referring to this home guidance, she notes that they have adopted an old-fashioned form of Japanese-ness and cites as an example, the negative way in which they refer to Koreans and Chinese. For Yukiko, their talk is racist, adding that 'they don't know that they sound very racist in today's Japan' (Yukiko, 17/5/2004).

In the end, her comments about these Mae and Keiko boil down to age and positioning *vis-à-vis* Japanese nationality. Yukiko is older and more experienced than these two young women. In addition, she positions herself in opposition to many aspects of Japanese culture and society, while showing a great deal of affiliation to English-language culture. Meanwhile, Mae and Keiko would like to know more about these things, as a way of bringing their expertise in line with their affiliation to Japanese language and culture. In effect, all three women meet up in the 'small Japanese society', but they come to this meeting point from diametrically opposed angles. Yukiko sums up matters as follows:

> For me [it] is getting more uncomfortable in a way because of Japanese mentality, Japanese behaviour. I have to behave Japanese, completely Japanese. But for them, especially Keiko, she mentions like: 'I needed to know I should have learned about Japanese society'... But I mean,... I don't have such a feeling because I think, I am 31 years old and I have had working experience in Japan and my working place, [the] school, and the hairdressing salon are completely different environments. I don't really want to work because I'm not interested in their working environment... and they are quite flexible because, I don't know, because of their age and because they don't have any working experiences. (Yukiko, 17/5/2004)

In common with the other informants in this study, Mie and Yukiko speak English with great confidence. They also position the English language as medium through which they can explore alternative femininities. However, unlike Motoko, Akira and Naomi, they are not bound to Japan in any way: neither has family commitments and neither seems particularly interested in returning to the English teaching jobs they left behind. There is no sense of urgency in either one as regards an eventual return to Japan, although both do recognize that being in their early thirties, they do have to consider their career prospects, which further diminish with each year spent away from Japan. It is perhaps for this reason that both have worked hard to be accepted on doctoral-level courses at London universities. A PhD would give them more options upon an eventual return. Still, unlike Motoko, Akira and Naomi, Mie and Yukiko do not seem to mind being slightly declassed, as regards their social standing, living an altogether more precarious existence in London than they would in Japan. This perhaps is the ultimate proof of their cosmopolitan spirit, developed in early adulthood.

Discussion

The Japanese community in London is the product of a relatively small and privileged migration, made up of middle class and wealthy Japanese citizens from what Spence (2003) calls developed 3C nations. In Faist's (2000) terms (see Chapter 2), it is driven at the macro level by economic and social forces. First, there is the emergence of Japan as a powerhouse in the global economy. The post–world-war boom eventually led to the spreading of Japanese financial institutions and corporations around the world and with this spread the migration of a financial and intellectual elite around the world. Second, the increasing internationalization of Japan, from without and within, has led more and more Japanese people to go abroad, not only as tourists, but also as students and more permanent residents in cities like London. In particular, as Kelsky (2001) notes, many women have left Japan seeking greater independence and opportunity in the so called 'west'.

Such movements have been facilitated by factors at Faist's meso level. On the one hand, there are by now well-established networks, set up by the government corporate Japan from the 1950s onwards, which make movement abroad for Japanese nationals relatively easy. At the receiving end, Japanese nationals are generally welcome, due to their associated high status as well-educated and wealthy individuals. Immigration officials in developed countries do not generally put up too many impediments to this migration, although in countries like Britain, they can be strict about individuals who overstay student visas. In addition, Motoko, Akira and Naomi, Mie and Yukiko all have the requisite social and cultural capital to make the move from Japan to London. All were from middle class (and even wealthy) backgrounds in which education was highly valued and all five had first degrees in English. In addition, Motoko, Akira and Naomi were all extremely proficient in English upon arrival and Mie and Yukiko have improved their English immensely since arriving. The former three, because of their cosmopolitan baggage and the latter two, because of their restless spirits, have had the where-withal to settle into London without too much difficulty.

As regards micro-level issues, these range from professional ambition, the desire for a better standard of living and, more recently, the desire to live new experiences abroad. In particular, for women like Mie and Yukiko, moving to London has been about finding greater opportunity both professionally and personally.

In many ways, Motoko, Akira, Naomi, Mie and Yukiko are what Kelsky (2001) calls 'internationalist women'. The latter is a broad term used by Kelsky to describe the growing number of women in Japan who live their lives with an international dimension and not entirely within the confines of traditional Japanese society. This international dimension can be lived inside Japan; indeed, Naomi in particular is able to satisfy her European tastes in fashion and food with no difficulty what-soever in Tokyo. However, internationalism very often involves leaving Japan and not going back, as seems to be the case with Mie and Yukiko. According to Kelsky, internationalization often leads to, or is associated with, what is known as an *akogare* – idealization or longing – for all things western (often meaning American or English speaking) and a rejection of all things Japanese. Among the five informants discussed here, there are no examples of this extreme form of internationaliza-tion. There are, however, varying degrees of a partial rejection of Japanese culture in four cases. Akira and Naomi claim third place identities as English speakers who have never felt entirely themselves in Japanese, while living in Tokyo. Meanwhile, Mie and Yukiko have effectively voted with their feet as they adopt a transnational subject position in London. They seek to construct themselves more and more as English speakers, but they do not reject outright their Japanese-ness.[6]

As I observed above, Motoko, Akira and Naomi position themselves in London as extremely cosmopolitan and knowing expatriates. By contrast, Mie and Yukiko seem to position themselves far more as transnationals and even immigrants. They effectively eschew the main-tenance of an expatriate identity and both seem motivated towards fitting into London life as much as possible. All of this can be seen in Mie's claims that she speaks little Japanese and that she progressively understands less and less the communication norms of Japanese speakers. It can also be seen in her involvement in different communities of practice associated with work, leisure and study, all of which take place in English. For her part, Yukiko has the intensive contact with Japanese life that comes with her work in the hair salon. However, as I suggested above, she manages to contain this contact, compartmentalizing it as a kind of Japanese transnational capsule embedded in her more important English-medium London life. Far more significant for Yukiko is that part of her life that she lives in English, in particular her studies.

Conclusion

In this chapter, I have discussed the lives of five Japanese graduate students, prior to and during their stays in London. In the context of London as a global city, Motoko, Akira, Naomi, Mie and Yukiko are members of a relatively small subgroup, subsumed under a larger Japanese community. This Japanese community, as I noted above, numbers about 30,000, enough to make it significant but not overly visible in London. Indeed, outside of the boroughs of Barnet and Ealing, the resident Japanese presence is not very notable at all. Still, it is almost completely middle class and wealthy in make up, and this gives it some economic clout. As for future prospects, I noted above how there has been a slight shift as regards the relative weight of private company employees (and their dependents) *vis-à-vis* other groups such as students, with the former going down and the latter going up. The net effect is for the population to stay more or less the same. However, this population is changing from one which is more bound to Japan, via company and government links, to one which is more hybrid and transnational in nature. In this chapter, Mie and Yukiko represent this trend. They started as students, already a non-private company category, and have now moved to something more akin to semi-permanent residents, both working and studying. Above all, they are acting as individual agents carving out new subject positions in London.

6
French Foreign-Language Teachers in London

When I go back to France, I like going back as a visitor. And I'm looking forward to going back and having all my French food and French family and all that routine. But, I just don't manage to get into the routine of all that 'cause I didn't have a very good experience of being independent there. So all my independence comes from living here on my own...

– Chantalle, 3/12/2001

I think that's enough with London. I want London to be a nice place, I used to love London, I no longer love London, so I have to do something...I'll probably come back to see my friends, because I still like the town, but I don't like the life I've got now....

– Nancy, 9/11/2001

I don't know anything about the future because last year, remember, we talked about the future and I still don't know anything about the future.... So, I don't know. I don't know what I'm going to do. Mystery...

– Laure, 11/11/2001

I think all of us have left our country and live here in some way we're a bit lost, aren't we? What do you think?...We don't really know where we are, where we're going, what we want, or we keep changing.

– Lise, 23/11/2001

These quotes are taken from interviews with four French nationals living and working in London as secondary school teachers of French as a foreign language. When these statements were made, all four women had been living in London for several years. The comments range from Chantalle's rejection of a future in France, as she has developed a more fulfilling life in London, to Nancy's forthright and outright expression of having had enough of London. Meanwhile, Laure and Lise capture the uncertainty that comes with living away from France, without knowing whether to stay in London, return to France or go elsewhere. Loving London or wanting to leave, and expressions of uncertainty about the future are two key themes running through the stories told in this chapter. Chantalle, Nancy, Laure and Lise all moved to London to broaden their personal and professional horizons and to do so via the English language. They all ended up enrolling on the same Modern Foreign Languages PGCE (Post Graduate Certificate of Education)[1] course in 1999 and subsequent to their successful completion of this course, they all got jobs in secondary schools in the London area. However, from the beginning, their plans were different and more importantly, their lives unfolded in very different ways once they began working full time.

This chapter is about the London experiences of Chantalle, Nancy, Laure and Lise, seen as members of the growing French community in London. I begin by providing some sociohistorical background in the form of a short history of French migration to Britain and London. I then examine each story in turn, before linking my findings with some of the general migration and identity issues outlined in Chapters 1 and 2.

The history of French migration to Britain and London

The history of French migration to Britain and London can be narrowed down to three major historical events. The first of these was the Norman Conquest of the 1066. The occupation of the French, led by William the Conqueror, imposed a more efficient feudal state on England, but it also allowed for the evolution of the English political system over several centuries. This political legacy contrasts somewhat with the human legacy, which by most estimates was minimal. As Winder (2004) notes, probably no more than 10,000 Normans actually moved to England to live permanently, representing some 1 per cent of the total population at the time. For the most part, these Normans were the support staff for the French administration, an implanted aristocratic layer to rule over the English masses. As Winder puts it, 'they were the *crème de la crème* [and] they arrived as, or became, bishops and barons, grandees and magnates' (Winder, 2004: 25). Over the years, these individuals intermarried with the local aristocrats, leaving behind what today are considered to be grand-sounding surnames such as De Mandeville, Lacy, Montfort, Mortimer and Mowbray (however, as Winder points out, even surnames considered to be more prototypically English, such as Sinclair, Neville, Gascoigne and Venables, are traceable back to French).

Politics and surnames apart, perhaps the most notable legacy of the Norman presence in England is the French influence on the English language itself. English-language historians, such as Baugh and Cable (2002), estimate that a great deal of the current lexical base of English is traceable to French. They cite clusters of vocabulary around government (e.g. state, empire, authority), the Christian church (e.g. sermon, baptism, communion) and food (e.g. dinner, supper, feast, beef, poultry), to say nothing of general vocabulary (e.g. action, calendar, metal). Important as the French influence on the English language has been, however, Winder questions whether the Norman Conquest should be considered the earliest example of French immigration. For Winder, a far clearer candidate is to be found in the Huguenots, who came to Britain after the revocation of the *Édit de Nantes* in 1685.

The *Édit de Nantes* had been issued in 1598 by Henry IV to end religious violence between Catholics and Protestants in France. The edict provided some protection for the Protestant Huguenots, granting them control over certain towns and above all legally respecting their right to practise Protestantism. Under pressure from the Catholic Church, wishing to convert the Huguenots to Catholicism, Louis XIV revoked the edict in 1685. The result was persecution of the Huguenots and what is surely one of the earliest documented examples of asylum seekers migrating en masse.[2] Exact numbers are hard to come by, but historians such as Easton (1970) suggest that perhaps as many as half a million eventually left France as a result of the revocation of the edict. The migrating Huguenots settled in North America, South Africa and countries in Europe where Protestants dominated, such as England, Holland and Prussia. The French economy suffered immensely as the result of this migration as the Huguenots were the primary practitioners of many important industries, such as textiles. As I observed in Chapter 2, the 40,000 Huguenots who settled in Spitalfields in London and the thousands of others who settled elsewhere in Britain are generally seen to have dynamized the English economy, in Winder's words, 'transforming an agricultural economy into an industrial one' (Winder, 2004: 63). Over the centuries, the Huguenots melted into the general population and the French language was lost along the way as well. Their legacy, then, is primarily an economic one, along with a few geographical landmarks such as Fournier Street in the heart of Spitalfields (Glinert, 2003).

The third historical event which led to significant migration of French people to Britain and London occurred more recently, in 1993. I refer here to the Treaty of European Union, also known as the Maastricht treaty, which was ratified that year. The treaty guarantees the free movement of people, goods, services and capital across the geographical borders of EU member states. In migration terms, it means that the citizens of one EU member state can live and work in another EU member state for as long as they choose to do so with no legal requirement that they register their stay. More concretely, it has meant a third wave of French migration to Britain and the most substantial of them all, in real terms.

According to Bernard Gentil (2003), prior to 1991, the number of French nationals living in Britain seemed to have stabilized, remaining within a 30,000–40,000 range: his estimate for 1984 was 34,134 and for 1991, only slightly higher in real terms, at 39,779. However, after the Maastrict treaty came into effect in 1993, French migration to Britain increased considerably and by 2002, the official number of French nationals residing in Britain was 85,823. This is more than a 100 per cent increase in just 11 years, but it is still likely to be a very conservative figure. According to the French Consul General, Louis le Vert, whom I interviewed on 8 November, 2004, a very large proportion of French nationals living and working or studying in Britain do not register with his office. Citing Maastricht as the principal reason, he suggests that official figures should be multiplied, perhaps as much as three times over, in order to obtain more accurate figures. Following this line of reasoning, the French population in Britain would be closer to 250,000. However, writing about the increasing French population in Britain in *The Observer* magazine in early 2005, Lucy Siegle cites an even higher figure. She states that '[t]he number of French nationals moving here is increasing by nine per cent each year and there are now some 300,000 French people living in Britain, predominantly in London, Kent and the Northwest, making Britain the home of the largest French expatriate community in Europe' (Siegle, 2005: 20).

Prior to Maastricht, the patterns of French settlement in Britain were similar to those documented for Japan (see Chapter 5). Thus in 1984, a large proportion of the 34, 134 French nationals in Britain were members of families headed by the holders of well-paying jobs with French and multinational companies. In addition, there would have been a substantial number of official posts, such as those related to government agencies. The French student population in Britain would have been proportionately smaller than the Japanese one, but this would have been made up by a large number of French nationals working in their own businesses, covering a variety of service sectors, such as the food trade (restaurants, wine merchants, grocers), fashion and clothing.

According to French Consulate figures, as of December 2003, the number of registered French nationals in London stood at 37,309. The biggest concentration of registered residents is to be found in middle class to wealthy areas of west and southwest London, such as Bayswater, Chelsea, Hammersmith, Fulham, Battersea, Kensington, South Kensington, Knightsbridge, Westminster and Chiswick. Indeed, the West (W) and Southwest (SW) postcodes alone account for 20,028 people, that is over half of the total number of French nationals. Typically, these residents are in family units with one or both parents earning high salaries with the traditional French and multinational business establishments in London. However, according to the Consul General, they progressively represent a smaller proportion of the total number of French nationals living in London.

The most notable new group of French migrants are as wealthy, if not more so, than the previously cited family heads in West and Southwest London. Over the past decade and half, there has been massive influx of highly qualified financial and IT specialists who find that they can make far more money in the City and Docklands areas of London than they can in France or anywhere else in the EU. Frequently graduates of France's *Grandes Ecoles*, these migrants tend to be young (25–35) single adults who in some cases live in London for a short period of time (several months), although many stay with no established exit date. As the Maastricht treaty means that there is no need for them to formalize their residence in London and that they are free to work anywhere they like, these individuals often do not bother to register with the French Consulate. The Consul General estimates that there are at least 20,000 French nationals who fall into this category living in London at present.

A second new group of French nationals in London is composed of individuals at the opposite end of the job market, from the highflying City and Docklands workers. The Consul General sees as perhaps the fastest growing group of French migrants those who come to London because they cannot find a job in Paris or any number of other large cities in France. These individuals generally have few if any qualifications and they can be found working in a variety of services, although waiting tables and working in retail seem to be the most common types of employment. Whereas the City and Docklands workers clearly profit from their residence in London, both financially and in terms of job experience, the low-level service providers are in a sense treading water, living in London until something better comes up either in London or back home in France.

The third group of French nationals is young adults. They work in the low-level services cited above, professional sectors, such as teaching, and as small business operators. They are generally university educated and they have chosen to live in London for an indefinite period of time so that they can improve their English, make some money and have a good time. This group of migrants, which is also growing at a rapid pace, is represented by the four cases to be examined in this chapter. As I will explain in a moment, Laure, Nancy, Lise and Chantale all had undergraduate degrees in English philology from French universities and all four had an interest in English language and English-language cultures. Most importantly, all four had decided to move to and live in London whilst waiting to see what they would do with the rest of their lives.

Meeting the French migrants

The story of my contact with Lise, Nancy, Laure and Chantalle begins in 1998, when I began to notice an increase in the number of articles published in the educational press in Britain about persistent teacher shortages in several subject areas in British secondary school education. Coming from a language teaching background, I was particularly interested in the shortage of teachers in the area of foreign languages. I noted that whereas shortages in subject areas such as Maths and Sciences had led to active recruitment in countries such as Australia, New Zealand, Canada, Barbados and South Africa, the shortage of foreign-language teachers was being resolved in an altogether more ad hoc manner: each year PGCE programmes were receiving an increasing number and proportion of application forms from foreign nationals, in particular French, German and Spanish nationals who had decided to take advantage of the opening of borders within the EU to take up residence in Britain. Published research such as Whitehead and Taylor (1998) and Adams (2000) confirmed this trend, pointing to the fact that by the late 1990s it was not at all uncommon on PGCE courses in London for over 40 per cent of the candidates to be foreign nationals, with a large proportion of these being from France, Spain and Germany.

Initially interested in exploring how these foreign nationals adapted to the educational system in Britain, in autumn 1999, I began a study in which I conducted periodic face-to-face interviews with French, German and Spanish nationals on the PGCE course for Modern Foreign Language teachers, run by the Institute of Education, University of London. After beginning with a cohort of 16 teachers, I ended the first year of this study with four French nationals, three German nationals and two Spanish nationals as participants. I maintained contact with these nine individuals over the next two and a quarter academic years, from September 2000 to November 2002, conducting a total of seven in-depth interviews with each. However, with this continued contact came a slow shift in focus away from these participants' development as teachers to how they lived their lives in London.

In Block (2001), I discussed the experiences of nine teachers, as they attended the aforementioned PGCE course. I charted their ambivalence as they moved among subject positions of national identity ranging from integrationist, where they manifested a preference for not being positioned as foreigners, to nationalistic, where they clearly invoked their national educational culture as a template when talking about British practices. In interviews conducted during this year, the teaching of grammar came up again and again, becoming a metaphor for academic rigour. To varying degrees, all of the teachers decried the lack of language awareness among British students.

Block (2005) picked up the story where Block (2001) left off, focusing on informants' post-PGCE experiences as NQTs (Newly Qualified Teachers). This time, however, I narrowed my coverage to the four French informants, Lise, Nancy, Laure and Chantalle, examining their talk about their dealings with students, parents and school staff and the differences between French education and British education that they continued to encounter. In particular, I focused on two aspects of their teaching experiences: (1) the National Curriculum as an idealized discourse of language education in England and Wales; and (2) the concept of student-centeredness in British education. In both cases, I matched Lise, Nancy, Laure and Chantalle's comments in interviews with the findings of research comparing official discourses of education in British and French (e.g. Broadfoot and Osborn, 1993; Alexander, 1996; Broadfoot *et al.*, 2000). I also explored the extent to which these teachers were expatriates, living as French people in London for a limited period of time, or immigrants, intending to stay perhaps for the rest of their lives.

It is this latter issue that came to prominence as the study proceeded. In effect, the more contact I had with these individuals, the more we talked about their personal lives. This evolution as regards the focus of interviews occurred in a very natural way, and it occurred without marginalizing talk about their professional development. Still, in interviews taking place from 2001 onwards, we often talked more about life in London than educational issues. In this chapter, my aim is to focus on the different subject positions these four individuals adopted when talking about their personal lives in interviews conducted over the period of over three years. In the sections that follow, I will recount the life stories of these four women in an attempt to provide glimpses of how they 'do being' a French person in London.

Lise: The restless one

Born in 1975, Lise grew up in a prosperous area of Paris. Both her parents worked in banking and she had a comfortable upbringing. She recalls that from an early age she showed a keen interest in languages and people from other countries:

> Looking back to the past, I've always been very very curious about what was going on abroad and I was very very keen on languages, on travelling...I remember asking questions about the language...and I remember wondering in my mind...why do foreign people speak another language if they have to translate it in their mind in French, anyway? I just couldn't work out the fact that there could be other languages...(Lise, 20/9/2000)

Lise also claimed to be different from most of the people she grew up with. While they have tended to stay in Paris, studying, establishing stable personal and professional lives, she has always wanted to travel. And, she has not found it difficult to uproot and leave her neighbourhood, city and country behind. Indeed, restlessness and a peripatetic lifestyle have characterized her life as a young adult. She explains how she is different from her childhood friends as follows:

> I think I am quite different when I talk with them, when I go back there...I'm just thinking, I wouldn't like to lead their lives...and I'm sure they wouldn't like to live my life. I'm sure they think I'm a bit crazy, being here, trying to teach French to English boys, young English boys...so I think I'm different, yeah. (Lise, 20/9/2000)

Lise recalls that one early influence in her life was a Canadian teacher of English she encountered when she was 12. This teacher showed her that leaving one's home country to live elsewhere is an option for young adults. More importantly, she inspired Lise to want to be a French teacher when she grew up. In recent years, Norton (2001), Kinginger (2004) and Piller and Takahashi (2005) have written about how language learners sometimes hold well-developed romantic or 'imagined' views about the cultures and speakers associated with languages they study. In Lise's case, this imagination covered several domains: all languages other than French, all things foreign and the dream of being a French teacher abroad. In a sense, all three domains came together in a grand romantic image that Lise followed when she moved to London just after finishing her undergraduate degree in English language.

Lise admits that at this time she was following a dream, qualifying herself as both idealistic and unrealistic. She lived a somewhat precarious existence in London, renting a room in a student residence and working in a fish and chips shop on Oxford Street. She recalls that she met a lot of people while working and was enjoying just living in London. However, after eight months, in August 1997, she went back to France.

Over the next 10 months, the pace of Lise's life picked up even more. She went back to London, but could not find a job. She went back to Paris, worked for a few months, but then decided to enrol on an MA course called 'Education and America'. This course had an exchange programme in New York and Lise took up this option in January 1998. However, once in New York, she decided to drop out of the course. She got a job in a French restaurant, but after four months, in May 1998, she moved back to Paris. She sums up this time in her life as follows:

> I was discovering, extremely enthusiastic. I decided to stop my Masters because I wanted to travel, meet people...that was a time when I was experiencing, achieving what I'd always wanted to do. You know you always think, oh yeah, you're an adolescent, then you get 20 years old, and you know people who went anywhere in the world, travelled and worked...And you always think, why not me? I can do that as well. So that was my first step. (Lise, 19/6/2001)

By the summer of 1998, Lise was back in London again, but this time she was thinking about more stable and better-paid employment. She recalls an all-important conversation which made her think for the first time about becoming a French teacher in London:

> I remember being in the summer of '98 in Wood Green [an area in North London], thinking, 'What am I going to do?' I went to the career advisor in the library of Wood Green. And she looked...I said,

'Can I do PGCE with a French *licence*?' And she looked and said, 'Well, yeah, apparently'. (Lise, 19/6/2001)

The PGCE course lasted for one year, during which time Lise learned about teaching in Britain. As I note elsewhere (Block, 2001), the biggest struggle during this time was learning about those aspects of British education that made it different from French education. Like the other three French informants in this study, Lise struggled with her students' lack of metalinguistic knowledge and she found anathema the notion of 'student-centeredness', which pervaded the National Curriculum. During this time, Lise dreamed of nothing more than getting out from under the PGCE course and having her own classes in a school:

I know that at the end of the PGCE, I was looking forward to being a real teacher, not being a student teacher . . . really excited about starting in this school, being a proper teacher and everything. (Lise, 20/3/2001)

At the end of her PGCE year, she managed to get a job at an academically achieving boys school in South London. However, two-thirds of the way through her first year of full time teaching, she was already having doubts:

I have reached a stage where I'm getting a bit bored. It's like in the last year, I've learnt so much. It's really hard and really challenging and now it's like when I teach, I'm a teacher now. . . . I want to do something else. In the last two months I've been thinking of so many things. I've been thinking of going back to study . . . changing [schools] or quitting at the end of this year and getting a job in London. Every week I change my mind. (Lise, 20/3/2001)

Lise soon after decided not to abandon teaching; however, her comment points once again to her restlessness.

One of the recurrent themes in our contacts was whether or not Lise saw herself as an expatriate French national living in London or something more akin to an immigrant, with plans to stay indefinitely. In one interview, I showed her a scale with the term 'expatriate' at one extreme and the term 'immigrant' at the other. I asked her which settlement option was nearest to how she lived her life in London.[3] She responded as follows:

I have lived here as an expatriate (pointing at the expatriate end of the scale). I would definitely be on that side. How far? I don't know.

Probably not too far, not too high, shall I say. Not too high, but definitely on that side. (Lise, 23/11/2001)

Still, she admitted that the years she had spent in London had had their effect, most notably in some of her behaviour and in her English-influenced French. Lise explained how when she went back to Paris, her friends and family noticed such changes:

> The fact that I drink beer now.... I've heard a few times, they say: 'Oh, look at how now she drinks beer.' Because before coming to England, I never drank beer. And in the language as well, my mum, every now and again says that, you know: 'Look at the *anglaise*... there's some expression sometimes that she can't say in French'. But I say: 'No, no, I'm very French'. (Lise, 23/11/2001)

Being 'very French' was related to the fact that most of her friends in London were French and that she maintained a 'French style of life'. She clarified what she meant by this French lifestyle with a description of her food and drink shopping and consuming practices:

> When I go shopping...I have a different...trolley to the people. I have a FRENCH trolley (laughing) I don't have any of these big drinks, weird colour drinks or this big burger bread and stuff...there's the way of cooking and the 'aperitif' that I still do every time when I have a friend at home. I drink wine very often...So I've got this typical French culture thing [but] it is mainly in food...(Lise, 23/11/2001)

As Paul du Gay notes, 'commodities...have importance as signs and symbols' that is 'they have "identity value" and not simply or primarily "use value"' (du Gay, 1996: 82). Here Lise tells us about who she is by telling us that she has a 'French trolley' as opposed to an English one, which I presume would have 'weird colour drinks' and 'big burger bread'. She also extends her shopping habits to her cooking and eating habits, citing the 'aperitif' and the drinking of wine as quintessentially French, and presumably, not an English custom. Thus, there is a semiotics of food consumption, involving what is bought and how it is consumed, that Lise invokes here to position herself as French. However, as I observed above, Lise also drinks beer, considered by her friends in France to be an English consumer identity marker. There is, therefore, a degree of ambivalence *vis-à-vis* English habits of consumption in Lise's comments: on the one hand, she rejects them; on the other hand, she embraces some of them. This ambivalence extends to how she feels when making her periodic trips to Paris, as she reported missing London when visiting Paris:

> But it's bizarre because when I was in Paris I was thinking of London but I am not in London and I was actually glad to get on the Eurostar on Sunday night and come back here. I was thinking that was really bizarre. One thing is it's always looking like that because I do like England and I like London and I'm not going to be here anymore.... I just feel like there will be a time in my life when I will want to go back and it will be hard anyway so I may as well do it now. (Lise, 10/4/2002)

In this comment, there is a sense that Lise is forcing her move from London on herself, as part of some kind of imperative that has governed her life, namely that she cannot stay in one place for too long. On one occasion, I asked her directly about her restless nature:

> *DB*: What if you're the sort of person who every three or four years you have to be adventurous?
> *L*: I will do it.
> *DB*: But it could mean going to another place.
> *L*: I know, I know.
> *DB*: Like New York.
> *L*: Yeah, I'll probably go back to New York. The thing is I would like to go away and far way, only if I knew it was for a year or two years. You know, if you know it is – you know for one year or two years. There's a limit. I wouldn't do like I've done here again.... Living a life and you don't know when – you have to take the decision really: Right. That's it. I have to stop this life here and leave. (Lise, 23/11/2001)

From autumn 2000, when she became a full-time teacher, leaving London was always a topic of conversation when we met for interviews. In a way, I began to think that Lise would never leave, that she would be, as she once told me, like a friend of hers who always says she cannot stand living in London, but remains nonetheless. Indeed, by the time of our last interview, in late October 2002, she still had not found her much-coveted job in an international school. However, in December 2003 I received an e-mail from Lise. In it, she explained that since October 2003, she had been living in Kenya, where she had found a job in an international school. At last, Lise the restless itinerant had escaped from London.

Nancy: Always leaving London

Like Lise, Nancy is also a great traveller, although she neither began her travels so young nor made as many moves back and forth as Lise did in such a short period of time. Nancy was born in Marseilles in 1967. Her father had immigrated with his Spanish parents to France as a child and this meant that Nancy had some exposure to Spanish as well as French as a child. Always interested in languages and speaking to people from other countries, she studied English at university, completing both BA and MA level courses. Unlike the other informants in this study, Nancy worked as an English teacher for three years in France before coming to live in London in 1997. This work experience was supply teaching, a source of income while she prepared for the CAPES (*Certificat Pédagogique pour l'Enseignement Secondaire*) exam.[4] After three years of teaching and studying, Nancy sat and failed the exam. At this point, she decided that she needed to improve her English. With no interesting professional prospects to keep her in Marseilles, she decided to spend two years in London to do just this, while studying for a second attempt at passing the CAPES. She worked for two years as an *assistant* in a private girls school for two years, and found little time to study. When asked about this two-year period of her life, she responded in the following way:

> It was great, it was great, I mean . . . it was new, I had the opportunity to meet plenty of foreign people, English people, American, Australian, it was great. . . . First of all, at school there were Spanish people and stuff like that. Afterwards, I went to a meeting where I was supposed to meet other assistants coming from all over the world. . . . And I don't know but after a fortnight I had so many 'friends', not *amis* as we call them in French, but [acquaintances] . . . (Nancy, 26/6/2001)

At the end of these two years, Nancy went back to France to sit the CAPES exam, which, unfortunately, she failed again. Her first reaction to this disappointment was to try to remain in London, but to upgrade her professional status from *assistant* to full-time teacher. However, despite her best attempts, she was not able to secure a good full-time job as French teacher; not sure what to do, she returned to Marseilles in the summer of 1999. She recalls that she spent this summer, which she terms 'awful', searching Marseilles for any job that she could find. However, she was considered over-qualified for many jobs and under-qualified for others, and the end result was that as the end of summer neared she was unemployed and beginning to feel very depressed. At this point, an English friend recommended the PGCE. Although Nancy had her doubts about a year-long course, fearing that she did not have the endurance necessary to complete it, she decided to give it a try. She moved to London again.

Two years later, Nancy told me that in some ways she wished that she had never made this move. She said that if she had stayed in Marseilles, her opinion of London would have been favourable, based on the fun period of 1997–99. Whereas during this period she only had positive experiences, now she was dealing with London as a place to both live and work. When I asked her about the phenomenon of loving a city, when it is a place of play, and hating it, when it becomes a place of work, she talked about how her first stay was marked by a certain period of euphoria and the feeling that everything was better in Britain than in France. However, with the second experience, she believes that she has become more nationalistic. She explains:

> The worst thing is that when I was here [the first time] I kept criticis-ing France and the system and I thought it was not fair and now I just can't stand when people are criticising French people and France, even if it's true... Yesterday somebody said like...'Oh, French people are like that...' and I said, 'Why do you generalize? Why don't you say that the French person I met is like that?' I'm quite defensive – I think it's because, you know, it's as if I was in front of the mirror. (Nancy, 26/6/2001)

Still, after more than four years in London, she admitted to having the same sensitivity about what she perceived as casual criticisms of Britain. In particular, she valued her life in London for what it has allowed her to do professionally. Nancy thus seemed to live a dual existence, her life a variation on Ong's (1999) 'flexible citizenship' discussed in Chapter 2. Flexible citizenship refers to the way that progressively more individuals with the requisite social, cultural and economic capital are making choices about where to situate their various work and leisure activities. In Nancy's case, this flexible citizenship meant that she lived in London because she worked there, but that she would prefer to live in Marseilles. She summed up her quandary by telling me the story of a French acquaintance, who at the time, had been living in London for 13 years:

> He's still complaining. He's always complaining. . . . Every time I meet French people who are teaching, they are complaining, they are frustrated people. So I think we are frustrated people living in another country. We keep criticising England, but we are bitter about France, because they didn't do anything for us. (Nancy, 26/6/2001)

Recognition of this good side of England has even led her to defend her adopted home on occasion, as she explains:

> I couldn't believe it, but the other day I was telling somebody – I was saying like 'I feel loyal to English people – to England. . . . At least I have the opportunity to do the PGCE'. And I had it, I didn't have to struggle like this bloody CAPES. . . . At least you know where you are going. If you follow your aim, you've got it. (Nancy, 26/6/2001)

However, when asked exactly why she did not like living in London, beyond her professional life, she replied:

> It's more a question of culture, probably, the reason why I don't want to stay here. Because probably like another French, I am really attached to my background, to my traditions, and more and more miss it. And the other day I was talking to a friend of mine – she's 50 . . . she's been living here for 30 years. And well, she keeps complaining . . . and for the first time I met her daughter and her daughter called her 'mum' instead of 'maman' . . . and it really shocked me. I don't know, perhaps you won't understand, but I think for me 'maman' is a magic word, whereas 'mum', it doesn't mean anything to me. (Nancy, 26/6/2001)

In this reference to the French form of address 'maman', Nancy invokes a highly essentialized model of core French national/cultural identity, which is tied to the French language. According to this model, one is socialized into French language and culture from birth and this becomes what Nancy calls her 'background'. However, she also allows that this French culture is not invulnerable and can be lost, as the story of her friend illustrates. Thus, one motive for leaving London would be to avoid being like her friend, with a daughter for whom French is an inheritance, but not the primary language of expertise and affiliation (Leung, Harris and Rampton, 1997).

Not surprisingly, when asked, Nancy positions herself very firmly as a French expatriate. Most of her friends are either French or foreigners, and this no doubt adds to her sense of not living an English life. Still, she holds steadfastly to the notion that she must conserve her French identity:

> I've got an idea about the culture, which I respect and about the tradition. It's just because I don't want to lose my identity. I'm not 'one of them', so why should I pretend that I am? (Nancy, 9/11/2001)

In an interview conducted at the end of her fifth year in London, Nancy told me that she could not imagine living in London beyond January 2003. However, when I next saw her in late October 2002, she was well into another year of teaching. When I mentioned her previous vow to be out of London by January 2003, she explained that she had not been able to find work anywhere in France or indeed countries further afield, such as Spain and Australia. Interestingly, by this time, Nancy had expanded the number of options she had to living in London, and talk of leaving the city generally included references to work in international schools in a variety of world locations.

In the midst of this resolve to leave London, Nancy had nevertheless found another advantage to living there: it is a city from which it is easy to travel, both inside and outside Britain. She explained her state of mind as follows:

> I'm still in London but I enjoy it and I think I take the most of it. I went to Cornwall thanks to the job I've got. I went to Thailand last September, last holidays. I'm going to Egypt. For Christmas. I just take the most of it. I know that I have to be patient little bit more. (Nancy, 28/10/2002)

She had therefore expanded her 'flexible citizenship' discussed above. Living in London was not only a work base, two hours from Marseilles, where she would prefer to live, but it also was a good place from which she could organize journeys to all corners of the world. As if to sum up her philosophy of life, she added:

> I think it's just being curious about the world. The world moves and I want to know everything. Yesterday there was something on television about the Sahara and I was thinking 'oh, I must go there'. (Nancy, 28/10/2002)

More than two years later, I caught up with Nancy. She was still working in the same school and seemed more integrated into its structure. She had set up a French-medium drama club, and more importantly, she had begun to work with a group of children with special education needs. She found the latter experience not only rewarding but also interesting from a professional point of view. In addition, because she was considered a 'key worker' by the school, she was provided a room in a flat near the school, for which she was paying rent at half the market rate. Her life through the school, therefore, had evolved into something both more interesting and comfortable. Most importantly, she now had more disposable income with which she could continue to satisfy her 'curiosity about the world'. Indeed, she had even been to Kenya to visit Lise.

Nancy shares with Lise both a strong self-image as French and a restless spirit that prevents her from staying in one place for too long. She is also like Lise in that she sees herself as different from people she grew up with and members of her family. Indeed, in the interview taking place in October 2002, she went into great detail comparing her globetrotting existence with that of her brother, who hardly ever leaves his neighbourhood in Marseilles. However, she seems unlike Lise in the way that she channels her desire to leave: while Lise took the first job she could find that allowed her to leave London, Nancy has been far more selective, turning down at least two offers she has had from schools abroad. It seems, then, that she continues in her resolve to leave London, but that she will do so only when the opportunity is right.

Laure: The indecisive

Laure was born in Annecy, in Southeast France, near the Swiss border and the city of Geneva. She was raised in a solidly middle-class family, in which the study of languages was highly valued. Like Lise and Nancy, she had always been fascinated with languages and once she started to study English in school at the age of 11, it became 'like a passion', as she put it. Echoing Norton's (2001) and Kinginger's (2004) discussions of imagined belonging in foreign language social networks, she explained her early interest in English language and culture, and how her dreams were fulfilled when she moved to London in 1997, as follows:

> I had always in mind that one day I would live in England, especially in London . . . because I was really really in love with the country and

I wanted to live there. And then when I got the opportunity I decided to come. (Laure, 8/12/2000)

Prior to her arrival in London, she did an undergraduate degree in English in nearby Lyon and then later enrolled for an MA in Economics at the Sorbonne in Paris. It was while doing the latter course that she came to London with her boyfriend in early 1997. From 1997 to 1999, she did research and wrote her MA report on the National Health Service. She also taught French in a secondary school in South Kensington at this time. As regards her first two years in London, she said the following:

It was great in fact. Everything was new.... Everything was different and in fact, it was like...I was where I wanted to be because when I started English I think that I thought about coming to London. English was like a passion back when I started it.... And in fact, yes, I thought that I was where I wanted to be. So I was with my boyfriend, which was great...Then I started working in a school. Then I did my PGCE.... (Laure, 28/6/2001)

At the end of the PGCE course, Laure found a job in an academically average comprehensive school in suburban Northwest London. From the beginning, she was not comfortable in this school. First, there was a strong xenophobic discourse among students (and in some cases, even parents) in the school, which arose, above all, in French and German classes. It is worth mentioning at this point that all four informants in this study had to deal with such anti-French and anti-German sentiments at one time or another. However, Laure reported far more such incidents than Lise, Nancy and Chantalle put together. In addition, the school's language department was never well organized or run, and she did not seem to get along with her colleagues, as Lise, Nancy and Chantalle seemed to do for the most part. The school's shortcomings were evident to Laure in her first few weeks on the job and the combination of these shortcomings with the break-up of her relationship with her boyfriend, made her seriously consider going back to live in France. However, she did not want to leave London and ultimately her indecisiveness meant that she never really made a serious attempt to go back to France. As for what such a move would have meant, Laure was not sure, as the following comment illustrates:

I've still got my friends and I'm very happy to see them when I go back.... But, in fact, I was not sure, in fact, if I could live in Annecy again, in a small town.... I really don't know. Sometimes, I really would like to go back... buy a flat, to have the life I had before... and sometimes, I'm just walking on the streets of London and I'm saying to myself that I would like to stay because... there are so many things to do.... But at the same time, it's really difficult to buy something here.... So, in fact, I have the feeling to sit between two chairs. I don't know, I don't know what to do. (Laure, 28/6/2001)

The metaphor of 'sitting between two chairs' captures very well the ambivalence emerging in Laure's ongoing account of her experiences over more than three years of contacts. While Lise and Nancy made very clear on many occasions that they considered themselves to be irremediably French and therefore overtly antagonistic towards what they saw as 'English culture', Laure's attitude was far more nuanced. Yet, she professed to being 'very French' and when asked if she saw herself more as an expatriate or as an immigrant, she emphatically claimed expatriate status. In addition, she could be very contemptuous of all things she considered to be typically English, criticising the binge drinking culture and even ridiculing the disciplined manner in which English people queued (she said that in many such cases, French people would be fighting with each other!).

However, beyond her French nationalism and her contempt for what she considered to be eccentric and unattractive English behaviour, there was a love of London as a city in which she wanted to live. Thus, she could make the most scathing comments about 'English people', but then go on to say, almost in the same breath, that she would find it very difficult to leave London. In a sense, it is almost as if she would like to live in London, but without the English people. Indeed, Laure confessed to me that she had no English friends. She said that she had Spanish, German and Chinese friends, but that with English people she found it difficult to find common points of interest. The following exchange makes this point. Laure describes an evening with a Spanish woman she met while doing the PGCE, who speaks French fluently:

L: ... Yes, we have exactly the same point of view. So, I suppose it is a reason why and maybe because... because it's good to talk French... because we've got the same values, because... we can share a bottle of wine with a good meal, things like that...

DB: You can't find any English people to do that?

L: ... Not really, because it's not the same value in fact... because they would drink in order to drink... (Laure, 2/4/2001)

When I asked her what 'drink in order to drink' actually meant in practice, she explained how when she was with her boyfriend, they would go to the pub with his colleagues, most of whom were English:

> We would go to the pub to meet his colleagues, but it was only because we had to.... I can remember that ... it's like after two glasses of beer, two pints, it's enough for me.... And they are drinking, drinking, drinking all the time. And I think that's a really strange attitude. You stop at one point.... If they are not drunk, they are not happy ... in fact, it's not, I have the feeling that it's not to socialize, it is to become drunk ... In fact, if they could drink on their own, in fact, it wouldn't matter. It's just for drinking. (Laure, 2/4/2001)

In this case, drinking beer 'in order to drink' is contrasted with the un-English habit of drinking wine with a good meal. Laure clearly positions herself as un-English. Still, despite marking herself clearly as French, Laure admitted that living in London was having an effect on how she viewed communication norms and practices in France. She explained an example of how she had changed as follows:

> And sometimes, I say to myself, 'Oh, my God, she's so rude!' ... And, in fact, it's because ... I'm used to the English way of talking ... And sometimes when I go back to France ... in the supermarkets, for example, I say to myself, 'Oh, my God, but they are so rude!' ... 'cause they never say 'sorry' etc.... (Laure, 2/4/2001)

However, it was not only to English indirectness that she was beginning to affiliate; it was also the English language itself. As she used English extensively on the job and in other communities of practice to which she could claim membership (the expectation being her social life with French speakers), she found that English had become her default language. In the following excerpt, she explains how she has even used English when in France:

> It's very strange when I go back to France sometimes I speak English ... but in fact I'm not thinking. But in a shop it happened to me. So in fact the sales assistant looked at me as if I was crazy. Yeah, sometimes just in English I'm thinking in English. Sometimes I'm trying to find the words in French. (Laure, 30/10/2002)

The latter quote is from the last full-length interview I conducted with Laure in October 2002. In the same interview, I asked the same question

I always asked of the four participants in this study: How long will you stay in London? Taking stock of her by-then almost six years in London, she commented wryly about her future:

> Every year I say 'oh, yeah, I will go back' and I'm still here. So maybe I will stay all my life. I don't know. [You might] yeah, I will be seventy years old and I will still talk to you and I will say 'Oh, I don't know if I go back next year.' (laughing) (Laure, 30/10/2002)

Laure eventually left the school where she had not been happy, taking a job in a secondary school in West London. At the time of writing, she continues to work in this school and still has not left London. Her prophecy in the quote above – 'So maybe I will stay all my life' – may therefore come true in the end.

Chantalle: The Anglophile

Chantalle was born in Bordeaux, in Southern France in 1973. Like Lise, Nancy and Laure, she was fascinated will all things foreign from an early age and this fascination with the foreign was most notable in her love affair with the English language. However, unlike her three compatriots, she never really felt particularly attached to the place where she grew up. In addition, she was the only informant to express a sense of rejection of France and even the French language, through which she experienced a relative lack of success in her school subjects. She explains how she associated French with failure and English with success as follows:

> You know in a way I think I've always associated the English language with success because it was MY subject, my favourite subject...That was my strongest point because everything else was average or below average....So everything in French is a bit associated to failure... and anything associated with English is success. (Chantalle, 26/4/2002)

Chantalle's success in her English classes led to such a strong affiliation to this language that she sought opportunities to develop her expertise whenever and wherever she could find them. In this sense, a nascent expertise led to a growing affiliation to English. Like the other three informants, she recalls always imagining herself in conversations with foreigners, speaking English, and at an early age, she acted on this imagined belonging to an English-speaking world. First, at the age of 14, she went on a three-week exchange to Bristol. Later, at the age of 16, she recalls that she went so far as to seek English language contact with Bordeaux football players who spoke English:

> And my way – where I could speak English was going there, seeing the football players training, and seeing Clive Allen, seeing Jasper Olson, and talking to them in English. What I did one day, because I wanted more English conversation, I said to one of them, I said to Wim Kift, I said my school is asking about professions and it's in English and would you mind if I recorded you? So, you know, language was driving me to do things like that. (Chantalle, 26/4/2002)

At the age of 18, she returned to Britain, this time to work as an *au pair* in Essex for one month. After that she began her BA in English, but she was always trying to find ways to get away from Bordeaux, or, when that was not possible, to spend time with English-speaking foreigners:

> And every summer I came back because I wanted to speak English and when I was at university, then doing English, I didn't like the atmosphere because I was just with French people. To me, they were boring because they had their little routine, you know.... So I was hanging around with the American students who were coming for, you know, study exchanges. (Chantalle, 26/4/2002)

By the time she was 21, she had an English boyfriend who lived in London. She recalls a difficult year of travelling back and forth between England and France so that they would be together. Tired of travelling, she decided to move to London and after applying to some 40 independent schools for the post of *assistant*, she finally got a job. In September 1996, she moved to London to take up a post at a highflying secondary school in South London. She describes the experience as follows:

> It was like discovering a capital, which was very exciting because it was different from Bordeaux, and this is what I expected. And lots of different cultural things to see, lots of people to meet... and funnily enough, lots of French people, sharing my experience with them abroad... as opposed to in France... (Chantalle, 11/6/2001)

In the cases of Lise, Nancy and Laure, the initial period in London was also lived with great euphoria. However, none of them saw their experiences at the time or even later as permanent in any way. Chantalle, by contrast, maintains that she knew very early on that she would stay in London and not go back to France, as the following excerpt illustrates:

> I never thought of leaving, I never ever thought of leaving, honestly... (putting on a dopey voice) 'I mean right, that's it, I'm going back to Bordeaux'. Never ever thought of that...cause I knew how my life was there. I was bored, I was living with my parents, I didn't have a car, I didn't have any money, was completely dependent on everyone. So when I left, it was just like free as a bird, and on my own... (Chantalle, 11/6/2001)

One thing that characterized her life during this period was moving from place to place. In just three years, she lived in Shepherd's Bush (1996), Dulwich (1997), Streatham (1998) and Brockley (1999). In between, her relationship with her boyfriend ended, although she soon met and began going out with the man she was to eventually marry in 2005. Importantly, in 1999, she began the PGCE course.

Chantalle experienced the PGCE course and the associated educational culture shock in much the same way as the other three informants. As I note elsewhere (Block, 2001, 2005), she could be just as critical as the others when it came to her students' lack of metalinguistic knowledge or child centeredness as a central plank of the National Curriculum. However, Chantalle distinguished herself from her compatriots by her willingness to compromise much more and accept the educational system and norms within which she was working. Thus, her complaints were by far overshadowed by her talk about how she might improve this or that aspect of her teaching. Upon completion of the PGCE course, Chantalle got a job in an academically achieving mixed secondary school in North London. During her first year of teaching, I recall that she agonized over her job far more than Lise, Nancy or Laure. By her own accounts, she certainly was working longer hours than they were. However, after one year on the job, she seemed to be moving towards a kind of equilibrium as regards her professional life. In the following quote, she talks about her professional and personal life simultaneously, and how she was developing a new identity:

> I think I'm just taking shape in a sort of English mode. I will always be French and I will always be a pain in terms of like being quite hands expressive and you know, waiting everything to be right... and you know, taking everything seriously...but I think I'm

going into the mode of adapting myself here and how it works...
(Chantalle, 11/6/2001)

As for her links with France and French culture, she said the following:

When I go back to France, I like going back as visitor. And I'm looking
forward to going back and having all my French food and French
family and all that routine. But, I just don't manage to get into the
routine of all that 'cause I didn't have a very good experience of
being independent there. So all my independence comes from living
here on my own and having nothing to do with people, to rely on or
whatever, really. (Chantalle, 3/12/2001)

As regards the expression of alienation towards the home culture,
Chantalle's accounts of her return visits to France sound very similar to
Mie's and Yukiko's accounts of their return visits to Japan. At the same
time, they contrast markedly with those provided by Lise, Nancy and
Laure in their interviews. Indeed, while they always could see themselves returning home to live (especially Nancy), Chantalle presented
her stays in Bordeaux as hard work. Part of this rejection of where she
came from is related to how she sees her childhood friends' lives. While
she always makes a point of meeting up with them, she nonetheless
erects a wall of sorts between their lives and hers, as the following
comment illustrates:

They're still stuck in their studies...all of them...hard to find a
job...sort of like delaying the professional life because we don't really
have that much support...because in France it's all about diplomas
and getting trained in specific areas...(Chantalle, 3/12/2001)

Ultimately, it this lack of professional opportunity, along with a dose of
restlessness, a need to be independent and a love of English language
that has led Chantalle to give up on France as a future home. She sums
up matters as follows:

When I was in France I'd never got as many opportunities as I have
had here...when I left university in France I was bored, you
know...I had no, you know, individual life I was living with my
parents. I didn't have a car I was just hanging around with the
foreigners I was bored I don't know it was not challenging enough.
And then I came here and then I worked in an amazing school you

know very traditional inside whatever however you know there's always disadvantages and advantages and whatever but that was fantastic and I would never ever have worked like that in France, never. (Chantalle, 4/11/2002)

Chantalle has many of the trappings of a classic immigrant, in particular as regards her desire to stay in her adopted country. However, like the more expatriate Lise, Nancy and Laure, she does not have a large number of English friends. She explains this situation as follows:

All the friends I have, ironically, are French. I've got one very good English friend, but apart from her, I don't really have that many English friends. And if I have English friends, it's through my boyfriend.... (Chantalle, 4/11/2002)

I caught up with Chantalle over two years after this interview, in January 2005. She had changed schools and was working in Southeast London, near where she was living with her boyfriend. Two major changes in her life were on the horizon. First, she was scheduled to move to Hong Kong with her boyfriend, who had been posted there by his company, in March 2005. Second, soon after arriving in Hong Kong, she and her boyfriend would be getting married. In this way, the most anglophile of the four informants, the one who seemed most likely to stay in London indefinitely, was to become the second to leave London.

Discussion

Across the stories told by Nancy, Laure, Lise and Chantalle, there are both similarities and differences. As regards similarities, there are certain macro-level factors that facilitated their respective moves from France to London in the 1990s. The first of these is related to what Faist (2000) calls the 'regulation of spatial mobility through nation-states and international regimes' (see Chapter 1). I refer here to the 1993 Maastricht treaty, which, as I noted above, allows for free movement across all EU nation-state borders. Lise, Nancy, Laure and Chantalle all took advantage of the new European order that allowed them to move to and live in London without any formal bureaucracy to deal with. A second important macro-level factor is related to employment opportunities and career prospects in France and Britain. Here I refer to the relative difficulty of becoming a fully qualified and employed English-language teacher in France compared with becoming a qualified and fully employed French-language teacher in Britain. Lise, Nancy, Laure and Chantalle all spoke favourably of the relative flexibility of the British educational system, in particular the transparent and relatively straightforward progression from first degree to teacher qualifications to first teaching post. Above all, they liked the fact that in Britain there was no CAPES exam.

At the meso level, there is no doubt that Lise, Nancy, Laure and Chantalle all had the requisite social and cultural capital to make the move from France to London. All were from middle-class backgrounds in which education was highly valued and all four had at least an undergraduate degree in English (Nancy and Laure had MA level qualifications). In addition, all four were highly proficient in English, which meant that, once in London, they had a broad range of employment and educational opportunities that they could take up. Ultimately, Lise, Nancy, Laure and Chantalle form part of a new and growing contingent of young European adults who can quite comfortably move across borders in the Maastricht age. They are therefore a part of a 'new form of collectivity' (Croucher, 2004: 35), taking advantage of a 'still fledgling conception of supranational citizenship' (Bauböck, 2002: 126).

At the micro, and more personal level, all four women professed a love for the English language, which went back to when they were children, and all four were drawn to London because it was an English-speaking city. In addition, London is not just any English-speaking city; it is a global city, which offers a vibrant cultural and social life to those who live in it. Indeed, all four informants said at one time or another that they would never consider living anywhere else in Britain. In a sense, they all see London as an un-English island, a place where they could live their hybrid Anglo-French lives without any distractions. However, it is instructive that all four, including the Anglophile Chantalle, professed to having few if any English friends, preferring, it seems, the company of French nationals and other foreigners living in the global city.

On the professional front, all four informants have followed an almost identical path. Nancy, Laure and Chantalle first entered British education via work as *assistants* and all four women decided to do the PGCE because it would allow them to obtain a full-time post as a language teacher. Once they began the PGCE, all four went through a period of educational culture shock; however, they have all moved from horror and dismay at educational practices and standards to working towards third place professional identities (Block, 2001, 2005). They have all described situations in which they invoked two very different strategies on their way to these professional identities: resistance and compromise (Block, 2001, 2005).[5]

All four informants are phenotypically White European, and not in any sense visible minorities in London. However, they have all, at one time or another, been subjected to nationalistic and xenophobic comments. These comments have come not only from pupils, but also from parents and even acquaintances encountered away from the workplace. All four found it tiresome in 1999 to have to explain the French government's ban on English beef. They have also found it wearisome to have to listen to stereotypes about French people eating frog legs and horsemeat. Finally, in the run-up to the war in Iraq, they all would have had to suffer anti-French comments from the more xenophobic section of the British population.[6] As I note elsewhere (Block, 2001), Lise, Nancy, Laure and Chantalle did not feel that they had to fly the French flag while living in London, preferring to be seen as free agents. Nevertheless, Lise, Nancy and Laure continually evoked in their conversations with me a strong sense of Frenchness. Tellingly, after the first round of the 2002 presidential elections in France, when Jean Marie Le Pen came second and therefore managed to get into the second round, all four women, who had always voted for parties on the French left, professed to feeling 'ashamed' and 'embarrassed'. Indeed, all four made a point of travelling back to their homes in France to vote for Jacques Chirac on 5 May, 2002.

While the various similarities I have cited thus far point to a common way of doing being French in London, there are important ways in which the four stories can be seen to be different. In my discussion of each individual case, I have made reference to a question I asked in interviews about each informant's migrant identity. In doing so, I used a scale ranging from expatriate, on one extreme, to immigrant, on the other. As I noted above, Lise, Nancy and Laure all fairly emphatically positioned themselves as expatriates. Fundamental in this claim was their decision early on to leave London either as soon as they could or after a period not exceeding a year or two. However, the three women acted on this determination to leave in very different ways. Lise did so by taking the first job that she found in an international school outside of Britain, leaving in the summer of 2003. Nancy, on the other hand, was being more selective: she would also leave, but she would do so without precipitation. Meanwhile, Laure was altogether more ambivalent about leaving. Unlike Lise and Nancy, she was not a great traveller or an adventurous spirit. She was not fed up with London, as Lise and Nancy professed to be, and in any case, leaving London for her would likely mean going back to her hometown of Annecy to settle down for the rest of her life. Not surprisingly, then, she was taking her time about making a decision that would be far more definitive than it was and would be for Lise and Nancy, respectively. Lise did not leave London to go back to Paris, and Nancy, while she expressed a desire to go back to Marseilles, was looking for a job in several different locations around the world, when I last spoke to her.

Notwithstanding their constant invocation of a strong French identity and their apparent determination to leave London as soon as possible, I do not see Lise, Nancy and Laure as expatriates. As I suggested above, in some sense, I see them more as 'flexible citizens' (Ong, 1999; Chapter 3), in that, as European citizens with the requisite social, cultural and economic capital, they have been able to choose London as the location of their personal and professional lives. However, this qualification only works to some extent for these three women. Crucially, it does not include what are perhaps the most crucial aspects of their lives, namely the way that they negotiate subject positions beyond 'French woman in London' and how they do a good job of fitting into their new environment. All three, therefore, are good cosmopolitans (see Chapter 3) and in my view, might more fruitfully be qualified as transnationals. They are, however, transnationals who often invoke strong nationality-based subject positions when talking about their lives.

In the case of Chantalle, there is also a degree of transnationalism, but more importantly, there is something more akin to an immigrant subject position. On the one hand, early on she had adopted a 'never-going-back' stance as regards France. On the other hand, she expressed a desire to take on board as much as she could of English life, both professionally and personally. In the workplace, Chantalle strove to become the best teacher she could in what she called an 'English mode'. In her personal life, she had a stable relationship with a British national, with whom she lived and to whom she would be getting married in 2005. Nevertheless, her British husband-to-be is the son of immigrants from Hong Kong and he has maintained strong contacts with the city all his life. In the end, via his job, he has found a way to 'return home' for a period of at least three years. As I noted above, it is ironic that Chantalle should be the second of the four women to leave London, given her strong ties to the city and English language and culture. It will be interesting to observe, from March 2005 onwards, the kinds of subject positions she will adopt once she has settled in Hong Kong. What will she do as a third-place Anglicized French national living in Hong Kong, where her European-ness will mean that she is positioned above all as foreigner?

Conclusion

In this chapter, I have discussed the lives of four French nationals living and working in London. Lise, Nancy, Laure and Chantalle represent one particular type of French national living in London at present: university-educated women working in education. Their lives no doubt are very different from those French nationals who work for multi-national corporations, the more recently-arrived highflying professionals who work in the City and the Docklands, or those who are in London because they cannot find even low paying jobs in France. However, all French nationals in London have in common the fact that they can come and go as they please. The Maastricht treaty has introduced the prospect of a new type of transnational migrant identity, one that affords European citizenship rights to all citizens of EU member states. Given this freedom of movement, the French population in Britain, and especially in London, is likely to continue to grow, as long as macro-level economic differences exist between Britain and France in the form of low British unemployment and high French unemployment. As regards long-term settlement, this will depend on the kind of transnational subject positions that French nationals adopt while living in London.

7
Spanish-Speaking Latinos in London

Introduction

It's obvious and it has even become noticeable in specific areas of London where...just walking down the street you hear music in Spanish, conversations in Spanish in specific areas of London. I think this space has grown in recent years because of, I don't know, sudden economic or political necessities in those countries.

Es evidente y incluso se está marcando en unas zonas específicas de Londres donde...solo pasas por la calle escuchas música en español, conversaciones en español, en áreas muy específicas de Londres. Yo creo que ese espacio ha crecido en los últimos años por cüestiones de, no sé, de las necesidades económicas de pronto o políticas de pronto en esos países. (Carlos, 12/9/2003)[1]

Carlos, a Colombian man in his early 40s, is responding to a question posed about the existence of a Spanish-speaking Latino (hereafter SSL) community in London. What he says here is consistent with what I have observed since I first moved to London in autumn 1996. Whether it is riding on the bus or a tube train, or simply walking on Tottenham Court Road, I will inevitably hear Spanish spoken on at least one occasion during my journey to and from work. And, if I go to one of the 'specific areas' referred to by Carlos, such as The Elephant and Castle in South London, I will surely hear even more Spanish spoken. Spanish, therefore, seems to have joined an ever-lengthening list of languages spoken regularly by more than 50,000 people in London and, indeed, it likely ranks ahead of more established languages such as Cantonese and even Greek. However, as of 2005, it is a grossly under-documented language: as I explain below, it barely merits a mention in the literature on multilingualism in Britain and there have been, to my knowledge, just two publications of note on SSLs.

This chapter is a modest attempt to remedy this lack of attention to SSLs in London. As I have done in previous chapters, I begin with a brief sociohistory of SSL migration to London. This done, I move to explore three distinct discourses of Spanish-speaking *Latinidad* (Latin-ness) in London. By 'discourses of Spanish-speaking *Latinidad* in London', I mean differentiated and perhaps even competing ways of describing, making sense of, analysing and evaluating the institutions and processes associated with being an SSL in London. The first of these discourses is the voice of the *marginado*, that is migrants living on the fringes of society, both socially and economically. The second discourse of *Latinidad* is the voice of the *asimilado* (assimilated), that is the migrant who intends to stay in London and does everything possible to take on local cultural norms. The third and final discourse of *Latinidad* is that of the educated expatriate, who lives at a midway point between the *marginado* and the *asimilado*. As I have done in the previous two chapters, I conclude by linking these stories to some of the frameworks and issues discussed in Chapters 1–3.

The history of Spanish language and SSLs in Britain and London

In publications devoted to the past and present of migration to Britain, there has been little or no information of Spanish speakers and SSLs in particular. Thus, in books on migration, such as Eades (2000) and Winder (2004), and books on multicultural Britain, such as Modood *et al.* (1997) and Parekh (2000), I have found no information about Spaniards or SSLs. An exception is to be found in Nick Merriman's (1993b) edited collection, *The Peopling of London*. Here there are two short chapters on Spanish speakers, one about Spanish nationals and the other about Latin Americans. Javier Pes (1993) argues that there is a long tradition of Spaniards in London, including Catherine of Aragon, who married Prince Arthur in 1501. From the Sephardic Jews, fleeing the Spanish Inquisition after 1492, to some 4000 Basque children, who arrived in the years of the Spanish Civil War (1936–39), there was for centuries a trickle of migration from Spain to Britain, primarily for political reasons. However, it was not until the 1960s and 1970s that Spaniards, mainly from Galicia, came to London in significant numbers.

More relevant to this chapter on SSLs is a short piece in Merriman entitled 'Latin Americans in London' (Merriman, 1993c). Here, there is a small amount of information about Chilean and Argentinian exiles who came after military coups in 1973 and 1976, respectively. There is also mention of labour migrations from countries such as Colombia and Bolivia from the 1970s onwards (more on this below). In the chapter, the population of Latin Americans in London is estimated to be 'about 17,500', a very conservative figure, as I explain below.

Elsewhere, in publications that specifically focus on multingualism in Britain and London, there is very little space devoted to Spanish speakers. In early publications, such as Campbell-Platt (1976) and Derrick (1977), Rosen and Burgess (1980) and Linguistic Minorities Project (1985), there is only passing mention of a Spanish-speaking community from Spain, said to number about 50,000, and no mention whatsoever of SSLs in Britain. Salvador Estebenez's contribution to Alladina and Edwards (1991a) focuses almost exclusively on the Spanish community making only passing reference to SSLs, as follows:

> In the British context, the Spanish speech community has an important Latin American component. As well as students from South and Central America, there is a small but significant popula- tion of Chileans who came to Britain as political refugees following the overthrow of President Allende in the early 1970s. By far the largest proportion of Spanish speakers in the UK, however, come from Spain and will therefore form the focus of the present chapter. (Estebanez, 1991: 241)

It seems odd that the only SSL groups mentioned here are students from South and Central America and Chilean political refugees, especially when Merriman (1993c) acknowledges explicitly the presence of other groups such as Argentineans, Colombians and Bolivians. Indeed, by the late 1980s, the Colombian population in particular had easily outstripped the Chilean and student communities in absolute numbers. However, I take Estebenez's omission as a sign that some 15 years ago, SSLs had yet to attract the attention of those interested in multilingual Britain.

Elsewhere, in Baker and Eversley (2000) there are several mentions of Spanish language; however, nothing is said about SSLs. In addition, the number of Spanish speakers in London seems to be shrinking rather than growing, as Marian Storkey (2000) estimates that there are 26,700 Spanish speakers in London. If one accepts that more than half of the 50,000 Spaniards cited above live in London (not at all unrealistic, I might add, given other European immigration patterns) and that the Chileans and Central Americans Estebanez mentions could number as many as 3000 in London, then Storkey's figure is surpassed without even counting a single Spanish speaker from Colombia, Ecuador, Bolivia, Peru or any other Latin American country. Clearly, even as recently as five years ago, researchers focusing on multilingual Britain had yet to take adequate or appropriate account of SSLs.

The National Census

As I have observed throughout this book, another source of information about ethnolinguistic groups in Britain is the National Census. Here, the situation is hazy due to the imprecision of ethnic categories, although there are three figures that I have found of interest. The first of these is 44,176, cited as the population of Londoners identified as 'South American'. The second is 62,181, listed as the population of Londoners classified as 'Other Caribbean and West Indies'. The third is 2605, for those Londoners classified as 'Other North American'. In the first case, I assume that the geographical term refers to all nation states falling between the northern coast of Venezuela and Tierra del Fuego, at the Southern-most tip of Argentina. If my assumption is correct, the census claims that all of the Brazilians, Colombians, Argentineans and so on living in London number fewer than 45,000. In the second case, the term 'Other Caribbean and West Indies' would seem to cover all of the countries in the Caribbean, and one might reasonably assume that among the 62,181, there will be some Cubans and Dominicans. However, as regards these 'Other Caribbean and West Indies' people, there is always the question: What about Haitians and others from the francophone Caribbean? Finally, as regards the 2605 'Other North Americans', I can only wonder if this number is meant to be not only North Americans, such as Mexicans, but also Central Americans such as Hondurans and Salvadorans.

Clearly, it is difficult to distil anything like a precise estimate of the SLL population from census data. Am I justified in speculating that in this total of 108,962 of the London population classified as 'South American', 'Other Caribbean and West Indies' and 'Other North American', there are perhaps 75,000 SSLs? Of course, such a number is possible, and if it were accurate, it would mean that SSLs are a significant minority in London. However, it seems somewhat on the low side when lined up against estimates made in the few studies to date which focus exclusively on SSLs in London. I now turn to two such studies.

Books focusing exclusively on SSLs in London

Dempsey and Lema (1998) is a research report about Colombians in London, based on interview and documentary data. In this report, the authors talk about three waves of migration from this country. In the first wave, taking place between 1975 and 1979, successive Labour governments responded to the shortage of workers in service sectors such as cleaning, restaurant staffing and nursing, opened the doors to controlled immigration and some 6000 Colombians and their dependants took advantage of this opportunity. According to Dempsey and Lema, these original settlers represent the current legal resident base of the Colombian community, although by now most would have British citizenship (and would by now be the parents of members of a second generation who have reached adulthood). In 1979, the Thatcher government imposed greater restriction on this migratory flow, although measures taken did not stop Colombians from coming.

The second wave of Colombian immigration, from 1980 to 1986, marked the beginning of widespread illegal immigration and the consequent problem of obtaining reliable figures. Dempsey and Lema make the point that the first wave of immigration set up a migratory flow that would not stop simply because the government decided that it should. Encouraged by family members already resident in the UK as well as an increasing number of unofficial residents, Colombians continued to arrive in the UK, as part of what has become, in effect, a chain migration (Sowell, 1996). A chain migration begins with an advance group of first-wave migrants who settle and establish themselves in their new home sufficiently to be able to provide adequate and appropriate local information and support to subsequent arrivals.

In the third wave cited by Dempsey and Lema, from 1986 to 1997, the chain migration continued and the number of Colombians arriving even increased. In addition, due to the unstable socio-political situation in Colombia – the combination of official and unofficial criminal and political violence – Colombians began to ask for political asylum in the UK. This trend grew during this period to the point that over one thousand official asylum requests were made in 1996 and 1997. However, as Dempsey and Lema point out, this particular recourse was to disappear as a change to the law in May 1997 meant that all Colombians needed a visa to enter the UK.

Elsewhere, Román-Veláquez (1999) outlines pretty much the same history of migration; however, she focuses on Latinos in general and not just Colombians. Román-Veláquez also differs from Dempsey and

Lema in that while the latter aimed to compile demographic data, she is primarily interested in the way that Latinos live in London and above all the making of Latin American cultural identities in London. To this end, she describes in detail how the Elephant and Castle shopping centre in south London has been transformed, and indeed saved from economic collapse, by Latinos who have been opening businesses there since the early 1990s. It has, as she puts it, 'become a social meeting point for Latin Americans in London' (Román-Veláquez, 1999: 54). In addition, it is a case of 'Latin Americans ... not only participating in the economy of the Shopping Centre, but transforming it and in this process creating a particular Latin cultural identity' (Román-Veláquez, 1999: 54). Román-Veláquez also sees the football matches played on Clapham Common at weekends as another example of Latino life in London. However, the main focus of Román-Veláquez is on salsa music and dance, specifically how despite its dislocation from its original geographical location in Latin America, it has come to constitute a highly visible way of Latin American identity-making not only in London but also globally. While salsa is not the focus of this chapter, there will be concern for how the Latinos who speak Spanish make sense of who they are in London.

Román-Veláquez also provides far more detail than Dempsey and Lema as regards the legal side of SSL migration to Britain. Specifically, she provides a history of the legal impediments placed on Latinos trying to migrate to Britain. However, these legal impediments have not stopped migration and she concludes that by the mid- and late-1990s, SSL migration not only had increased but had also become diversified, including more Central and South American and Caribbean countries than had previously been the case. The increase in and diversification of SSL migration together have meant that it has become almost impossible to estimate with any confidence the actual number of SSLs in London. For example, Dempsey and Lema note a huge discrepancy among three different sources: what they are able to venture based on their research, that is, 30,000–50,000 Colombians in London; official estimates from the Home Office, amounting to approximately 10,000; and estimates provided by the Colombian consulate, that is 20,000–25,000. The latter figure suggests that there are a good number of Colombians who have officially registered as residents. However, 20,000–25,000 is necessarily a conservative figure, if one takes into account two factors. First, there are by now many participants in the first wave of migration with children born in the UK, who will be classified as British and therefore will have 'disappeared' from official tallies of Colombians. Second, and far more important, there are Colombians who enter via travel visas or even falsified documents such as EU member-state passports, before effectively 'disappearing'. Meanwhile, Román-Veláquez (1999) cites information gathered from Latin American organizations, which estimate that the population of Latin Americans in London fluctuates between 60,000 and 100,000.

The SSL community

Although the estimates proved by Dempsey and Lema and Román-Veláquez are enlightening, they are by now about a decade old. Not surprisingly, then, they fall well short of accounts I have been able to gather from informed sources during the years 2003 and 2004.[2] For example, in an interview with the Peruvian Consul General in November 2003, I was told that SSLs probably numbered between 200,000 and 300,000 in London, and that Colombians alone probably accounted for over 100,000 of this total. Elsewhere, in a newsletter published in Spanish for Spanish-speaking Catholics living in London, I read that 'Colombians alone numbered some 150,000 four years ago, and it is calculated that Latin Americans in general cannot be less than double this figure, that is 300,000' (San Eufrasio, 2003: 4; my translation). Finally, in an interview with Oscar Silva, head of the Colombian Refugee Association (November 2004), I was told that the figure of 300,000, for the total number of SSLs in London, was certainly possible and that Colombians probably numbered at least 100,000.

In my view, the figures provided by informed sources are probably more accurate than those provided by researchers and National Census, although one must be cautious when trying to provide exact numbers for groups of migrants that are, in a sense, invisible. The invisibility of SSLs arises for several reasons. First, there is the precarious legal status of many who will figure neither in censuses, nor indeed in research, for fear of being deported. A second factor is the geographical dispersion of SSLs over several boroughs in London. Thus, while Román-Veláquez (1999) writes of the Elephant and Castle and football tournaments in Clapham Common, a walk around London reveals nothing that approaches the self-defined Latino communities in North American cities such as Los Angeles, Miami, New York, Houston or Chicago. Third, SSLs come to London with a broad range of social and cultural capital. Thus, a large proportion of migrants arrive in London with little formal education, and they generally move directly into low-level service jobs such as cleaning. On the other hand, university graduates are generally able to obtain employment consonant with their qualifications once they are proficient in English. Fourth and finally, the invisibility of SSLs arises from their multiracialism. In National Census terms, some SSLs will fit into the 'Other White' category while many more will fit into the 'Mixed Race' category.[3] However, for now there does not seem to be any handy label to refer to SSLs, as there is for the better-documented minority ethnic groups discussed in Chapter 3.

Apart from the paucity of firm and reliable population estimates, I have also found lacking in-depth studies of the lives and language practices of individual SSLs, Román-Veláquez (1999) being the exception. Thus in the remainder of this chapter, I explore who these SLLs in London are. Using life-story interviews, in addition to some field data collected by one of my informants, Carlos, I focus on three individuals who represent three very different discourses of Spanish-speaking *Latinidad* (Latin-ness) in London.

The first discourse of Spanish-speaking *Latinidad* is that of the *marginados*, that is the marginalized class of individuals living and working on the fringes of society. These individuals are neither visible minorities nor visible individuals. They are cleaning the windows of the big stores on Oxford Street in semi-darkness at seven in the morning in December. And they are members of crews of workers who do odd jobs for all kinds of business establishments all over the city. In this chapter, the *marginados* are represented by Javier, a man who works in several office buildings in central London as a cleaner.

The second discourse of Spanish-speaking *Latinidad* is that of the *asimilados*. These are Latinos who have come to London for work or study and who have ended up living as classic assimilated immigrants. In many cases, these individuals hardly move in Latino circles and after years in London, they may well profess a greater ease in talking in English than in Spanish. In the cases I have encountered, these Latinos are working in either the professions, such as education and medicine, or the service sector, often running their own small businesses, such as restaurants. In this chapter, I present the case of Luis, a Cuban man who has settled in London.

The third and final discourse of Spanish-speaking *Latinidad*, the educated expatriate, falls somewhere in between the *marginados* and the *asimilados*. This is the discourse of well-educated migrants who were professionals, or in any case, middle class, in their countries of origin. They are in London either voluntarily or as exiles and they live their lives in London as expatriates or transnationals more than immigrants. They maintain Spanish language as a strong marker of their identity. Carlos is the educated expatriate in this chapter.

Javier, the *Marginado*

Here Latinos – call them Latino or whatever – go like unnoticed.

Aquí el latino – llámele latino o lo que sea- pasa como desapercibido.
(Javier, 22/12/2003)

These are the words of Javier, a Colombian man in his mid-40s who had
been living in London for three years when I met him. Javier worked as
a police officer in Colombia for 20 years, but in the late 1990s he
decided to take early retirement. In effect, the level of violence had
risen to such a high level in Colombia that he had begun to fear that he
would be killed while on duty. Indeed, he told me that he had narrowly
escaped death on three occasions. Javier also wanted to spend more
time with his wife and children. Unfortunately, the pension he was
paid upon retirement was not enough to support his family (Javier's
wife was not in paid employment). For this reason, he decided to
emigrate in search of work. In this way, a career move meant to allow
him to feel safer and to spend more time with his family turned into a
long period of personal instability away from his family. This is especially
sad when, as Javier freely admits, keeping his job as a police officer for
ten more years would have meant a far better pension.

In his interview, Javier gives voice to what I have described above as the
discourse of the *marginado*. He is a part of the underground economy,
living on the fringes of official society, both socially and economically. In
effect, *marginados* are invisible and therefore the thousands of Javiers
living and working in London do not figure in any census statistics or any
other official register, such as consular records. Javier's marginal status is
reflected in just about every aspect of his life that I have learned about,
even in the difficulty I encountered when trying to arrange a meeting
with him. Indeed it took me a week of false starts and missed meetings
before I was finally able to conduct a lengthy interview with him. I was
immediately struck by Javier's cheerful nature and his disarming honesty
and openness. His rather precarious status in London was immediately
symbolised in confusion over names that occurred at the beginning of the
interview. I had been told that his name was Javier Rojas; however, he
gave me a different name, explaining the situation as follows:

The thing is that here we Latinos have lots of names, right? . . . Do
you understand? Given the conditions to enter this country, that
they deny [entry] to just about all Colombians, right? So, you
sometimes have to try to enter through another country. For example,

I came in through Spain. In Spain I had to buy a passport with the name Javier Fernandez. I don't know who this man might be but he exists. This guy exists and with that passport I entered this country. With that passport, I work. With that passport, I opened two bank accounts.... So here my name is Javier Fernandez. In one job, my name is Victoria. My name is even Victoria!... In another job I use the papers of a Colombian friend, who is a legal resident in this country, and I work under the name Lorenzo Acosta....

Lo que pasa es que nosotros los latinos aquí tenemos muchos nombres, ¿sí?...¿Entiendes? Con las condiciones de la entrada a este país que nos la niegan a casi todos los colombianos, ¿no? Pues, uno está a veces por entrar por otros paises. Yo, por ejemplo, entré por España. En España me tocó comprar un pasaporte con el nombre Javier Fernandez. No sé quién será el señor pero existe. Existe el tipo y con ese pasaporte entré en este país. Con ese pasaporte trabajo. Con ese pasaporte abrí dos cuentas en el banco....entonces aquí yo me llamo Javier Fernandez. En un trabajo me llamo Victoria, !hasta Victoria me llamo!...En otro tengo los papeles de un amigo colombiano, que este tiene residencia en este país, y trabajo con el nombre Lorenzo Acosta. (Javier, 22/12/2003)

However, adopting different names is only a part of the marginal and unstable way that Javier lives in London. He explains further what he has done to get to London and why:

Why do I do it? I wanted to work but when I arrived in this country, I spent one year living illegally with a Spanish passport. Then I became a refugee. I asked for refugee status in this country with my name, but they didn't give me a work permit because the new law is that they won't give you the work permit from 2000 until now...You come here because you are interested in working. Why? To provide for your family in Colombia.

¿Por qué lo hace uno? Yo quisiera trabajar pero cuando yo llegué en este país estuve un año ilegal con el pasaporte español. Después me refugié, pedí un refugio en este país con mi nombre pero no me dieron un permiso de trabajo porqué la nueva ley es que no dan permiso de trabajo hasta el año 2000 para acá...uno viene aquí es por el interés de trabajar. ¿Por qué? Para mantener a su familia en Colombia. (Javier, 22/12/2003)

Not surprisingly, Javier is somewhat bitter about his current situation. He works as many as three different jobs, seven days a week, and he does so within a timetable ranging from 5 am to 11 pm. Despite so much work, he barely makes enough money to live on, which of course frustrates his plan to send money back to his family in Colombia. In addition, because he generally works with other Spanish speakers and seldom has any opportunity to interact with English speakers, he has learned practically no English during the three years he has been in London. Thus, when I asked him about his English, he told me that he knew 'about 20 words', what he had learned 'in the street'. He explains his frustrated attempts to study English formally as follows:

> I was in a school here learning English . . . I had been here about eight months [when] I registered at a school, Remington College, as a Spaniard so that they wouldn't charge me because if I registered as a Colombian they were charging me 500 pounds and I didn't have that. I had to leave after three months, you know why? Because I needed to work. And that's the problem for the Colombians here. We spend all of our time working working and we don't study . . . Of course there's no time to study. You either study or you work so if you study there's no money.

> *Estuve tres meses en una escuela aquí aprendiendo inglés . . . llevaba como unos ocho meses de estar aquí [cuando] entré en un colegio el Remington College como español para que no me cobraran un peso porqué si entro como colombiano me cobraban como quinientas libras y aquello no tenía pero me tocó salir al cabo de tres meses ¿sabes por qué? Porqué necesitaba trabajar. Entonces esto es el problema de los colombianos aquí. Nos dedicamos a trabajar trabajar y no estudiamos . . . Lógico, no hay tiempo para estudiar. O se estudia o se trabaja, entonces si se estudia no hay plata.* (Javier, 22/12/2003)

There are three interesting points arising from Javier's comments above. First, they represent a direct challenge to many stories propagated by much of the British press that labour migrants in Britain are heavy users of public services, giving nothing back in return. Javier appears to be a minimal user of public services, such as the National Health Service, whilst spending most of the money he earns (and therefore supporting the local economy). It is true that he does not pay taxes, but then he probably does not earn enough to find himself in a taxable income bracket. A second matter of interest emanating from these comments is the recognised importance of English. Javier says he can get by with his '20 words', but he also acknowledges that it would help his situation if he could study and learn more English. In any case, his comments here challenge another myth about many migrants, namely that they do not want to learn English. Javier certainly does, but he cannot, which leads to the third interesting point arising from this comment. Javier lays out the clear options of 'you either study or you work'. However, he makes it clear that because he has to work so many hours, studying is not really an option. He therefore is caught in a vicious cycle of marginality: in order to scratch out a living in London, he has to sacrifice his English studies which would, in the long run, help him to find better employment.

As if to emphasise the harshness of this life, Javier responded as follows to a question about whether or not there is a unified SSL community in London:

> Latinos tend to go their separate way. They are very guarded with their things....it's not very Latino to tell you 'now I have this problem'. Never, they never tell you the truth. There is no problem. There is no lack of unity. Rather, there is envy. This exists in all Latinos. Envy is when suddenly they see you with a good job [and] they want to get you out of there so they can have it.

> *El Latino tiende a irse cada uno por su lado, es muy celoso con sus cosas.... es muy poco latino que te comente 'ahora tengo este problema'. Nunca, nunca te dicen la verdad. No hay ningun problema. No hay desunión. Hay más bien envidia. Esto existe en todos los latinos. La envidia es de pronto te ven con un trabajo bueno, quieren sacarte de allí para ellos entrar.* (Javier, 22/12/2003)

Here Javier describes a rather bleak dog-eat-dog world of SSLs in London. However, envy would appear to be just one part of the *marginado's* life; outright exploitation by fellow SSLs is another, as Javier goes on to explain:

> I've spoken a lot with a friend who has been in this country for fifteen, twenty years. When the first Latinos arrived here they made a lot of money because the English are very honest. That's what I say, the English...are honest. But the Colombians themselves, the few who in the beginning could speak English, they took jobs in the companies. Then they said say: 'No, no, no. Don't pay them seven pounds, they are happy with four pounds'. So the Colombians themselves, the Latinos themselves, they fired him from the job....

> *... he hablado mucho con un amigo que lleva quince, veinte años en este país. Cuando los primeros latinos llegaron aquí, ganaron mucha plata*

porqué el inglés es muy honesto. Eso lo digo yo, el inglés . . . es honesto. Pero los mismos colombianos, los pocos que al principio hablaban inglés, entraron a trabajar en las companies. Entonces dicen: 'No, no, no. No les paguen a siete libras, con cuatro libras están contentos.' Pues los mismos colombianos los mismos latinos le tiraron del trabajo . . .
(Javier, 22/12/2003)

Javier thus paints a picture of an SSL community in which individuals are driven by envy, machiavellianism and greed. He does not talk of a community of support and he sees himself as a victim of his circumstances, although he does recognise that his current state is primarily due to his – in retrospect – bad decision to take early retirement in Colombia.

In his short story 'La frontera de cristal' ('The glass border'), the Mexican author Carlos Fuentes (1995) describes the meeting of the invisible world of migrants like Javier and the world of 'real people doing real jobs', such as banking, accounting, city planning and so on, against the backdrop of New York as a global city. Lisandro Chavez, a migrant sent to great altitudes on a wooden platform so that he can clean the windows of the skyscrapers of New York, finds himself face to face with Audrey, an advertising executive. The pair are invisible to one another, Lisandro tending to the task of cleaning the windows, while Audrey ponders an ad she is preparing for Pepsi. However, first Audrey and then Lisandro actually see each other through the window. Fuentes describes a slow build up of looks and gestures which lead to a kiss, eyes shut, lips separated by the window. But the kiss is as fleeting as the meeting of the eyes and the recognition of mutual existence. Audrey opens her eyes to find that Lisandro has disappeared, no doubt descending to clean a window on the floor below hers.

Like Lisandro, the Javiers of London are invisible (or 'unnoticed' as he puts it) to the 'real people who do real jobs' in London. Yes, there is the occasional meeting of the eyes, perhaps even a short conversation (or even an interview with a researcher!); however, for the most part Javier does not exist in any census or in the mind of anyone who matters as he slips in under the cover of night to clean an office that will be ready for the activity of the 'real people' the following morning.

Luis, the *asimilado*

In Europe I think it's the most cosmopolitan city ehrm . . . I think partly because of how selfish it is, as in you know, it's not that people allow you to do what you want to do. I feel more like they don't give a shit so if you want to do whatever with your life, I wouldn't do it the same as you, but it's your life. (Luis, 27/1/2004)

In this way Luis, a Cuban who has been a legal resident in London since 1997,[4] describes the life of the migrant in London. Unlike Javier, the *marginado*, Luis presents in his life-story interview a far more positive version of life in London and above all the possibility that he will stay. In the context of this study, I classify Luis as an *asimilado*, primarily because of the way he positions himself as having reached a point of no return to his native Cuba and therefore as someone living in London as an immigrant more than a temporary sojourner. Linguistically, he does not deny his status as an SSL; however, given a choice of languages in which to conduct the interview, he told me that he had no preference and then proceeded to speak almost exclusively in English. He thus manifests a high degree of affiliation to and expertise in English.

Luis was born in Havana in 1972, the son of a psychiatrist and a journalist. When he was nine, his journalist father was posted to Hungary and Luis was thrust into the Hungarian education system in a sink-or-swim fashion. Although he was offered his father's translator to help him, he recalls that he did not want this help and that he just got on with the task of learning Hungarian. By the time he went back to Cuba five years later, Luis claims that he had, in effect, 'lost Spanish' as a language of education and communication with his peers. Still, he recalls that it did not take him too much time to re-join his old friends after his return to Cuba.

Luis describes a contrast that existed between his family's high status in Cuban society, with contacts in the government, and the fact that they lived in one of the more impoverished areas of Havana. Perhaps because of his middle-class cosmopolitan upbringing, Luis decided to study English when he went to university. As he puts it, he was good at languages and he liked to show off his linguistic skills.

Before finishing his university degree in English, Luis met Claire, the woman he now identifies as his 'ex-wife'. Claire was an 'English volunteer' during her gap year and by the time that year was over, she and Luis were a couple. Over a period of three years, there was a good deal of to-ing and fro-ing between Havana and London, and it was during a year Luis spent in London in 1995–96, that he decided he wanted to live in London. He applied himself more to his university studies and finally got his degree in English. In 1997, he and Claire got married and Luis moved to London to live with her.

From the start, Luis adopted a strong affiliation to the English language. As a general rule, he avoided Spanish speakers in London, spending a lot of time with his wife's circle of friends. However, he was eventually tired of people whom he saw as 'middle class kids', who after discovering another world in Cuba, had begun to question their 'capitalist' values. He also did not like the way that they wanted him to take them to salsa bars, poetry readings and other Cuban-associated activities. Luis explains his position as follows:

> They used to go out to salsa places and tried to go to, you know, and poetry readings that the [Cuban] embassy would invite them, stuff like that. And from day one I said I'm not going to do any of those. And there was an element of friction at the beginning, but I suppose I won and that severed the link with Cuba. (Luis, 27/1/2004)

Luis's rejection of contacts with the embassy was coupled with a strong desire to learn English and get on with his life in London, leaving his Spanish-speaking Cuban side behind. In particular, he saw a need to think more in an English way, leaving behind his Cuban way of expressing himself:

> some people that I was relating to ... found it a bit [inappropriate] and you know you put a point across in a different way. And I sort of needed to learn how the English one worked, not necessarily to adopt it but to be able to relate to it and to produce it whenever I needed to ... (Luis, 27/1/2004)

However, there is a certain ambivalence about what he is and what he will end up being:

> I've never seen [living in London] that definite. Perhaps I'm scared of seeing that as definite ... It's very strange I suppose I realise that I'm not going to be English and I'm not that Cuban either. So I want to hang on to that little one that I have. I don't want to lose the whole thing. (Luis, 27/1/2004)

When asked about settling down in London, Luis became philosophical, telling me how just about all of his friends from Cuba have ended up settling in countries around the world:

> I suppose it's where responsibility catches up with you there you stay. It's just strange because from a very close-knit, very big group of

friends, we all went to very different places. We've sort of got extremely different lifestyles but also age and responsibility and bank accounts and stable relationships caught up with us at the same time. And suddenly you look around and say: 'Hang on a second, I really wasn't planning for this'. But on the other hand, you know it's just the way it worked. And I became English as much as one of my closest friends became Chilean. And you know we all have you know standing orders to charities and you know...very similar lifestyles. But with the same kind of abiding to the same social contract if you like. But I'm abiding to the English social contract, where he's abiding to the Chilean one, and another one is not very well abiding to the Californian one. But you know that we all have in some way signed up to comfortable responsible living... (Luis, 27/1/2004)

This comfortable responsible living is now carried out without Claire: the couple eventually divorced. Over the years, Luis has moved from jobs in bars and restaurants, even selling chocolate for a period of time, to a more white-collar job in language teaching. Eventually, he took a desk job working in the administration of a London university. He later left this job to work as a plumber. All of this work experience has given him confidence in himself as a Londoner and it has allowed him to make his own set of friends:

Because finally you get the confidence, which I think I got from working in bars and restaurants and relating to some migrants, but also some normal English people. I moved away from the kind of family cocoon or friends' cocoon that I had lived in...I started making my own friends which eventually finished my marriage, but I started crafting my own life and making my own decisions. (Luis, 27/1/2004)

By the time Luis and I met for this interview, he had become an Anglophone to the point that he carried out most of the interview in English. Looking back on what he has done with his Spanish-speaking side, he says:

I suppose it was a race, you know, to adapt to the new environment and I saw relating to Spanish-speaking people as a drawback to the adaptation. (Luis, 27/1/2004)

However, now he is moving towards a more balanced view of things. While rejecting a lifestyle whereby he would try to *conservar lo cubano* (conserve the Cuban), he does not see himself as becoming English either. He seems to enjoy a third-place identity in the global city:

> And I suppose I had that choice but... I didn't want the English one either and I kind of like the ability to be jumping from you know one to the other. I had a party on Saturday and while I was sober I started looking around and there were people from all over the place and not that I've picked them out to be from all over the place. So I can have kind of [a] comprehensive sample of identities. but it's more like, you know, it's the way it happens. You find interesting people around here who could be from here or not here or anywhere else and... I don't know... it gives me more freedom and I suppose living in London has allowed me to do that more than anywhere else but then I don't have the experience of anywhere else. (Luis, 27/1/04)

Luis provides us with the more hopeful discourse of an *asimilado* in London. Although he worked a variety of service sector jobs in his first three years in London, his ability to speak English meant that these jobs, such as barman, were at the higher end of the sector. His situation, therefore, contrasts markedly with Javier's. Javier spoke no English when he arrived in London and he has hardly been able to make any progress since, due to the type and intensity of the jobs he is forced to take. He is therefore denied the possibility of developing expertise in and an affiliation to the English language. Meanwhile, Luis came to London with a university degree in English and he has generally associated with university-educated people, both British and non-British. The London that he has experienced, not surprisingly, is a cosmopolitan city in which, as he suggests in the quote reproduced at the beginning of this section, people do not 'give a shit'. London provides a backdrop against which he can pretty much live the life he wants to live. Under such circumstances, assimilation is the most natural course to take, and one that Luis has taken at what is apparently very little personal cost.

Carlos, the educated expatriate

> There is an amazing number of Hispanics, above all Latinos. So they come and a lot of people don't know me but they go asking for Carlos. So 'my friends told me that you can help me with this...' Or 'they told me to get you to get permission to get this'. Or 'your wife speaks Spanish too and she can write us a letter we need fast because they won't pay us because they reduced part of my working hours...' And

there are people we don't know (laughing) and they ask you to do these things. And Kelly and I are, let's say, conscientious about that and we can't say no. And we do it, either when we are working or we find time for them during our lunch hour, which means that we don't have lunch; rather, we are there solving little things for people. But it makes us feel good. It makes us think about all of these people, there are people who exist, but they don't appear and they hide because they are aliens or they need a letter or they want to phone.... They are going about their lives, but without the language, it's hard, it's difficult, I don't know (laughing) We are going to open a social assistance agency one of these days.

Hay una cantidad de hispanos impresionante, sobre todo latinos. Entonces vienen y mucha gente no me conoce y ya van preguntando por Carlos. Entonces 'mis amigos me dijeron que usted me puede ayudar con esto... O 'me dijeron que usted me haga el permiso de sacar esto' O 'que su señora también habla español, que ya de pronto nos hace una carta que necesitamos porqué no nos pagan porqué me quitaron tantas horas de trabajo'... Y hay gente que no conocemos (riéndose) y te piden estas cosas. Y Kelly y yo somos, digamos, muy exactos en eso y no podemos decir no. Y lo hacemos o mientras trabajamos o les buscamos espacio en la hora de nuestro almuerzo, lo cual significa que que no almorzamos, sinó que estamos por ahí resolviendole cosillas a la gente. Pero nos hace sentir bien. Nos hace pensar en toda esta gente, hay gente que existe pero que no aparece y que se esconde por alien o necisitan una carta o quieren llamar... Está haciendo su vida pero sin el idioma es muy duro, es difícil, no sé (riéndose). Vamos a abrir una agencia de ayuda social un dia de estos. (Carlos, 4/12/2003)

Carlos is talking about how he and his wife, Kelly, have become fix-it-alls for SSLs suffering varying degrees of economic and social exploitation in London. At the time of the interview, they were both working in and around the reception area of a university building – Carlos as a porter, Kelly as an administrator – and for this reason it is easy to imagine people coming in off the street to ask them for help. In the context of the story of SSLs in London, Carlos is an interesting case, falling somewhere between the *marginado* status of Javier and the *asimilado* status of Luis: he is neither living on the fringes of London society nor is he overly concerned about assimilating in a conscious manner.

Carlos grew up in a working-class family in a small city located in the southwestern part of Colombia. He studied philosophy and eventually became a philosophy lecturer at a university in Colombia. By the late

1980s he was married and he had two children from this marriage, which ended in 1991. In the late 1980s and early 1990s, Carlos was very active in leftist political movements working in opposition to the Colombian political establishment. On more than one occasion he was imprisoned and on two occasions he visited friends in London to get away from 'hot' situations. During his second visit, in 1991, he met Kelly, whom he soon after married. Their son, Eduardo, was born in 1992. Carlos, Kelly and Eduardo lived in Colombia together from 1992 to 2001. Their life was middle class: Carlos was a philosophy lecturer at a university and Kelly worked as a Spanish/English translator. After more than eight years in Colombia, Kelly wanted to be close to her family in London again and there was some concern that Eduardo would never learn English, given that the couple spoke only Spanish at home. So they moved to London in autumn 2001. As I explain below, Carlos left behind in Colombia considerable social and cultural capital. He also left behind his two children from his first marriage. However, upon his arrival in London, he immediately began to explore ways to bring them to live in London, having reached an agreement with their mother. Eventually, he was successful and the two children, then aged 14 and 16, settled in London in the summer of 2004.

As he explained in his first interview with me, throughout his formal education he had studied French, almost as a manner of protest against what he perceived as the imposition of English as the international language by the US. As a result, upon his arrival in London, Carlos spoke hardly any English and this meant that he could not find any employment beyond that of a manual labourer. In this sense, he was effectively declassed when he arrived in London, falling from professional middle class to unskilled low-level service provider in one fall swoop. However, he recalls that ultimately he was lucky to some extent: his declassing could have been worse had he not found an old friend from Colombia, who was already established in London as an area manager for a cleaning company. This company provided outsourced cleaning services to businesses in London; the majority of the workers on the crews sent by the company were *marginados* like Javier. Although his English was poor at this time, Carlos was immediately put in the role of manager of these workers by his friend, acting mostly as a liaison between the English-speaking managers, who had hired the cleaning company, and the SSLs workers, supplied by the company.

Accepting this job and then later the porter job at the university, meant far lower pay and status than Carlos was used to. However, the latter job allowed Carlos access to English in a variety of contexts. At the same time, Carlos had begun to experience English as a language at home for the first time. For most of the first two years in London, Kelly, Eduardo and Carlos lived with Kelly's mother and Carlos found that at home he always had ready interlocutors in English, if and when he was willing. In addition, he began to study English on his own and Kelly also helped him in his efforts to learn. Finally, when Eduardo began to get on his feet with English in school, he brought more and more English home. Carlos describes his homelife at this time as '*un medio muy bilingüe*' (a very bilingual medium) with Kelly continuing to speak with him in Spanish, but with her family – mother, sisters- and brothers-in-law – speaking English to him. When asked to describe in detail this situation, he responded as follows:

With my brothers-in-law, Charlie would arrive, say hello and he would ask me how my day had gone. And I would try to tell him: 'Fine, I'm tired...Tomorrow I start at such and such a time'. It wouldn't go any further than that. However, he would try to make more contact with me by talking about the news or seeing a film. And I wouldn't be able to take all of this in because it seemed boring, right? After coming home from a day's work, I wouldn't want to do anything. And I would choose the easy way. Kelly would intervene as interpreter and (laughing) at the same time she would be with Eduardo [in Spanish], even though Eduardo was of course responding very well to the demands of English after the first five months. With my mother-in-law, I can speak more easily, I don't know, because I trust her a lot and this means I don't feel ashamed if I make a mistake and she corrects me, although with Kelly it's the same: she corrects me and I take notes. But with her sisters, my sisters-in-law, they don't correct, but they understand. I mean we can communicate. And one of them wants to start speaking Spanish and so she has bought books and sometimes I teach her and there we go, talking. Their husbands are Scottish and it's a lot more difficult (laughing)...Good thing they aren't Irish because I would understand even less! That's it. Now I know I can communicate. I can get my ideas across to them now. I can get my ideas across and I've chosen to operate with two tenses in English, which are the present and the simple past, and that has helped me a lot.

Con mis cuñados, Charlie llegaba, saludaba y me preguntaba como me había ido. Y yo trataba de decirle: 'bien, estoy cansado...Mañana empiezo a tales horas.' No pasaba de allí. Sin embargo, el trataba de hacer mas contacto conmigo a traves de comentarme las noticias o ver una pelicula. Y yo no asimilaba eso porqué me parecía pesado, no? Después de venir de un dia de trabajo no quería hacer nada. Y optaba por lo fácil. Kelly se ponía en medio de intérprete y (laughing) al mismo tiempo estaba con Eduardo [en español], aunque Eduardo logicamente después de los primeros cinco meses respondía muy bien a las exigencies en ingles. Con mi suegra hablo mas facilmente no sé, porqué tengo mucha confianza con ella y eso hace que no tenga pena si me equivoco si ella me corrige, aunque con Kelly igual pasa: ella me corrige y yo hago apuntes. Pero con sus hermanas, mis cuñadas, ellas no hacen correcciones pero entienden, o sea nos podemos comunicar. Y una de ellas quiere empezar a hablar espanol y entonces ha comprado libros y yo a veces le enseño y allí vamos haciendo, vamos conversando. Los esposos de ellas son escoceses y es mucho mas difícil (laughing)... menos mal que no son irlandeses porqué entendería menos!... Es eso. Ahora sé que puedo comunicar. Comunico mis ideas con ellos a este tiempo. Comunico mis ideas y he optado por manejar dos tiempos del inglés, que son el presente y el pasado simple, y eso me ha asistido mucho. (Carlos, 12/9/2003)

Having so many potential interlocutors proved to be useful to Carlos until Kelly, Eduardo and Carlos moved to their own home in late 2003. This move, not surprisingly, meant that the family unit could go back to speaking exclusively in Spanish, as had been the case prior to their arrival in London in 2001. However, English had established itself as a language used in the home, even if it was still a distant second to Spanish. This slight change in language practices at home was due to three factors: Kelly's settling into life in London again; Eduardo's virtual immersion in English, which had, by then, turned him into a proficient English speaker; and Carlos's increasing use of English, both in social contexts and work contexts. Still, to this day Carlos maintains an ambivalent relationship with English and how it might fit into his sense of self. On the one hand, he regrets, to some extent, not having studied English when he was younger; however, on the other hand he admits that he will always try to use Spanish if and when this is possible. When asked if he could ever 'be himself' in English, he responded as follows:

You should know, David, because when I found out that you could speak Spanish, from then on we always tried to speak in Spanish. Or at least I know I can speak with you in Spanish and carry on perfectly...

Tu lo puedes pensar, David, porqué cuando descubrimos que tu hablabas español de allí en adelante siempre tratamos de hablar más en español o yo por lo menos sé que puedo hablar contigo en español y definitivamente seguir... (Carlos, 12/9/2003)

Speaking Spanish as much as possible is not, of course, an assimilationist migration strategy. Importantly, it leads us to the question of the extent to which Carlos seeks to maintain a strong Colombian identity. However, even here I found ambivalence to be the dominant feeling. For example, when asked about his affiliation to his Colombian nationality, Carlos relativised his situation as follows:

I consider myself Colombian even if I might have the advantage of participating, let's say, in English 'legality'... as much as I might define myself as a citizen of the world since... I have been here and there... When I think about Colombia, I see it a different way, a view I didn't have when I lived in Colombia.

Yo me considero Colombiano aunque pueda tener la ventaja de participar, digamos, en la legalidad inglesa... tanto como me pueda definir como ciudadano del mundo porqué... he ido por allí, por acá.... Cuando yo pienso en Colombia la veo diferente, una mirada que no tenía antes cuando vivía en Colombia. (Carlos, 12/9/2003)

However, the experience of having been able to examine Colombia from the inside and from the outside, does not, in itself, explain his relationship to Colombians and other SSLs in London. Above all, it says nothing about his relative reluctance or lack of desire to socialise with Colombians and other SSLs in London. When asked about his contact with Colombians and other SSLs, he responded as follows:

It's funny, David, because I work in contact with Colombians basically, and Latinos in general. But away from work, and being at home, we don't want contact with more Latinos, supposedly because we wanted to develop more my English or so that our son also could speak English. But I think that [the contact with SLLs] doesn't really work at the end of the day [because] they are people with specific objectives. For example, they need to work a certain number of hours a day, which does not allow time to have a very broad social life either. And then I'm not interested in the type of social activities that they go to, for example, going out drinking, going out dancing and going out to eat a type of food that I have eaten every year of my life. I can't share this type of things just because they just aren't enough.

Es curioso, David, porqué trabajo en contacto con Colombianos basicamente, y latinos en general. Pero por fuera, y estando ya en casa, no queremos el contacto con más latinos, supuestamente porqué queríamos desarrolar más mi inglés o porqué el niño también hablara mas ingles. Pero creo que [el contacto con SSLs] no está funcionando al final del dia [porqué] son personas que tienen objetivos muy precisos. Por ejemplo, ellos necesitan trabajar un numero de horas por dia, que no les permite hacer una vida social muy amplia tampoco. Y luego, ya el tipo de actividades sociales a que ellos acuden, a mi no me interesan, por ejemplo, que es ir a beber y ir a bailar y ir a comer una comida que he comido durante todos los años de mi vida . . . no puedo compartir este tipo de cosas porqué no, o sea no me llegan . . . (Carlos, 12/9/2003)

On the one hand, Carlos cites the desire to build up English as home language, when explaining why he does not socialize with the SSLs with whom he works. However, he goes on to cite a more important reason, his social and cultural capital that is very different from the majority of SSLs with whom he comes in contact at work. Most of these SSLs, to whom Carlos refers to in third person, would fall into the category of *marginados*. Carlos's political consciousness, manifested in the quote that opened this section, pushes him towards this community when he attempts to help them solve some of their day-to-day problems. However, his background as a philosophy lecturer in Colombia, along with his more cosmopolitan lifestyle, pushes him in a diametrically opposed direction, away from the majority of his compatriots and towards better-educated, middle-class Spanish speakers. He explains:

Some Spanish friends come round who have professions, who are engaging in another type of activities, different from the Latinos and obviously it's a slightly more interesting level. Some Argentinian friends also come round who work in psychology and some of them are teachers. So it's little different . . .

. . . por casa vienen unos amigos españoles que tienen profesiones, que están desarrollando otro tipo de actividades, diferente a los latinos y claro es un nivel un poquito más interesante. También vienen a casa unos amigos argentinos que trabajan en esto de psicologia y algunos son profesores. Entonces es un poquito diferente. . . . (Carlos, 12/9/2003)

Carlos, thus, is an individual who is comfortable carrying out his life as much as possible in Spanish. In this sense, he adopts a form of cultural and linguistic maintenance. However, this maintenance is more cosmopolitan in nature, a kind of transnational community of university-educated Spanish speakers, than more classically pan-SSL. In other words, it is transnationalism more related to social class and language than to nationality and language.

Carlos's social and cultural capital works both in his favour and against him when it comes to his interactions in English outside of the home. As regards contacts with professionals, such as doctors and lawyers, Carlos positions himself as a competent interlocutor who can say what he wants to say, and who can participate fully in the conversation. In the following excerpt, I have reproduced Carlos's side of a telephone conversation with a barrister. The topic is the appeal of a Home Office decision to deny his two children from his first marriage, still in Colombia at the time, permanent resident status in Britain.

Carlos: Recording 1

Good morning sir (.) can I speak to Mr Fulham please/ (.) oh right good morning sir/ (.) I'm Mr Carlos Sanchez/ (.)/Carlos Sanchez / (1)/ yes (.) you was on my flat yesterday/ (.) in our place yesterday/ (.)/ you was yesterday in my place in <provides his address>/ (.)/ no/ (.)/ ah (.) yes/ (.)/ I received the notice/ (1)/ erm/ (.)/(xxx)) yeah OK <laughing>/ (.)/ yeah erm/ (.)/ yes/ (6)/ sorry Mr Coram/ (.)/ yeah/ (.)/ yeah/ (.)/ yes sir/ (.)/ yeah/ (.)/ yes sir/ (3)/ but I yes I yes yesterday we were in erm erm hearing because I / (.)/ in the court/ (.)/ yes sir erm/ (.)/ yes sir erm we were in an appeal we made erm (.) with the erm (.) home office/ (.)/ yes and we spent all the day there because/ (.)/ yes we started at 10 o'clock and we spent all the day there/ (1.)/ yeah/ (12)/ yes that's fine/ (10)/ yes please/ (4)/ yeah/ (8)/ yes sir/ (12)/ yes/ (4)/ yes/ (4)/ OK could you let me know when exactly? because in that in that/ (1)/ no/ (3)/ yeah/ (5)/ yeah

Transcribed in this way, Carlos's side of the conversation shows the odd grammatical anomaly (e.g. 'you was on my flat') and lexical fault (e.g. 'notice' for 'news'), but on the whole it seems very coherent and to the point. Listening to the recording, I was struck by the confidence that Carlos conveyed during the call: he seemed very calm and assured throughout. When asked about why he seemed more at ease in such conversations than, for example, with his English-speaking colleagues at work, he responded as follows:

> ...my previous experience, let's say academic...gives you confidence to go to the doctor, for example, to kind of do things in your normal life. But it's a little like feeling strengthened by that intellectual situation that allows you to gain confidence. And I have thought about this and I have seen how the people who don't have, let's say, this support...are weaker, more vulnerable.

> ...*la experiencia mia anterior, digamos academica...te da confianza para ir al médico, por ejemplo, para hacer un poco las cosas en tu vida normal. Pero es un poco sentirse como afianzado en esa situación intellectual que te permite como ganar la confianza. Y he pensado también o he visto que la gente que no tiene, digamos, ese sustento...es más débil, es más vunerable...* (Carlos, 4/12/2003)

However, most of Carlos's contacts with English speakers did not take place in the company of doctors and lawyers; they took place at the university where he worked as a porter. And on the job, his ability to come across as a confident, competent speaker of English varied considerably.

Carlos at work

Carlos's job as a porter required not only contact with fellow workers, but also people asking for information at the reception desk. In general, he found it easy to carry out the day-to-day tasks he was assigned, such as mail deliveries or acting as a liaison between the Spanish-speaking cleaning crew and his line manager. Conversations around this part of his work were both routine and easy. In addition, Carlos encountered a good deal of spoken English when he was stationed at the reception desk. In this case, he had to deal with people coming into the building to make deliveries or to attend functions. Carlos again had few problems with such exchanges: providing information, giving directions and taking requests became so routine that he did not have to think very much. Where he did have problems was with English-speaking colleagues engaging in non-work related talk.

Sociolinguists such as Janet Holmes (2000) have noted how a good proportion of workplace conversation is not about work-related topics, strictly speaking. A large part of doing one's job, of being part of a group at work, is engaging in informal conversations around topics ranging from football to one's personal life. In the English, male-dominant atmosphere in which he worked, Carlos found that one of the few things he had in common with his fellow workers was a passion for football. However, he often found that even when engaging in talk about this topic, he often was not able to follow what was going on. As regards other non-work conversations, which might be about illness or leisure activities, he felt even more lost, particularly when he had to deal with more than one interlocutor. In the following excerpt, Carlos describes the experience of taking part in a conversation with two of his colleagues:

> I'm listening and there is a part of the conversation, that I tell you, I lose it because the other person he is talking to... he has this problem, he stutters, and then his diction, how he pronounces, its very sharp, and I lose spirit, interest, in the conversation. So, I just leave them there, to talk between themselves. I'm there but... (shrugging)

> *Estoy escuchando y ya hay una parte de la conversación, que yo te digo, la pierdo porqué la otra persona con quien habla... tiene el problema, es tartamudo, y luego su dicción, la forma de pronunciar, es muy cortante, y pierdo ya el ánimo, el interés, en la conversación. Entonces los dejo ya entre ellos allí. Yo estoy allí pero... (encogiéndose de hombros)* (Carlos, 6/2/2004)

However, far more important than the comprehension of his English-speaking colleagues' accents was the issue of whether or not, football notwithstanding, he actually had anything to talk with them about. As I noted above, Carlos was more than conscious of how he was carrying out a job for which he was over-qualified. However, to make matters worse, he was working with people he did not find particularly stimulating as conversation partners. On the one hand, he had trouble following his immediate White British colleagues, even when the conversation turned to football. On the other hand, in his contacts, with other workers, including SSLs, he found that due to differences in their educational background, he did not always find anything interesting to talk about.

Still, he did talk to all of his co-workers on a regular basis and when possible he attempted to structure conversations around issues that interested him and he thought should interest them, such as poor work conditions, low wages and lack of status in the organization. However, he often found that his more immediate White British colleagues were not interested in talking to him about such matters. In a sense, there was a gap between Carlos and these colleagues, which had to do with language, educational level and possibly, racism: Carlos spoke English with an accent, he was too well-educated and he was the only non-White employee in his section at work. To illustrate the gap between Carlos and his colleagues, I reproduce below a conversation that took place between Carlos (C) and his line manager, Bob (B). In it, the two men are talking about future plans.

Carlos: Recording 2

1. C: in ten years I will be living in Colombia again/
2. B: <expressing surprise> would you like to live in Colombia again?/
3. C: yes B/ (.) yes I like living there/
4. B: you [know
5. C: [and I miss a lot to my country/ and I I miss everything I was doing before =
6. B: = yeah but the only thing is/ it's very poor environment isn't it?
7. C: no:o it depends B/ because erm (.5) people are in some difficulties/ but we were living in a very good situation (.) very good level/ (.) yeah (.) well it's not erm it's not erm it's not a normal way for all the population =
8. B: = no no [no
9. C: [no it's [not
10. B: [lots of [people
11. C: [but you can live with commodities there with/ (.2) obviously you're never =
12. B: = you can't [compare
13. C: [with the first world/ nah nah nah =
14. B: = it won't it doesn't compare with living in Europe (.) does it?
15. C: no/ it no/ (.) you can't compare except if you are one of the erm erm rich ones in the country/ (.) (.) you are the one of the biggest man in the country or you are one of the big [politicians
16. B: [well those/ (.) well I mean/ (.) I suppose it's like when you were a lecturer there/ it was you were the sort of/ I suppose above average income weren't you? for people there =
17. C: = yes (.) I was making good money and my income was very [good
18. B: [in relation to =
19. C: = and also Kelly/ (.) she was working and (.2) we had very good level and standard of living/ but it's not the common/

20. B: no/
21. C: no/
22. B: a lot of the people like the guys who come and work ((xxx))/ (.) most of them come from poor areas don't they?
23. C: yeah ((xxx)) most of them they come from very very poor areas erm/ (.5) they have not many erm level education/
24. B: no/
25. C: but from there they come to pay for everything for their families that's =
26. B: = so all their [money
27. C: [they use to do/ (.) they send the money for buying houses for food for . . .

<B changes the subject at this point, mentioning a friend has moved to Thailand, where he will be able to buy a home very cheaply.>

In this exchange, the lack of understanding between his line manager and himself is patent. First, he is positioned as fortunate to be in Britain, as Colombia is a 'very poor environment' (turn 6). It is interesting that Carlos then has to explain how he in fact did not have such a bad life in Colombia, especially when, as Bob reveals in turn 16, it is common knowledge that Carlos was a university lecturer there. Still, in turn 19, Carlos acknowledges that his situation was not typical, thus in a sense admitting Bob's argument that Colombia is a lot poorer than Europe. In turn 22, Bob mentions that most of the Colombians at work come from 'poor areas', which prompts Carlos to shift the topic to that of labour migrants who can barely support themselves in London whilst still trying to send money home. However, his colleague does not follow his desire to discuss economic exploitation, moving to the new topic of his friend's home purchase in Thailand.

Not all of Carlos's workplace recordings involved his immediate colleagues. Yet another type of workplace conversation took place when Carlos met up with members of staff working in the food services at the university. These workers are responsible for preparing and delivering sandwich lunches and coffee and biscuits to offices and classrooms in the building. The group is made up of at least 12 members of staff, some eight of whom are Brazilian and at least one who is Polish. The conversation that follows is fairly typical of these encounters. Carlos (C) and Ricardo (R), a Brazilian university student, by his own admission 'hanging out' in London for a year, spoke fairly frequently and they had developed a kind of code that drew on Spanish and English and sometimes Portuguese. However, in this case, just about all of the conversation is in English. This is probably due to the fact that Jozef (J), a Polish national who speaks no Spanish or Portuguese, is present.

Carlos: Recording 3

N.B. This conversation takes place amid constant background noise of machinery. Spanish portions are in **bold** with translations immediately afterwards in brackets: {xxx}

1. C: do you know Lonnie the cleaner?
2. R: ah yes =
3. C: = the black guy /(.5) always his happy happy face/
4. R: nahh/ (.) with you/
5. C: yes/
6. R: **me he peleado algunas veces con el y con el otro** {I've fallen out with him a few times and with the other one}/
7. C: why? **por que peleaste?** {why did you fall out?}
8. R: **quería que que quería que yo li <sic> pase las aulas con la basura conmigo (.5) y que uhh pusharse (?) conmigo y ponía lo lo la basura dientro <sic> de esta mierda y** {he wanted he wanted wanted me to go through the classrooms with the rubbish with me and that uhh 'push it' with me and he was putting the the the rubbish inside this piece of shit}
9. R: I said, no, no <Carlos laughs> I'm sorry/ (.) it's not my work/
10. J: he always complains/
11. C: yes?
12. J: yes/
13. C: but with him I have good relations/
14. J: but actually he always complains <imitating Lonnie> oh, don't put boxes in there ohh <Ricardo and Jozef laugh>/
15. C: well, he was the same with me but I didn't pay attention at that/ I said take it easy <Ricardo laughs>/ yes/ (.) life's short/ (.) yeah don't worry about that/
16. J: [yeah, yeah
17. R: [yeah, yeah
    <Jozef and Ricardo think Carlos is talking to them about their current work>
18. C: NO/ (.) that I told him to Lonnie (.) just relax be calm/
19. J: he said are you fucking kidding? <laughing>/
20. C: yes/ (1) they use to employ that people because they are very good workers (.) you know and very cheap you know/ (.) four pounds per hour/

21. R: [how
22. C: [four pounds =
23. J: [four
24. C: [four pounds/
25. J: ((xxx))/
26. C: he starts it at six o'clock and he finish eight/ fourteen hours a day/
27. J: Jesus Christ man/
28. C: Monday to Saturday/
29. R: fucking hell/
30. C: erm?
31. R: much work/
32. C: and [that way
33. R: [how much per hour?
34. C: four pounds/
35. R: huh?
36. C: FOUR POUNDS/
37. J: ((xxx))/
38. C: yes/ (1) he was living here in this country for maybe three years/ and in that way he bought the house (.) big house in Kenya (1)/
39. R: he bought the house?
40. C: yes it's hard/ (.) it's hard
41. R: ((xxx)) <loud noise of meal tray trolleys moving around>/
42. C: huh?
43. R: he's quite intelligent/
44. J: four pounds/ ((xxx))/ making only two pounds/ ((xxx))/
45. C: at the end of the day they (.) the rate is three seventy five after tax/
46. J: after tax/
47. C: yeah (.) more or less/ (1) and it's peanuts/

This conversation begins in English, with Carlos talking favourably about Lonnie, a cleaner from Kenya. First Ricardo, and then Jozef, express negative feelings about Lonnie, the former telling a story about a run-in with him (turns 6, 8 and 9) and the latter imitating him (turn 14). Carlos, however, attempts to be more balanced, saying that he had problems with Lonnie, but that he was able to resolve them. Eventually Carlos manages to move the conversation to where he wants it, when in turn 20, he introduces the topic of low wages. After clarifying what Lonnie's hourly wage might be and adding that he works fourteen hours a day, six days a week, Carlos then surprises his interlocutors by telling them, in turn 38, that after three years of hard work, Lonnie has managed to save enough to buy a house in Kenya. This revelation causes surprise in Ricardo and Jozef, and Ricardo seems to have changed his opinion of Lonnie, as in turn 43, he says that 'he's quite intelligent'. When asked to comment on this exchange, Carlos offered the following analysis:

> We are four people from different 'backgrounds', as they say in English, and different interests. In the case of the Brazilian, he is very young and takes his life easy. He doesn't have any worries yet, he doesn't have any obligations. So...he takes whatever life throws up. The Pole is just as young, but he is thinking about getting married at this time and...he has a different view. So in that situation they see our friend from Kenya as inferior because he makes less money and his job is a lot harder. And they try to take advantage of that situation, so they kind of transfer their work to him. And obviously...he has realised this and of course they are on a collision course. But this happens because of the type of migration, the type of interests... that there is always a tendency to underestimate people a little... especially if the colour of your skin is different from theirs.

> *Somos cuatro personas de diferentes 'backgrounds', que se dice en inglés, y con diferentes intereses. En el contexto del 'Brasileiro', es muy joven y va muy tranquilo por el mundo. Todavía no tiene afanes, no tiene compromisos. Entonces...lo que le llegue va bien. El polaco es igualmente joven pero está pensando en ese momento en casarse y...tiene otra visión. Enonces en esa situación ellos ven en inferioridad al amigo de Kenya porqué el gana menos y su trabajo es mucho más difícil. Y tratan...de tomar ventaja...de esa situación, entonces le transfieren como su trabajo a el y claro...se ha dado cuenta y por supuesto viene el choque entre ellos. Pero pasa eso, por el tipo de migración, el tipo de intereses...que siempre hay una tendencia a menospreciar un poco la gente de otra...especialmente si el color de tu piel no es como el de ellos.* (Carlos, 3/9/2004)

One interesting aspect of this conversation is the way that Carlos acts as a tutor for his younger colleagues. He talks them down from explicitly insulting Lonnie to seeing him as multidimensional and a more sympathetic character. In doing so, he manages to turn their contempt for Lonnie to admiration by inserting in the conversation the concept of hard work in the face of exploitatively low wages and overall hardship.

As Carlos states in his analysis of this conversation, he sees Ricardo and Jozef as young and Ricardo, in particular, as carefree. Importantly, he makes the point that racism might be behind both how Ricardo and Jozef treat Lonnie (trying to shift their work to him) and how they talk about him (making fun of him). Ricardo and Jozef are phenotypically European in appearance, while Lonnie is Black. As Carlos puts it, 'there is always a tendency to underestimate people a little...especially if the colour of your skin is different from theirs'.

The conversations and interview excerpts I have presented here provide us with a complex picture of the different subject positions that Carlos adopts as he 'does being' an SSL in London. On the one hand, he engages with more marginal SSLs in London, taking on a mentoring and counselling role, writing letters and trying to get things done for people who cannot do these things themselves. On the other hand, he eschews further contact with *marginados* and indeed makes little or no effort to participate in the kinds of activities that many SSLs participate in (e.g. he does not frequent salsa bars).

Carlos clearly positions himself as a transnational, educated Spanish speaker, finding his ideal company in Spanish-speaking professionals living and working in London. However, while his social and cultural capital allows him to join this cosmopolitan group, it is not an effective resource in his workplace. Indeed, his most immediate White British colleagues are impressed by neither his academic qualifications nor his more highbrow interests. At the same time, other colleagues, such as Ricardo and Jozef, do not offer him the kind of intellectual stimulation that he apparently needs. Surrounded by colleagues he does not find particularly interesting, Carlos has opted for acquiescence, on the one hand, and a form of political mentoring on the other. In the former case, he just gets on with his job, doing the tasks he is asked to do and socialises as best he can, talking about football when possible. In the latter case, when he can, he steers conversations towards topics that he finds interesting, such as worker rights, social injustice and economic exploitation. However, one has to wonder if, in such situations, he is doing identity work that is appreciated or even registered by others. In a sense, on the job, he is ultimately a porter, just like his colleagues.

In late 2004, Carlos left his job at the university and took up a post in a London hospital, as the ward manager of 16 cleaning employees. This new job has meant an increase in status and salary, but is not likely to provide the kind of intellectual and professional stimulation that he would like.

Discussion

In the first part of this chapter, I discussed whether or not there is an SSL community in London to speak of. In my view, whether one takes the census-inspired estimate of 75,000, or the larger figure of 300,000, gleaned from informed sources, there are still enough SSLs in London to merit the term 'community' as a demographic description. However, as regards community in Bauman's (2001) sense of the word, that is as a metaphorical space in which people feel a sense of belonging and trust, the picture is mixed. Surely the existence of *asimilados* like Luis suggests that some SSLs effectively opt out of the community, preferring to become part of the ethnic mosaic of London, with no strong ethnic or language affiliation. Javier's depiction of dog-eat-dog world, in which SSLs compete with and exploit one another, also does not bode well for community spirit. However, as Carlos noted in his statement reproduced at the start of this chapter, and as Román-Veláquez (1999) claims in the most extensive account of the SSL community to date, there are a significant number of Londoners who self-identify as SSL and who organize their social lives around this notion.

As regards how individuals 'do being' SSLs in London, the stories told by Javier, Luis and Carlos are representative of three distinct discourses of SSL existence in London. Javier's *marginado* story is probably the most common among SSLs in London, although one should not underestimate the number of *asimilados* and individuals with more nuanced and ambivalent subject positions, such as Carlos. All three cases point to a large and varied community which nonetheless remains relatively invisible. As I explained above, invisibility comes in different forms, from the invisibility of doing the cleaning jobs that no one sees to the invisibility of being racially indistinguishable in the mass of multiracial Londoners.

Most importantly, there is every indication that for the time being the SSL community in London, loose as it is in definition, will continue to grow. This growth is guaranteed by the combination of Faist's (2000) macro, meso and micro conditions, which condition and shape migration. At the macro level, there remain for the foreseeable future massive differentials between Britain and countries like Colombia and Cuba, as regards income, unemployment and political stability. In addition, there are fewer and fewer impediments for those wishing to leave these countries, and control at the receiving end is become increasingly difficult. This difficulty is in part due to the increasing strength of meso factors that favour SSL migration to London. On the one hand, there are

intermediaries who facilitate entry, often by providing illegal documen-
tation, as I noted in Javier's case. However, perhaps more important are
the ties to the family already living in London and information about
job prospects in London. One Colombian woman I interviewed told me
a long story of how her brother had settled in London in the 1980s and
then, over the next 20 years, made arrangements to bring her over as
well. An additional incentive is the growing number of agencies set up
to help SSL migrants, such as the above-cited Colombian Refugee
Association. Finally, at the micro level, there is the simple desire to
improve and secure survival, which is driving millions of migrants each
year away from Mexico, Central America, the Caribbean and South
America to all corners of the developed world.

Another factor which guarantees the growth of the SSL community –
or in any case its maintenance – is the unfulfilled dream of return. For
most SSLs, the initial intention is to stay in London for a few years and
then go back home with enough money to buy a house or open a business. However, circumstances almost inevitably conspire against the
fulfilment of this dream. Children are already in school, studying in
English. Job prospects back home are worse than they were when the
migrant left. And, against all expectations, the migrant begins to carve
out a new identity in London: he/she is not the same person who left
Colombia, Ecuador or Bolivia five or ten years ago. Oscar Silva, head of
the Colombian Refugee Association, describes this frustrated dream as
follows:

> Everyone wants to go back but nobody goes back . . . Everyone, every-
> one arrives here, they say: 'I'm going to save money so I can go back.
> I'm going to buy my house in Colombia so I can go back'. They don't
> go back. And they are not going to go back.
>
> *Todo el mundo quiere volver pero nadie vuele . . . Todos, todos llegan aquí,*
> *dicen: 'Yo voy a ahorrar para volver. Yo voy a comprar mi casa en*
> *Colombia para volver'. No vuelven. Y no van a volver.* (Oscar Silva, 3/11/
> 2004)

Silva is talking about Colombians here, but what he says applies to all
SSLs, and indeed Brazilians, who are perhaps the largest Latino group in
London at present. This being the case, members of this migrant group
begin to experience a transformation from expatriates to transnationals
and immigrants. In the three cases discussed in this chapter, there is a
very clear division along these lines. Javier is an expatriate, maintaining

his sense of self as a Colombian as much as possible. Importantly, however, he is not an expatriate in the same way as the Japanese graduate students and French teachers, discussed in the previous two chapters, might be: his agency is surely curtailed considerably by the conditions in which he lives as a marginalized labour migrant.

In marked contrast to Javier are both Luis and Carlos. Luis, as I explained above, is moving towards a definitive immigrant status, seeing London as his home for the foreseeable future. He speaks English effortlessly and feels comfortable moving from job to job, all the while settling into life in London. Meanwhile, Carlos is not as convinced about staying in London, but he certainly is able to live a more cosmopolitan experience than Javier. This is due to his contact with well-educated middle-class professional Spanish speakers who have settled in London, as well as his sustained contacts with English speakers, both at work and via his wife's family. He lives an ambivalent existence, between his former job as a philosopher lecturer and his current one as the manager of a small group of service staff in a hospital ward, and the social and cultural capital differentials that these two professional subject positions entail.

Conclusion

In this chapter, I have discussed the lives of three SSLs living and working in London. In the context of London as a global city, Javier, Luis and Carlos are members of a rapidly growing multinational migrant group, consisting of individuals representing virtually every Spanish-speaking nation state in the Americas, from Mexico to Argentina. However, several factors have come together to make what is by now one of the larger migrant groups in London practically invisible both to researchers – sociologists, anthropologists, sociolinguists – and official entities, such as the ONS. These factors include their physical dispersion around London; the variability of their physical appearances; the wide range of social and cultural capital they bring with them to London; and the illegal migrant status of many SSLs. However, as I noted in the previous section, the current global economic, social and political conditions serve as a guarantee of sorts that the SLL population in London will continue to grow in coming years. My prediction is that a transnational and immigrant community will eventually develop, one which will come to be a recognized and accepted part of the ethnolinguistic landscape of London.

8
British Asian Undergraduate Students in London

Siân Preece

English I would say is my everyday language, I think in English as well...it's part of my everyday. Urdu is...part of my everyday as well...I communicate with my parents in Urdu [and] the rest of my family. So English and Urdu are both equal in my mind...And Punjabi I hear everyday anyway because my parents talk it at home.

(Aisha, 7/12/2001)

When I speak Urdu I think of my parents...when I speak Punjabi for some reason I think of Sikh people, the language belongs to them...When I speak English I don't think of English people, I think of me. I think of me in England. When I think of Arabic I think of religion because that's what I was there for. I went [to] Saudi Arabia and MAN it's...just like 24-7 religion out there.

(Tahir, 7/11/2001)

The good thing about English is...everybody else speaks it as well so...I am able to...communicate with them...Plus I like the music as well...With Gujarati...I'm basically able to communicate with my family and all my uncles...I also have some friends who are Gujarati as well so I am always able to...speak to them...Swahili, I don't know what to say about that one because I don't know anyone who speaks Swahili...that is something different.

(Geet, 11/11/2001)

These quotes are taken from interviews with Aisha, Tahir and Geet, three British Asian undergraduates studying at Millennium University,[1]

171

one of London's post-1992 universities. They are responding to a question concerning the associations they make with the different languages in their life. Their answers show that they live in a 'multilingual' world comprised of English, in which they experience much of their daily life in London, and the language(s) associated with their heritage culture. While they are 'multilingual' in the sense that their language repertoire embraces varieties of English and 'community' languages common in Britain (Martin-Jones and Jones, 2000), this in no way determines either their 'expertise' or their 'affiliation' (Leung, Harris and Rampton, 1997) to their ancestral languages. In fact, unlike the participants in Chapters 5–7, their greatest expertise is in English and not their 'mother tongue'.

In this chapter, Aisha, Tahir and Geet talk about language by telling stories about their lives, in which they relate language to experiences and relationships. Many of these stories are concerned with 'home', which at times refers to London and at other times denotes ancestral homelands. However, 'home' does not only refer to a physical location, but also to the complex realm of the emotions as a place where we feel we belong and can pursue our most intimate relationships. As was observed in Chapter 2, for people who have migrated, there is frequently an inner 'tug of war' that involves dealing with the ambivalent feelings arising from attempts to reconcile new surroundings with remaining attachments to an 'imagined homeland' (Anderson, 1991). The data presented here suggest that these feelings remain, to a greater or lesser extent, for the children of migrants. For while Aisha, Tahir and Geet are unlike the other participants in this book in that they are British nationals who have grown up and been educated in London, they all go through a process of positioning and re-positioning themselves in relation to their British nationality and the maintenance of links with the people, customs, practices and language(s) of their ancestral homelands. In this chapter, therefore, I set out to explore these issues and consider whether Aisha, Tahir and Geet can be said to live their lives as 'transnationals', as described in Chapter 1.

Additionally, the young people in this chapter are part of a steadily growing number of British Asians, that is people of South Asian heritage, entering London universities. Perhaps this is not so surprising given that, as was observed in Chapter 3, British Asians represent the largest ethnic minority group in London. However, while many London universities are recruiting large numbers of British Asians, together with members of London's other ethnic minorities, the issue of ethnicity is still often discussed in terms of 'essentialized' ethnic groups based on the National Census categories. There is, as yet, little discussion of ethnicity among higher education students in terms of 'identifications, subjectivities and positions'. In this chapter, therefore, I aim to make some contribution to the debate on the student body from this latter standpoint.

The 'communities of practice' framework, discussed briefly in Chapter 2, postulates that individuals develop a sense of 'who they are', their identity and place within the social order, through participating in the practices of social communities. While Jeanne Lave and Etienne Wenger (1991) focus on the individual's identity inside a community, Penelope Eckert and Sally McConnell-Ginet (2003) argue that identity is constituted in the 'process of balancing the self' both within and across the 'central' communities of practice in an individual's life. In this chapter, therefore, I consider Aisha, Tahir and Geet's attempts at 'balancing the self' across key 'communities of practice', which for the purposes of this research I have interpreted as family, peers and the University. I begin by providing some background of the research setting and project. Following this, I explore each story in turn before discussing my findings in relation to some of the issues outlined in Chapters 1 and 2. Unlike Chapters 5–7, I do not discuss the history of migration, in this case of South Asians, to Britain. This seems unnecessary for setting the scene in this chapter as the participants are all British nationals whose families either migrated to London before their birth or while they were small children. Furthermore, as Chapter 3 provides a concise historical background of the migration of South Asians to London, here I intend to focus on the stories of their children, as the second generation.

Setting

The data on which this chapter is based come from a research project into issues of undergraduate identity and identifications in higher education within the context of widening participation in British universities.[2] All the data were collected in the physical location of Millennium University over a two-year period, while the participants' main occupation was study. Millennium University has an ethos of widening participation in London, where it recruits over 70 per cent of its student population. As was observed in Chapter 3, as a global city, London is a site of multiple and massive migrations of people from all over the world. This has resulted in a great diversification of London's population which now has several million inhabitants from ethnic minority communities (see 2001 Census figures in Chapter 3). It is not surprising, therefore, that as Millennium continues to recruit actively in the London area, the number of ethnic minority students has risen to well over 50% of the overall student body, with some courses attracting a much higher proportion (see e.g. Adia, 1996; Bird, 1996; Modood and Acland, 1998; Farr, 2001 for discussions of issues relating to ethnic minority students in British universities).

Many Millennium students have grown up and been educated in London in what Roger Hewitt calls a 'polycultural' setting, which he describes as encompassing 'cultural entities that are not...discrete and complete...not "intrinsically equal"; and...active together and... bound up with change' (Hewitt, 1992: 30). Much of the student body is accustomed to mixing with people from a wide range of ethnic and religious backgrounds. In their eyes there is nothing particularly noteworthy about this; it is a normal part of London life and being a Londoner. Additionally, many Millennium students use varieties of London English with their peers, which have been referred to as, for example, 'local multi-ethnic vernacular' or 'community English' (Hewitt, 1992). This is in keeping with Leung, Harris and Rampton's (1997) claim that many British children, whether from ethnic minority or majority communities, are affiliated to the local vernacular. Among these students there is a wide range of expertise, both spoken and written, in the home language(s) and in the *literate English* used by academic communities, which Catherine Wallace defines as a variety of English, both spoken and written, which is 'most like [the] formal written English... [encountered] in broadsheet newspapers, quality novels and non-fiction texts' (Wallace, 2002: 105).

Millennium University has established various measures to support this diverse student body, including an academic literacy screening programme that refers some incoming undergraduates to an academic writing course (see Preece and Godfrey, 2004, for a discussion of the student profile on this course). This writing programme, on which I was a teacher, provides the setting for the first stage of the research. During this first phase, I collected data in the classroom on issues of language, gender and ethnic/linguistic identity. I kept field notes of the teaching sessions, gathered questionnaire data and audio-recorded small group discussions in the classroom, related to language practices of the academic community, their peer groups and their families. I discussed the research in class and used data concerning the students' preferred reading practices and their thoughts on 'posh' and 'slang' English, their terms for 'literate English' (Wallace, 2002) and 'peer-group English' respectively, for classroom discussions and activities. The second phase of the research took place in the students' second year at the University. I approached former class members to see whether they would be prepared to meet with me for a series of interviews. Aisha, Tahir and Geet are three of the participants who agreed to this.

In the following sections, I draw on the peer-group discussion and interviews I carried out with informants to explore the ways in which Aisha, Tahir and Geet 'do being' young British Asians in London and to consider whether there is any evidence to suggest that they live their lives as 'transnationals', as described in Chapter 1. I focus on the ways that negotiating identity involves a continual process of positioning the self in relation to the (language) practices of key 'communities of practice' (Lave and Wenger, 1991), in which the 'old' and the 'new' interact and transform each other. As Aisha, Tahir and Geet negotiate 'difference' (Papastergiadis, 2000) between London and their parental homeland, they take up 'culturally intelligible' (Butler, 1990) subject positions within the discourses to which they have access. In addition, as they position and re-position themselves within these discourses, there are moments where the interaction of gender and ethnicity becomes evident. While there are many examples in the database of the participants positioning themselves in relation to their family communities, it was beyond the scope of the research to collect spoken data from the family setting.

Aisha: At home in London and Pakistan

Born in 1982 in London, Aisha is the oldest child of an Urdu and Punjabi-speaking Pakistani family and has two younger sisters. Aisha lives with her parents, sisters and one of her uncles in the parental home in London and maintains regular contact with her relatives in Pakistan through visits and letters. With her mother, Aisha primarily speaks Urdu, while with her father she code-switches far more between English and Urdu. When talking about herself in relation to her parents, Aisha frequently positions Urdu as her 'mother tongue':

> My parents are from Pakistan. My dad knows English very well but my mum isn't...too well...at speaking English...because Urdu is her first language. I've learnt it from them, it's my first language as well...It's much easier communicating with my parents [and] everyone else in the family. And also my parents want me to speak this language because...it's their culture...so...they wanted me to learn it. (Aisha, 7/12/2001)

In the example above, Aisha seems to be trying to reconcile two positions. In one, Urdu is the 'first language' learnt in the normal course of growing up in an Urdu-speaking home. In the second, there is a suggestion that Urdu needed to be learnt in order to fulfil parental expectations and do being a dutiful daughter. In this latter position, Aisha also suggests a rather more distant relationship with Urdu and her heritage culture through using 'their' to refer to her parental culture, rather than 'my' or 'our'. Interestingly, this is one of the few places in the data in which Aisha creates some distance between herself and her ancestral heritage. This may have arisen through the social setting of the interview, in which Aisha was positioning herself in relation to me, an outsider to the British Pakistani community, while trying to explain the language practices of her family.

Aisha reports that she finds it easier to talk with her siblings in English. However, she also comments that the setting influences their language choice. On visits to Pakistan or in family gatherings, for example, they use much more Urdu. The context also affects her language choice with friends. At Millennium, they generally use English but when her friends visit her home, they use Urdu mixed with English. The variety of English is again determined by the setting, with 'formal' English reserved for class presentations and 'slang' among her peers. As the following interview excerpt illustrates, Aisha adapts her language according to the 'environment' in order to facilitate her inclusion in group relations:

A: [The language] depends on the environment...When we're all in Pakistan we all communicate in Urdu but then here (i.e. London) we all communicate in English...

SP: And when you have family gatherings and...there's lots of people together, do you find that you are talking more in Urdu or more in English?

A: More in Urdu definitely because everyone else is speaking Urdu... so you don't want to feel left out...you want to be a part of it...

SP: What about with your friends?...Do you speak most of the time in English with your friends?

A: Yes, all the time...It's the same thing as my sisters...it's...the environment like in uni, it's English [because] everyone speaks English, so you want to be part of it...

SP: And is it the same with friends who would speak Urdu?

A: Yes...but if they come round my house...there's a different environment so then maybe we would speak Urdu sometimes and mix it in more with the English. (Aisha, 7/12/2001)

These comments suggest that Aisha associates talk with building solidarity and intimacy with family and friends. Her ability to switch between Urdu and English, according to the setting, facilitates her participation in talk with friends and at family gatherings in London and Pakistan. Perhaps her anxiety about being 'left out' and excluded have acted as an impetus for her to develop her expertise in Urdu. Certainly there is a large body of literature (e.g. Rubin, 1985; Gouldner and Strong, 1987; Coates, 1996, 1998; Hey, 1996; Johnson and Aries, 1998) documenting the central role of talk in establishing and maintaining friendships and close relationships for women. This may partly explain Aisha's motivation to learn Urdu so that she can be included in conversation with her family and maintain these social relationships. Stephen Frosh, Ann Phoenix and Rob Pattman (2002), for example, discuss female talk as doing 'interpersonal work' (p. 100) focused on the 'relational' rather than 'individuation' (p. 121). While there is a danger of over-generalizing about women focusing on achieving 'rapport' (Tannen, 1990) through talk, Aisha frequently presents a self that is concerned with social relationships, fitting into the 'environment' and working to maintain cordiality. This persona is highly oriented to traditional discourses that position women as 'naturally' disposed to co-operative relationships, which, in Aisha's case, she relates to through frequent references to adaptability to the 'environment'. This enables a presentation of self, in effect, as a confident young woman positively oriented to her Pakistani cultural heritage and the British popular youth culture of her peers. This adaptability is reminiscent of Pia Pichler's (2001) findings on ways in which British Bangladeshi teenage girls negotiated 'bi-cultural' femininities with their peers through adopting subject positions intertwining traditional and popular discourses.

For Aisha, adaptability to the 'environment' means orienting to discourses popular among her peers as well as those in her family; one such discourse is 'girl power'. Defined as a 'self-reliant attitude among girls and young women manifested in ambition, assertiveness and individualism' (OED, 2001), 'girl power' appears to constitute femininity in terms of sassiness, youth, glamour, consumerism and individualism enacted through doing being a 'ladette'. Although this involves orienting to the laddish norms of having a laugh, acting cool and being tough and aggressive, doing being a ladette also values the interpersonal aspects of female friendships and encourages young women to have greater aspirations in life. However, 'girl power' discursive subject positions, as Imelda Whelehan (2000) points out, are based on a consumerist 'manifesto' (p. 48), divorced from social and political movements for change, ambivalent at best and hostile at worst to feminism. Consequently, while ladettes can emulate lads' bad behaviour, they are still expected to collude with female objectification as a way of 'having a laugh'. As Imelda Whelehan (2000) comments, there is a very thin dividing line between ladette as 'sassy, intelligent and independent' and ladette as 'glamorised "tomboy" ' (p. 51).

One way in which orientation to 'girl power' is noticeable is through appearance. Aisha, like many of her female peers, is highly concerned with glamour and young women's fashion. She closely follows the latest trends not only through reading magazines for teenage girls and young women, but also in her own appearance. Another way that identifying with 'girl power' becomes noticeable is in the talk of all-female discussion groups. The following excerpt is from the all-female group discussion data from the classroom. In it, Aisha is interacting with three other second-generation British Pakistanis, Davinder, Saba and Zarina, who are all female. Davinder and Saba are close friends and core members of this group while Aisha and Zarina have peripheral group membership. Their talk begins with an overt 'othering' of the mainstream student body at Millennium which sets the tone for much of the remaining discussion.

S = Saba, D = Davinder, A = Aisha, Z = Zarina

1. S: okay/ (.) now then/ <tape paused> girls/ (.) HOW do you SEE YOURSELF in RELATION (.) to a) other student in your year? <reading aloud>

2. D: erm/ (.) okay/ erm there's like loads of different people/ and it's completely different/ because (.) they're not all the same age as us/ because it's like/ at the end/ (.) you're talking about/ <laughs> same age as us/ [<laughs>

3. S: [thank you Davinder/ (.) Aisha?

4. All: <laughter> (4) <tape paused>

5. A: I think there are a lot of students/ that are mature/ (.) so that we can't/ (.) relate to 'em/ <laughs>

6. S: thank you Aisha/ <laughs> <recording turned off/on> (2) okay/ right in relation to the other/ (.) member/ I mean =

7. Z: = YEAH/ I agree with the points that are made/ (.) that's what I would say as well/

8. S: all right/ (.) I think that erm/ (.) there's different type of people around/ and =

9. D: = it's LOADS of people we hardly/ (.) [mm/

10. S: [yeah/ it's [difficult/

11. D: [we're only
        about two out of the whole university/
12. All: [<laughter>
13. S: THANK YOU <laughs> DAVINDER
14. All: <laughter> <tape turned off> (Group discussion, 26/2/2001)

In this part of the discussion, Aisha works to fit in with Saba and Davinder, the dominant members of the group. In turn 1, Saba positions them all as 'girls'. Her utterance has a humorous tone, suggesting she is inviting them to have a laugh. It also appears to be an inclusive move; the other participants can be included through cooperating. Davinder develops her friend's utterance through drawing attention to 'age' differences in which she adopts a position in opposition to other Millennium students (turn 2). Her reply appears playful and is collectively responded to with laughter. At this point (turn 5), Aisha is nominated for the floor. Not wishing to take her turn too serioulsy, and risk upsetting group relations, she presents a youthful, carefree persona. Collaborating with Saba and Davinder, she clarifies the reference to 'age' by positioning Millennium students as 'mature' and claiming that this is a barrier to social relations. Saba and Davinder then provide the conclusion to this part of the discussion through further collaborative turns which reinforce the youthful and sassy 'girl' tone.

Throughout this section, the talk is punctuated with laughter, which orients the participants to 'girl power' and enacting ladette femininity, which, according to Imelda Whelehan, is constituted through a lack of seriousness in which 'normal "girls" like nothing better than a laugh with their mates' (Whelehan, 2000: 40). As Jennifer Coates (1996) comments, laughter also serves as a minimal response in the co-production of the collaborative floor. However, it also positions Aisha within the power relations of the group. It is questionable whether she laughs because she is having fun or because she is working to maintain face with Saba and Davinder. As Deborah Cameron suggests, smiling and other 'expressive' sounds and intonation patterns are construed as 'symbolically feminine behaviours' (Cameron, 2000: 334), which can function as signs of deference and appeasement, or as gestures 'offered upward in the status hierarchy' (Henley, 1986: 171).

From this excerpt, we see Aisha adapting to the 'environment' by orienting to 'girl power' in order to co-operate with her peers, in a playful, stylish and sassy 'girl' rendition of self. Despite the frequently pejorative naming of women as 'girls', Aisha and her peers appear to embrace this gendered identity in a way which suggests identification with youth, lack of responsibilities and a carefree existence. As Whelehan comments, when women name themselves 'girl', it can be to recall youthful and untroubled times before the 'travails of womanhood set in' (Whelehan, 2000: 39). However, despite orienting to the norms of 'girl power', Aisha also takes advantage of opportunities that arise with her peers to present herself as positively oriented to the (language) practices of her parental culture. In the excerpt below, taken from later in the same peer group discussion, Aisha positions herself as having both expertise and affiliation to her parental languages. In her exchanges with Zarina (turns 3–10), she makes a bid for a more serious conversational floor in which they can display this identification. However, as the excerpt illustrates, Saba and Davinder resist this move, perhaps because it threatens their control of the group proceedings and their strong identification with doing ladette femininity.

S = Saba, D = Davinder, A = Aisha, Z = Zarina, F = unknown

1. S: how do you see yourself in relation to these languages? <reading aloud> Davinder?
2. D: okay I'm quite good at English/ as in speaking and stuff/ but er Punjabi/ I'm not that good (2)
3. A: okay I can speak Urdu quite well/ and read it/ and write it/ (.) and er I keep in [touch with my cousins as well/ so that I can practise Urdu
4. F: [wow
5. A: that way =
6. Z: = that's really [good/
7. A: [and (.) I'm okay at English as well/
8. Z: I'm okay with English but Urdu/ (.) I can't write it that well =
9. A: = can you read it?
10. Z: yeah/ I can read it/
11. D: RAH =
12. S: = basically ME/ (.) I'm okay in English/ and Punjabi/ I cannot read it AT ALL/ (.) so that's about it/ (.) all right moving onto number six/ (.) HO:W do you THINK you are/ ah:::: (3) <laughs> we're finished now/ thank you very much/ and er Davinder wants to say 'bye'/
13. All: <laughter>
14. S: everyone say 'bye' now
15. All: BYE:: <laughter> (Group discussion, 26/2/2001)

In the interview setting, Aisha discusses the (language) practices of her home in more detail. She recalls learning to speak Urdu with her mother as a small child. Her mother also taught her the Urdu alphabet and spent time reading children's stories in Urdu to her. Later Aisha studied Urdu formally during her secondary schooling, taking Urdu for GCSE and A-level. She presents her London school in a positive light, claiming that one way it paid attention to the multicultural composition of the student intake was by offering home languages and treating home languages and English equally.

These interview data suggest that Urdu facilitates the mother–daughter relationship for Aisha. She frequently links learning and speaking Urdu with her mother and presents Urdu as marking intimate moments with her mother since early childhood. Part of the motivation for studying Urdu for GCSE and A-level may also have been to please her mother by displaying her identification with her 'mother tongue'. This is suggested in data where Aisha reconstructs conversations in which she enacts her 13-year-old self in dialogue with her mother over whether to study Urdu at school. These associations may also colour her attitude to her other parental language, Punjabi. For while her parents can speak both Urdu and Punjabi and use Punjabi between themselves, as the following excerpt from her interview shows, Aisha makes a great distinction between her parental languages, in which she distances herself from Punjabi.

A: My family background is Punjabi so mainly my parents actually speak Punjabi with each other. But with us it is in Urdu because I don't like Punjabi.

SP: You don't like it?

A: No...I think it just seems like you're arguing when you're talking [Punjabi].... Urdu I think is really sweet...when you talk it...whereas when you speak Punjabi, it seems like you're fighting. It's not very formal...it's like slang but I don't like it...My parents [and] my family elders they all speak in Punjabi but with kids it is Urdu.

SP: So do you think that your parents are equally fluent in both?

A: Yes, definitely...

SP: Have they always spoken to you in Urdu? Do you think they spoke to you in Punjabi at any time?

A: No, Urdu always. Because I have told them I don't like Punjabi, so don't talk to me in Punjabi.

SP: Where do you think that you formed that opinion that you didn't like Punjabi? Do you remember what started that off?

A: I think...when I went to Pakistan (laughs) because all my family there speak Punjabi there...but I didn't like it much...I decided at a very early age that I liked Urdu more.

SP: You like the sound better?

A: Yeah, Urdu...seems...more polite whereas Punjabi it sounds as though you're just being rude.

SP: When you go to Pakistan and you're with your relatives...are they speaking...to you in Punjabi?

A: No, Urdu...they speak both [but] with us they speak in Urdu... But mostly all my cousins communicate in Urdu. It's just maybe once or twice that their parents say to speak Punjabi...It's like...maybe a generation gap, the older generation speak Punjabi and the younger generation speak Urdu. (Aisha, 7/12/2001)

Aisha seems to make several associations with her parental languages which enable her to favour Urdu over Punjabi. Firstly, she 'genders' both languages, positioning Urdu at the 'feminine' pole, by constructing it as soft and 'really sweet' and 'polite', and Punjabi at the 'masculine' pole, through associating it with aggression, 'fighting' and being 'rude'. These associations seem to have arisen during trips to Pakistan, which began when Aisha was a baby and have occurred on numerous occasions since then. Perhaps Aisha associates Urdu with her home life as a small child in London in contrast to Punjabi, which she seems to associate with trips 'back home' to her extended family in Pakistan. As a small child, perhaps she found these family gatherings in Pakistan a little chaotic and unsettling and began to associate Punjabi with these feelings. Secondly, she associates Urdu and Punjabi with life stage and age, in which she positions Urdu as the language of her contemporaries and Punjabi as the language of her elders. This coupled with her linking Punjabi with 'slang' and Urdu with speaking more formally may suggest that she associates Punjabi with older and less educated Pakistanis, who may be more traditional in outlook, and Urdu with a more youthful, educated and 'modern' Pakistani generation, who have moved away from traditional village life to become city dwellers. This presents an interesting contrast to 'slang' and 'posh' English in which Aisha, like the other participants in the research, associates 'slang' with doing being 'cool' and youthful Londoners, who represent a generation 'on the move', and 'posh' English with doing being mature and serious. As one participant commented, their generation associates 'posh' talk with the 'elderly', which within the context of Millennium, appears to denote those identifying with the (language) practices of academia.

To conclude, it seems that Urdu facilitates the intimacy of the mother–daughter relationship for Aisha and enables her to develop relationships with her Pakistani contemporaries, whom she positions as 'modern', and possibly a modernising influence in Pakistan. While at 'home' in London, she maintains written correspondence in Urdu with these contemporaries and keeps up to date with Pakistani news, through reading a daily Urdu newspaper, and Pakistani lifestyle, through Urdu women's magazines. Through familial and social networks which connect Britain and Pakistan, Aisha has found ways of affiliating to both her 'homes'. While London remains her primary home, in which she participates in peer group practices, she has also discovered ways of feeling 'at home' in Pakistan and with her Pakistani cultural heritage.

Tahir: Only at home in London

Born in 1979 in London, Tahir is the second child of an Urdu and Punjabi-speaking Pakistani family who also use Arabic to practise Islam. Tahir has eight siblings, six younger sisters, one elder and one younger brother, who live in the parental home in London and have regular contact with members of the extended family in London and Pakistan. With his parents and elders Tahir uses a mixture of English, Urdu and Punjabi. However, he frequently comments that he finds it difficult to maintain a conversation in Urdu or Punjabi. As the excerpt below from the interview data illustrates, this can result in the disapproval of relatives and occasions when he is silenced in family settings:

> Me and the little ones, my sisters and brothers, we [speak] mixed innit?...My mum and dad they can speak Punjabi and Urdu, they understand both...They're quite similar...Urdu and Punjabi... have words...that mean the same in both languages...My mum and dad...can understand both Punjabi and Urdu. They can speak Punjabi [and] Urdu and read it whereas we can't. We just pick up a little bit here, pick up a little bit there [and] just speak as we go along. My parents don't mind...[but] I think relatives do sometimes. Relatives think [we] should speak proper Urdu or Punjabi... When I speak in front of my mum and dad I say what I want but when I speak in front of relatives and they're speaking Urdu or Punjabi, in that case I just don't talk. (Tahir, 7/11/2001)

While Aisha distinguishes between Urdu and Punjabi, Tahir frequently conflates them with claims that they are similar and with frequent substitutions of Punjabi for Urdu, and vice versa, throughout the data. As Tahir has little knowledge of his parental languages, it seems likely that this has arisen through the 'mixed', or hybridized, variety of language used at home, in which Urdu and Punjabi words and expressions have become embedded in English. As Tahir has discovered, while this acts as a means of communication among the immediate family, it is not transferable to other settings. The data suggest that there are few situations when Tahir uses Punjabi or Urdu out of choice. One of the few uses he reports in this way is his use of Urdu for giving his sisters commands when there are visitors present in the house. However, as he claims that he only uses Urdu in front of visitors who are non-Urdu speakers, this appears to be a face-saving device in case his sisters do not comply and he loses face. Tahir draws on his cultural heritage to explain community social relationships in which he positions elders as needing to guide, protect and provide for younger and more vulnerable members of their families and communities. In turn, it is the responsibility of those who are younger to accept this guidance as the following excerpt illustrates:

> My brother is older than me so obviously there's something that I can say in front of him and some things I can't…I'll speak to him with respect, he speaks to me with respect [and] I'll call him brother…He talks to me and I'll follow his instructions…but when I'm speaking to [my sister] I'm the older one and she has to talk to me with respect and I'll give her guidance and then she'll follow it. (Tahir, 13/2/2002)

Throughout this section of talk, Tahir relates family and community practices to gender in ways which suggest that men are in a position of authority and have a duty of care while women are in a position of vulnerability and need protection. An illustration of this comes from a narrative in which Tahir tells the story of an 'Urdu woman', unknown to him, who was lost on the London underground and asked him for help. As he was unable to explain directions in Urdu and she was unable to speak English, Tahir felt it was his duty to escort her to her destination, a journey which involved him in a detour. Other examples of this traditional masculinity oriented to his family community arise in talk about his sisters' progress at school. He takes pride in their confidence and achievements, for which he takes part of the credit with his older brother through, for example, ensuring that their sisters have the latest educational computer software. He also appears to be responsible for representing his family at school events in which his youngest sister is a participant. At these moments, Tahir appears to enact a somewhat old-fashioned and chivalrous masculinity oriented to the practices of his home community. These stand in marked contrast to his performances of laddish masculinity, which I will discuss later in this section.

As Tahir becomes older, he is expected to take on adult responsibilities, not only for representing his family at British institutional events, such as his sister's school, but also community gatherings, such as weddings and funerals. As the following excerpt from his interview illustrates, he is part of a network of social relations in which he is expected to fulfill his role as a son by giving a good account of himself and his family with his elders; it is not acceptable to remain silent:

> Actually going to weddings and stuff at first... they [would] say, 'Oh look! That's Mr T's son' [and] I was quiet. But then recently, because I'm older now, ...someone passed away so I had to go down [to pay respects] because you have to go down...So I went down on behalf of my father and my family and I walked into the room [but] before I sat down, my uncle's going, '...Do you know who this guy is?' And everyone looked [and my uncle said] 'Tell them who you are' and I go 'I'm Mr T's son...' [and they said] 'Ah! You're Mr T's son! What do you do?' [and I replied] 'Oh I go to university' [and then they asked] 'What are you studying?' [and]...'How's your father...[and] mother?' And you've got to learn to speak...You can't just sit there...You can't escape it. (Tahir, 13/2/2002)

Because of his low levels of expertise in Urdu and Punjabi, Tahir constantly presents himself as having difficulties in these family situations. One strategy he adopts is to allow his interlocutor to 'speak first' and then attempt to 'use those words back' while keeping the pace of the conversation 'slow'. However, there are times when this strategy does not work, particularly on visits 'back home' to Pakistan, or on occasions when his parents have just returned from Pakistan. At these times, the 'new' and the 'old' (see Chapter 2) come into conflict for his parents and relatives who worry about the fact that their British-born children do not speak 'beautiful' Urdu. According to Tahir, this results in 'a lot of problems' and 'nerve-racking' family situations in which he resorts to positioning himself as a 'native speaker of English' and/or 'keeping [his] mouth shut'.

These 'nerve-racking' situations do not seem solely related to language, however. On visits to Pakistan criticism of his inability to speak fluent Punjabi and Urdu also provides a way for his relatives to probe into deeper issues related to doing 'acceptable' masculinity (Coates, 2003) as a Pakistani male. For it seems that members of Tahir's family do not consider that he displays sufficient identification with his Pakistani heritage and accuse him of being one of 'these guys (i.e. British Pakistani males) who have forgotten their roots'. Tahir does not deny this charge but attempts to defend himself by claiming that he is misunderstood by his relatives in Pakistan who do not understand what it is like to live in England. For Tahir, therefore, contact with 'back home' appears to raise conflicting subjectivities which are difficult to resolve. He fluctuates between a self-presentation in which he displays concern for maintaining 'face' within family social relations and a persona who is unconcerned with enacting 'acceptable' masculinity within his family.

A further example of these conflicting subjectivities arises in relation to maintaining religious practices. Tahir discusses several experiences relating to religion in which he positions himself passively, as a spectator, rather than participant, and as fulfilling other people's expectations. This is illustrated in the way he depicts his family's visit to Mecca, in Saudi Arabia, for the purposes of *Hadj*.[3] He presents this pilgrimage negatively, describing it in terms of '24–7 religion' in which he was surrounded by 'really mean' and 'aggressive' people who 'go mad' while practising their faith. He also shows little identification with the six years in which he spent ten hours per week learning Arabic in the mosque after school. According to Tahir, while his sisters were having a 'good laugh' learning Urdu poetry and stories, he was required to do the serious work of reading the whole Koran in order to do ' "acceptable" maleness' (Coates, 2003) in his family, particularly in relation to his father:

> [In the mosque, my sisters] would read poetry...they knew all the poetry...I can remember vaguely about 2 birds [that] would come alive...it was really exciting. So [they] would sit there singing out all this poetry. It was a good laugh but I never got to do it. My dad made me read the 30 chapters [of the Koran]...whilst my sisters got to do all the poetry...I'd prefer to do [the poetry]. (Tahir, 7/11/2001)

For much of the time, Tahir presents himself as weakly oriented to the practices of his parental cultural heritage, particularly those which prescribe the norms of hegemonic masculinity. Much of this ambivalence appears to be based on a perception of Pakistan as old-fashioned and Pakistanis as uninvolved in the practices of popular culture, with which he shows a strong identification, as we shall see. An example of this perception arises in the interview excerpt below, in which he tells how his sister, while on a trip to Pakistan, met a young woman who expressed an interest in popular music:

> I was really shocked because [when] my sister went [to Pakistan] she got off the plane and this girl walked up to her and said...'Do you

know Livin' La Vida Loca?' My sister goes, 'WHAT! Livin' La Vida Loca! The Ricky Martin set! What are they doing listening to that?' She come back and told me and I was like, RAH shocked. (Tahir, 7/11/2001)

In presenting himself as 'shocked' by this episode, Tahir reveals the way in which he constructs an archaic and old-fashioned image of Pakistan as a place where there is little youth culture and where young people are not interested in Western music or lifestyle. As he recounts his experiences of life in London, this contrast between life in Pakistan as traditional and old-fashioned, and life in London as modern and 'cool' continues. This becomes particularly noticeable when Tahir talks about his interest in computer games, particularly those based on Manga, in which he shows a strong affiliation to aspects of Japanese culture. Tahir's interest in Manga and computer games developed through his friendships with Chinese boys at school with whom he spent much time in London's China Town. During these China Town trips, Tahir claims to have met several Japanese 'geezers' who were 'renowned' for their 'class stuff' in the computer games industry. Tahir eulogizes the work of these men claiming that they are 'legends in Japan' and 'masters' who 'set goals' and 'standards' that have resulted in 'people looking up to' and 'respecting them'. As the following interview excerpt illustrates, Tahir identifies strongly with the 'cool' youth aspects of Japanese culture to the point where he can imagine himself as Japanese:

I always wish that if – if I wasn't, well I'll ask a stupid question, 'If I wasn't Pakistani, what would I be?' And I'd probably want to be Japanese because...I'm interested in their culture,...they're nice people, they have rough[4] stuff (laughs)...You've got to respect them. (Tahir, 7/11/2001)

Interestingly, Tahir often does not seem sure if his school friends and the China Town 'geezers' are of Chinese or Japanese heritage, frequently conflating the two. However, this does not seem to matter for Tahir as he is drawn to the tough hegemonic masculinity enacted in the world of Chinese and Japanese film, comics and computer games in which men earn respect not only for being tough, hard and streetwise, but also because they are capable of coming up with 'cool' ideas under pressure. This world provides alternative subject positions to that of his family, positions which he frequently adopts when talking about himself in relation to his peers and the University. In addition to these Chinese/Japanese 'hard men', Tahir constructs a world peopled by other males in popular culture to whom he aspires, such as Michael Schumacher (Formula One racing driver), Tiger Woods (golfing celebrity) and Han Solo (fictional character in *Star Wars* movies). Interestingly, he claims that he identifies with Han Solo because he is 'solo', in other words, because he has 'no parents' and is therefore 'free' to act as he wants. These role models also provide Tahir with a world in which he claims he can 'disappear for a while' to live vicariously, disconnected from 'reality'. When orienting to this world with his peers, he is no longer tongue-tied. Instead, he engages in fast-moving and witty repartee in which he is frequently centre stage and through which he accomplishes being 'one of the lads'. As Imelda Whelehan (2000) comments, being a 'lad' has become widely associated with adolescent male behaviour, embedded within popular culture and linked to the practices of having a laugh, acting cool and/or tough. In his peer group, his verbal displays facilitate his domination of the conversational floor and encourage his peers not only to defer to him, but also to look to him to provide laddish entertainment in the classroom. While Tahir enjoys this attention, he can also find this onerous, as he explains in the following interview excerpt:

> I've got no problem if someone tells me to do a presentation, I can do it...Last week we had to do one [in class]...and all the boys said, 'You've got to do it'. Anyway it annoys me sometimes because I always do it...it does my head in sometimes [but] I can sit there and laugh because when I get up there they start smiling and laughing. (Tahir, 13/2/2002)

In group discussions Tahir collaborates with his peers in the construction of fast-moving dialogue based on series of in-jokes. In class, he is the core member of a peer group consisting of Randeep (male), Vritti (female) and Geet (male), who are all British Asians. Tahir, Randeep and Vritti collaborate to form a close-knit in-group, from which Geet (who is the subject of the following section) is largely excluded. Sometimes, Tahir and Randeep make Vritti do 'serious' talk on their work while they provide tongue-in-cheek laddish commentaries designed to entertain each other, largely at Vritti's expense. At other times, their interactions with Vritti are flirtatious as they vie for her attention with ever-wittier and/or daring remarks. At other times, all group together and turn their attention on Geet, as I will discuss in the following section. Some of this talk fuses together elements of their parental heritage with other cultural traditions. The following excerpt from the group discussion data is typical of the co-construction of the floor, in which the talk is designed both to entertain and to see which of the males can outperform the other in front of Vritti. Geet remains silent throughout this exchange.

T = Tahir, R = Randeep, V = Vritti

1. T: If you could choose any language =
2. R: = now?
3. T: yeah/
4. V: I want to speak Italian =
5. T: = why are you? (.) don't copy me [plea:se/ don't copy/ you know
6. V: [no NO NO<laughs>
7. T: what I mean <humorous tone>/ [maybe ((xx)) seriously in my blood (.)
8. V: [NO NO
9. T: you know/ (.) I have got slight Italian =
10. V: = oh: okay =<disbelieving tone>
11. T: = WHAT do you know? WHAT do you know? [WHAT do you know? <humorous tone>
12. V: [<laughs>
13. R: [<laughs>
14. T: I shouldn't have said anything/ you know my great great great granddad?
15. R: mm mm: <ironic tone>
16. T: he made spaghetti back in =
17. R: = Brick Lane⁵
18. V: [<laughter
19. T: [I'M NOT JOKING <humorous tone>
20. V: [laughter
21. R: [laughter   (Group discussion, 26/2/2001)

Overt attention to gender and sexuality frequently occurs when Tahir is relating stories of his life in London. In the interviews, he discusses the way his peers objectify women in men's magazines such as *FHM*. Interestingly, this talk also functions as a way of enacting heterosexual masculinity with his male peers, which, as Cameron (1997) points out, young men in all-male groups are often at pains to do. Heterosexual masculinity is further reinforced by the importing of traditionally 'feminized' subjects on celebrities, sex, fashion, lifestyle and relationships into men's magazines in which men are given advice on these subjects in relation to maintaining heterosexual relationships. Tahir comments, for example, that one of the functions of *FHM* is to provide discussion material on subjects such as 'how to satisfy your women in a hundred and one ways' and 'how to impress your girlfriend'.

As the excerpt below shows, he also narrates imaginary incidents concerning violence against women in which he positions himself as giving expert advice to his male colleagues on 'acceptable' ways of portraying male violence against women in video and computer games:

> Let's say I'm working for [Johnson's[6]]...they might move to their branch in Highbury and Islington and I go there and I meet a few people and I go, 'I'm from [Johnson's] in Tottenham Court Road' and they go, '...will you just help us out on this bit?' And I go, 'Yeah, this is how you...edit it. DO NOT SHOW THE GUY punching the woman in the face cos you can't show that on television, obviously on a computer game, but you can't show a guy hitting a woman or breaking a woman's arm or anything like that'. And they'll go, 'Oh yeah'. Whereas if that was Geet [referring to fellow group member], he'd go there and he'd...stand outside for half an hour before he walked in and he'd just hide from everybody (laughs). (Tahir, 7/11/2001)

In narratives such as these, Tahir positions himself as having expertise, authority and as being in control. The gender relations he depicts suggest that Tahir is constrained by the norms of hegemonic masculinity which, as Jennifer Coates (2003) comments, require displays of 'heterosexuality, toughness, power and authority, competitiveness and the subordination of gay men' (p. 196). While Tahir does not discuss homosexuality overtly, he is at pains to portray himself as heterosexual and tough in contrast with his friend, Geet, who is frequently positioned as a 'wimp'.

With his peers and while talking about his peers in the interviews, Tahir frequently enacts laddish masculinity that is rooted in London as a global city, a setting in which aspects of 'cool' cultures from around the world can become fused with British popular youth culture. In contrast, he appears more ambivalent about doing 'acceptable' masculinity in the setting of his family, frequently discussing this in terms of family obligations and duties. While Aisha has discovered ways of feeling at 'home' in both London and Pakistan and with a 'bi-cultural' self, Tahir only really seems at 'home' with his London laddish self. Unlike Aisha, who uses family and social networks to forge her own links with Pakistan, Tahir shows little inclination to use the networks of his family and community to develop his own links with Pakistan.

Geet: 'Rootless' in London?

Born in 1982 in Kenya, Geet is the third child of a Kenyan Asian family who are Gujarati speakers. Until the age of eight he lived with his parents and three siblings (one older and one younger brother and an older sister) in Kenya and attended an English and Swahili-medium school. He remembers using Swahili both at school and in everyday encounters with 'people outside in Kenya' while home life, at that time, was exclusively Gujarati speaking. As was noted in Chapter 3, however, many Kenyan Asians were forced to leave the country as a result of the Kenyan government's Africanization policy from the 1960s onwards. Consequently, when Geet was a small boy, his family migrated to London where they joined other family members. Geet currently lives at home with his mother, younger brother and sister, who is also a university student, and he is in regular contact with his uncles. At home, he primarily speaks Gujarati with his mother, who he describes as 'learning English', and a mixture of Gujarati and English, with his siblings, depending on the topic. With his peers, he primarily speaks English.

For much of the time, Geet presents himself as a shy and nervous young man who is oriented to both his Gujarati cultural heritage and the popular youth culture of his peers. Like Tahir, Geet peoples much of his world with males but, unlike Tahir, Geet frequently adopts a position, and is positioned, on the margins of his peers' social networks. This feeling of distance and otherness appears to have begun with the move to London, the transition into London schooling and the need to use English. While Geet could understand English, through his prior schooling in Kenya, the experience of suddenly finding himself in a new school in London was, not surprisingly, stressful. Additionally, his accent positioned him as different from other children:

G: In Kenya...in the school there was Swahili, the Kenyan language, and we also had English...so we had two languages, we studied Swahili and English. So when I came here I could speak English... but it was a bit different...the accent...and the words...it was just getting used to it, it was like another level...

SP: So do you remember when you first...came to school in England? What was it like?

G: Well, it was a bit scary to me because...the people here are different people and then just getting used to their English...So it was quite...difficult. (Geet, 11/11/2001)

Geet constantly refers to the feelings of anxiety he experiences with English, both the 'literate English' (Wallace, 2002) of academic communities and the 'slang' of his peers. He frequently positions himself as an inexpert English speaker who becomes agitated when called upon to speak because of his difficulties in expressing himself. Interestingly, this facilitates Geet in adopting the position of a 'native speaker' of Gujarati, in which he is able to contrast his hesitant and nervous English persona with a Gujarati self who is able to relax and enjoy himself in his 'mother tongue'. This is illustrated in the following interview excerpt in which Geet presents himself as strongly affiliated to Gujarati, a language in which he can express himself, whereas he seems much more ambivalent about English despite 'always speaking it' with his peers.

> G: I have noticed as well when I am...with my friends, say at work,...if they speak Gujarati then I will speak Gujarati as well. When I'm talking [in] that, I'm more calm and I'm actually more easy going...When I speak with people just with English, I sometimes stutter...I might not...really have the words to say, they are difficult...
>
> SP: So sometimes it's actually more comfortable for you to speak Gujarati than English you think?
>
> G: Yeah, I do.
>
> SP: What about at university here?...Do you have Gujarati friends here that you speak Gujarati to, or do you speak in English most of the time?
>
> G: Well [at university] I have Gujarati friends but they don't usually speak Gujarati that much so...I'm always speaking English... so I can improve my English [with them]...I mean...if I always speak to people [in] English, I'm able to improve my English. But at home...I have my Gujarati mother tongue language. (Geet, 11/11/2001)

In a sense, Geet still relates to English as a language learner, despite the fact that he has greater expertise in English than his 'mother tongue'. Not only does he repeatedly refer to his lack of oral fluency in English, but he also consistently adopts a deficit position *vis-à-vis* his peers. For example, Geet spoke very highly of an oral communication skills course he had attended at the University. What he seemed to value most was participating in discussions, in which the goal was for students to pay close attention to each other's contributions and to create opportunities for nervous and quieter members to speak. While Geet claims his self-confidence is developing as a result of this course, this carefully controlled setting for discussion seems a far cry from his everyday experiences in the classroom, in which he often appears marginalized and silenced. As discussed in the previous section, Geet operates on the fringes of a peer group in which Tahir, Vritti and Randeep collaborate closely in generating laughter and/or behaving flirtatiously. As Geet cannot participate in their fast-moving repartee, he remains silent for much of the time. He also does not signal his involvement in the talk through minimal responses. Consequently, moments arise during the group discussions in which Geet becomes the focus of attention. He is made to occupy the position of 'fall guy', in which he finds himself the butt of peer group humour, a position from which he does not derive much, if any, satisfaction. This is illustrated in the excerpt below from the group discussion with Tahir, Vritti and Randeep in which Geet, as yet, has made no attempt to participate. At this point, his silence becomes the focus of attention as Tahir nominates Geet for the floor in a move which appears highly face threatening:

T = Tahir, R = Randeep, V = Vritti, G = Geet

1. T: hello/ are you going to speak or? <addressing Geet>
2. R: <laughs>
3. T: or are you gonna be like a silent partner?
4. V: [<laughs>
5. R: [<laughs> yeah/ he's just going to do the notes in the/ (.) <laughs>
6. T: I think we should put the next question to Geet =
7. V: = okay (.) how do you feel about studying the language used in these texts and using it yourself? <reading aloud> ((xx))
8. G: ((xx)) = <very hesitant>
9. V: = GO ON/ (.) ANswer (.) the QUEStion/ (Group discussion, 26/2/2001)

While male students usually pay little attention to female students who do not participate in group discussions, prolonged silence for males with male peers appears to cause discomfort. The accomplishment of hegemonic adolescent masculinity necessitates an 'insouciant sharp-wittedness' which is evidenced through displays of being 'fast, cool and never a dupe' (Frosh, Phoenix and Pattman, 2002: 81). Tahir uses Geet's silence to make a joke and challenge him to speak (turns 1, 3 and 6). Vritti and Randeep collaborate through belittling Geet, positioning him in the feminized role of a secretary whose role is 'just...to do the notes' (turn 5). Vritti takes up Tahir's invitation for someone to question Geet (turn 7). Following Geet's hesitant and inaudible answer (turn 8), she demonstrates no sympathy or encouragement. Instead she adopts a coercive and hectoring tone, shouting at Geet to 'answer the question' (turn 9). Perhaps Vritti is not feeling particularly sympathetic as this comes after a lengthy section of talk in which Tahir and Randeep have conspired to make her do serious talk on the task at hand while they make jokes at her expense. It also seems likely that the re-focusing of attention on Geet presents her with an opportunity to re-position herself within the power dynamics of the group. Geet finds himself positioned in a weak and feminized position, emphasized by his loss of face at the hands of the only female member of the group. While he does nothing to remedy this loss of face when it occurs, when he is next nominated for the floor, he draws on his Gujarati cultural heritage as a strategy to increase his status in the group. As the excerpt below from the group discussion illustrates, he positions himself as a 'native speaker' of Gujarati who, by implication, is more competent in his 'mother tongue' than his peers can claim to be:

T = Tahir, R = Randeep, V = Vritti, G = Geet

1. V: so Geet/ (.) what kind of languages do you use at home?
2. G: I just use my national tongue Gujarati/ (.) my friends it's English/ and at school I did French at school as well/ (3)
3. V: mm <prompting Tahir>
4. T: well I'd like to say we speak Urdu/ but we don't/ we speak Punjabi mixed with English/ (.) so/ (1) if I were to go back home/ I don't think I could speak it properly/ but (.) what I speak with my parents is ((definitely)) Punjabi but mostly it's mixed with English =
5. R: = and French =
6. T: = I had wicked French but er [(.) y'know I gave it up/
7. R: [<laughs> (Group discussion, 26/2/2001)

The three-second pause following Geet's claim to be a 'native speaker' of Gujarati (turn 2) suggests that his response to Vritti's question has temporarily silenced his peers. Perhaps most importantly, it has forced Tahir to show respect for someone who has much greater expertise in his home language. However, this generally more positive mood is soon deflected by Randeep, whose interjection of 'French' (turn 5) as a home language for Tahir facilitates Tahir shifting back into another section of jocular repartee (turn 6). The short utterances in this excerpt are the total of Geet's participation in the group discussion with his peers. Both result from Geet being forced to take the floor through direct questioning. Following this, he lapses back into silence and is ignored.

Perhaps because of these difficulties in maintaining social relations with his peers, Geet presents himself as working hard to maintain his peer group networks by keeping up to date with the latest developments in popular culture involving football, soaps, gadgets and cars. He reports spending several hours every week carefully reading publications, such as *Which* (a consumer affairs magazine), various car magazines and the sports pages of tabloid newspapers, such as the *Sun*, in order to be able to participate in discussions on these topics and give helpful advice to family and friends. Importantly, ensuring that he is not ignorant of the latest technological advances in popular gadgets also appears to be a way of maintaining face among peers as it allows him to project an image of street credibility and coolness. Deliberately keeping abreast of what is discussed in the press is suggestive of good language-learner strategies, in which learners study aspects of the host culture in order to improve their language skills and develop their understanding of the target culture (see Byram, Nichols and Stevens, 2001). This impression is developed further in parts of the interview in which Geet reports keeping up to date with popular shows on television, in case these become the subjects of discussions among his friends:

> I like watching TV basically. I like watching all these different shows and ... soaps, ... keeping up to date with your weekly TV news as well [because] if you go somewhere with your mates ... I'm sure someone will ask you, 'What happened on EastEnders?' [and] 'Did you watch what happened?' (Geet, 27/02/2002).

Geet contrasts this quiet and anxious self among his British peers with a more comfortable and relaxed Gujarati self at home where he seems to spend much of his time with his younger brother watching football, East Enders and Hindi movies. They talk in a mixture of Gujarati and English, using English for topics such as sport, but code-switching for everyday home events, such as discussions about meals. When asked about his relationship with his siblings at home, Geet makes overt references to gender as a factor in determining the closeness of these:

> I'm more close to my little brother than my sister when it comes to talking. I think it's because ... he's a guy ... he's into sports ... just like me and he supports the same team as me and he likes watching the same ... programmes as me ... Yesterday we were watching a

film, ... me and him sitting down watching the film, and my mum and sister were like doing something else. So that's one way of putting it; I'm more close to my little brother. (Geet, 27/02/2002).

Later he reinforces this closeness with his younger brother with further comments about his relationship with his brother and sister, in which he presents a picture of family life oriented to traditional discourses on gender in which his sister, as a 'girl' is more disposed to 'chatting' to their mother while he and his brother occupy themselves with stereo-typically male activities, such as watching football.

Although he positions himself as a 'native speaker' of Gujarati, Geet sees little point in developing his literacy in Gujarati beyond the stage he reached in the Gujarati Saturday school he attended in his early teens. He also has little interest in reading a Gujarati newspaper or following any Gujarati news, seeing Gujarati as a spoken language in the private sphere but as having little relevance for him in everyday life. One reason for this appears to be the low cultural capital of Gujarati within mainstream British society and institutions, as is indicated in the excerpt below:

> College was basically if you want to do [Gujarati] for A levels or a GCSE, then you can ... but there were too few people. I didn't do that [because] I didn't want to get a degree or a qualification in Gujarati. For me I didn't see a step forward in that unless ... I was going to be a Gujarati teacher, ... but I wasn't. I didn't see any point in actually doing Gujarati at that level. (Geet, 11/11/2001)

A further reason for his lack of interest in developing his expertise in Gujarati appears to be an absence of links with social networks connecting India, as his ancestral heritage, and Britain. As was noted in Chapter 3, while many Kenyan Asians did not have Kenyan nationality, many could, in fact, trace their roots in Kenya for at least one generation. It may be, therefore, that his family have had little contact with India, as an ancestral homeland, for some time. In fact, besides speaking Gujarati with his family, the only cultural activity related to India in which Geet appears actively involved is watching Bollywood movies. Nevertheless, despite the absence of a 'transnational' network, Geet consistently positions Gujarati as his 'mother tongue', while showing ambivalence about English. Perhaps this positioning is less an issue of affiliation with his ancestral language and a strategy for coping with the social relations of his peers and the Millennium academic community.

Discussion

Despite a tendency in institutions such as universities to discuss students in terms of homogeneous groups, such as 'ethnic minority', 'Black', 'Asian', 'White' (see Chapter 2), these brief glimpses into the lives of Aisha, Tahir and Geet illustrate that there is no single way of coping with the daily lived experience of 'cultural hybridity' (Hall, 1992) or doing being British Asian. Aisha and Tahir, for instance, are both British Pakistanis whose families have retained strong links with Pakistan as their 'homeland'. In both cases, their families are part of a 'transnational community' which have settled in Britain but retained links with Pakistan. Fouron and Glick Schiller (2001), cited in Chapter 2, argue that 'transnational communities' are developed through their participants organizing networks 'across the borders of two nation-states', which actively encourage and facilitate connections between the host and heritage community. Both Aisha and Tahir's families encourage them to continue these links through involvement in social relations and cultural practices. In Tahir's case, he is also encouraged to maintain religious practices.

Aisha shows a strong sense of identification with her 'transnational community', identifying with both London and Pakistan and seemingly 'at home' in both. Aisha's expertise in language, in both speaking and writing, seems to play a role in facilitating this. She also appears motivated to learn language as a means of becoming included in the key 'communities of practice' (Lave and Wenger, 1991) in her life. Through her interactions with the members of her immediate and extended family, she appears to have negotiated a positive sense of self which encompasses both London and Pakistan. She maintains connections with Pakistan through regular visits and correspondence, through the media and through reading. She presents herself as well informed about life in Pakistan and as involved with her 'generation' of Pakistani relatives, who she presents, like herself, as secular, modern and educated.

Tahir, on the other hand, appears more ambivalent about his 'transnational community'. He identifies strongly with London and shows much less affiliation with Pakistan. While he is 'at home' in London, he presents himself as ill at ease on trips 'back home'. Tahir spends his time with peers in London enacting a laddish masculinity oriented to popular youth culture. This subject position enables him to imagine himself as a 'free agent' within the 'global city' of London. Nevertheless, Tahir attempts to maintain his social relations in his family through participating in practices which fulfil his parents', in particular his father's, expectations of him as a dutiful son. However, his lack of expertise in his 'home' languages appears to hinder this while his relatives accuse him of forgetting his roots. These issues also seem bound up with age. While performing laddish masculinity, Tahir can concentrate on 'having a laugh' with his peers and is relatively free from adult responsibilities. As he becomes older, however, he is under increasing pressure to take on the responsibilities of an adult male in his community and maintain links with his 'transnational community'. Nevertheless, Tahir seems more disposed to 'cool' aspects of popular culture from around the globe which have become fused into popular youth culture in the London scene.

Geet is in a different situation to Aisha and Tahir in relation to his heritage community. He is a member of a refugee community in which trips between the 'host' and the 'heritage' homeland are difficult, if not impossible. It does not seem surprising, therefore, that Geet lacks iden-tification with Kenya and shows no desire to visit there. His early childhood memories of life in Kenya are constructed in terms of an opposition between his family life, lived in Gujarati, and the external world, lived in Swahili and English. Given the circumstances surround-ing the exodus of Asians from Kenya (see Chapter 3), his family does not seem to have an 'imagined' homeland (Anderson, 1991) to which to return. Furthermore, although Geet's ancestors are Gujarati Indians, there are no references in the data to networks linking Geet with the Gujarati community in India. While Geet can speak fluent Gujarati, he is not particularly interested in developing his literacy beyond his achievements in Gujarati Saturday school. For Geet there seems no purpose in this. It will not facilitate employment or help him main-tain links with a 'transnational community'. For while Geet posi-tions Gujarati as his 'mother tongue', it seems likely that there is no place for him to call 'home' apart from London. In his case, it seems more likely that he will construct a sense of his identity in London in which he and his family will eventually construct 'roots' as they develop a 'strictly London space for themselves'. As was suggested in Chapter 2, this is more in keeping with the processes of assimilation rather than transnationalism. Nevertheless, Geet rarely seems com-pletely at 'home' outside the private sphere of his family life, or away from his London Gujarati friends. This seems to stem from his shyness and anxieties not only about expressing himself in English with his peers and in the formal setting of the academic community, but also about coping with the 'rough and tumble' social relations of his peers.

Conclusion

In this chapter, I have explored the lives of three British Asian under-graduates who, as British nationals, live, study and work in London as their primary 'home'. Two of these young people, Aisha and Tahir were born in London and have grown up and been educated in London state schools. Geet, on the other hand, arrived in London as a young boy after his family left Kenya. All of them represent a new generation of undergraduates, as 'non-traditional' students, who have partly been encouraged to participate in higher education through the University's active and continuing efforts to widen participation from a wide variety of London communities. All three found themselves on an academic literacy programme designed to improve their writing skills and presumably their prospects in higher education. While they are catego-rized as British Asians, Aisha, Tahir and Geet clearly do not experience this ethnic subject position in the same ways, or have the same identifi-cations and affiliations with the languages and practices of the main 'communities of practice' in their lives. While Aisha seems likely to maintain a 'transnational' subject position, it remains to be seen to what extent Tahir is prepared to maintain links with Pakistan as his heritage community, or whether he, like Geet, will negotiate a sense of self within a 'strictly London space'.

9
Taking Stock: Where to London?

Introduction

In the first three chapters of this book, I presented a theoretical framework for the stories told in Chapters 5–8. I discussed globalization, migration, multiculturalism, identity, London as a global city and the history of migration and multilingualism in Britain and London. My argument was that in order to understand micro-level individual stories, one must consider the global social and historical forces which form the backdrop to these stories. Chapters 5–8 were then devoted to the stories of Japanese graduate students, French foreign-language teachers, Spanish-speaking Latinos and British Asian undergraduate university students. In no way were the stories presented as typical of the migrant groups that they putatively represent. However, they were meant to illustrate how some of the denizens of London today bring to life membership in these migrant groups in London. In this final chapter, I would like to revisit the themes covered in Chapters 1–3 and examine how the stories relate to them. In effect, I will attempt to answer the third question outlined in the Preface: What do the stories tell us about migration as a global phenomenon; multiculturalism and multilingualism; migrant identities in the early 21st century; and London as a global city?

What do the stories tell us about migration as a global phenomenon?

First, in all of these stories I see the strength of Faist's (2000) multi-level model as a means of understanding migration. Macro-level factors, such as the economic power of Japan, the Maastricht treaty in Europe and the economic and political instability of much of Latin America, go a long way towards explaining why migrants from Japan, France and

Latin America have ended up in London in significant numbers. As regards the undergraduate students in Chapter 8, they are the children of two very different migrations of South Asians to Britain – one more economic in nature, originating in Pakistan in the 1950s, and the other more political, coming from Africa from the late 1960s onwards. Meso-level factors which figure highly in these stories include the social and cultural capital of more middle-class migrants from Japan, France and Latin America, the family and social support that form part of the chain migration from Latin America and the transnational cultural and family contacts of Siân Preece's undergraduate students. Finally, as regards micro-level values and expectations, these include the desire for a different life, manifested by Mie and Yukiko in Chapter 5; the need to travel, manifested by Lise and Nancy in Chapter 6; Javier's quest for money to send back home in Chapter 7; and the desire of Geet's parents to escape from an uncomfortable life in Kenya in Chapter 8.

However, beyond confirming the usefulness of Faist's multi-level model, the stories also enter what I think is relatively uncharted territory. As I noted in Chapter 3, a great deal has been written by migration researchers about the post-colonial migration to Britain of people from the Caribbean, Africa and South Asia.[1] These publications follow a general trend in the migration literature, where there is a tendency to focus on migrant groups which number in the millions when viewed worldwide. But what about smaller migrations, such as the 3C nationals from Japan and the EU citizens from France? In the case of the former, increased wealth has meant that more Japanese nationals are not only travelling to all parts of the world as tourists, but also settling abroad as short, medium and long-term sojourners. To date, the Japanese abroad are members of an under-researched migrant group worldwide, notwithstanding the efforts of anthropologists like Kelsky (2001) and applied linguists like Kanno (2003). Meanwhile, French nationals who take advantage of the Maastricht treaty to set up a new life in another EU country are in a similar situation to the wealthy Japanese. While theoretical discussions of what the EU means in terms of citizenship are welcome (Weiner, 1999; Weil and Hansen, 2002), what is really needed are more studies along the lines of Chapter 6, in which there is a glimpse of how Europeans do being European citizens.

However, more studies of the Japanese and the French, or other East Asians and Europeans, would not actually be about national migrant groups *per se*; rather, they would be about subgroups within these larger categories. They would be about what David Conradson and Alan

Latham (2005) call *'middling* forms of transnationalism'. Conradson and Latham describe *'middling* transmigrants' as follows:

> They are often, but not always, well educated. They may come from wealthy families, but more often than not they appear to be simply middle class. In terms of the societies they come form, and those they are travelling to, they are very much in the middle. (Conradson and Latham, 2005: 229)

Middling migrations are often centred on one particular activity that is carried out in the host country. This activity might be leisure, as in the case of retirees from Northern European countries who migrate to resort communities located on the Mediterranean coast. However, it might also be educational or academic in nature, as in the case of adolescents and adults on gap years or the Japanese graduate students. Or, it can be professional, as in the case of the French foreign-language teachers. In a sense, larger, more traditional migrations have always had subgroups that occupied particular labour niches in host societies (Castles and Miller, 2003; Jordan and Düvell, 2003). Indeed, Javier in Chapter 7 can be seen as representative of this type of migration, given that he works in the cleaning trade, which has become the domain of SSL migrants in London. However, as Conradson and Latham make clear, middling transmigration is very much a middle-class affair. Among other things, middling transmigrants are individuals with near or total control over their movements, who go somewhere to live with one particular general purpose in mind. In addition, they do not subject themselves to poor living conditions, awaiting a better future for their children, as labour migrants generally do; rather, they make the most of their stay in the host country. They are cosmopolitans, as conceptualized by Hannerz (1996; see Chapter 2), and to a degree, flexible citizens, as conceptualised by Ong (1999; see Chapter 1). They are also an under-researched type of migrants, which means that there is a need for more studies into how middling migrations are lived and what the consequences are for both host societies and the migrants themselves.[2]

What do these stories tell us about multiculturalism and multilingualism in general?

Following Benhabib (2002) and other authors, I made the point in Chapter 2 that multiculturalism should not be seen as a 'mosaic' of fixed and well-defined communities living side-by-side, getting along as best they can. Communities do not come in neat packages and indeed, it is far more realistic, to say nothing of intellectually rigorous, to adopt a processual view whereby they are seen as ongoing dialogic practices. The same applies to groups defined according to an assumed language inheritance. In short, there is no mosaic of fixed languages for migrants; rather, shifting and changing language affiliations, expertises and practices mean that the multilingualism of a city like London is in constant flux. The stories told in this book contribute to a de-essentialized view of multiculturalism and multilingualism as they all show a great deal of intra-group diversity.

For example, in the stories told by Motoko, Akira, Naomi, Mie and Yukiko in Chapter 5, I see no evidence that they lived their experiences in London as part of a larger Japanese community. None of these women gave any indication that they actively sought to spend their time with Japanese people living in London, and indeed, Mie and Yukiko claimed to avoid such contact.[3]

As regards the Japanese/English bilingualism practised by these five women, there are considerable differences. Due to their *kikokushijo* experience, Motoko, Akira and Naomi arrived in London already extremely proficient in English and above all confident in themselves as English speakers. Nevertheless, they did see their MA course in London as an experience that would allow them to polish up their English. By contrast, Mie and Yukiko were in an entirely different situation. They were, to be sure, proficient English speakers when they arrived in London; however, for them the London experience was much more a language-learning experience.

In contrast to the Japanese students, the French nationals discussed in Chapter 6 all seemed to seek out the company of French compatriots. However, these compatriots were much more like themselves, that is well-educated 25–35 year olds with moderately well-paid jobs. None of the four women ever mentioned connections with other subgroups of French nationals in London, such as the City and Docklands workers or the professional class of South Kensington described in Chapter 6. They therefore did not position themselves as forming part of a larger French community, even if three of them strongly claimed a French expatriate subject position.

As regards their French/English bilingualism, all four women told stories of their adolescence and student days, when they dreamed of being proficient English speakers. And, when I met them in September 1999, all four were highly proficient and confident speakers of English. However, by this time, much of the romanticism they had at one time attached to English seemed to have disappeared. In its place was a generally utilitarian attitude towards the language: it was what they needed to communicate in most contexts in London. Thus, whereas Mie and Yukiko seemed self-conscious about the languages in their lives, Lise, Nancy, Laure and Chantalle took a far more prosaic stance. Indeed, they practised what might be termed a 'relaxed' and even 'banal' (to borrow a term from Billig, 1995) bilingualism, using French and English naturally and with no problems, as and when appropriate.

While the Japanese and French nationals discussed in this book are part of a more privileged and wealthy migration to London, the Spanish-speaking Latinos are a more mixed socio-economic group. First, they are from a variety of different nation states. Second, there are huge wealth differentials between the mass of labour migrants like Javier and the better-educated middle-class migrants like Luis and Carlos. As was noted in Chapter 7, Román-Veláquez (1999) makes the case for an emergent Latino community (which includes Brazilians) in London and in his comments, Carlos more or less confirms this judgement. Notwithstanding factors which work against the formation of a full-fledged SSL community, such as their dispersal around London, my view is that this migration will continue to grow and that eventually SSLs will go through a stage of what Friedman (2004) calls 'ethnification', that is they will gain official recognition as an ethnolinguistic community in London. In this sense, they will follow a long list of groups identified by nationality and language, ranging from Gujarati-speaking Indians to Greek Cypriots.

As regards their Spanish/English bilingualism, the experiences of the three men could not be more different. First, Javier does not really qualify as an English speaker given his extremely limited linguistic repertoire, which he himself estimated to be about 20 words. He is therefore a monolingual migrant who does not speak the dominant local language. By contrast, Luis has become a fully functioning English speaker with little interest in using his first language, Spanish. Finally, Carlos has developed his English expertise for work purposes to the extent that he can do his job; however, he has yet to develop a positive affiliation to English. He is an unbalanced Spanish/English bilingual who has found a way to keep his first language and use it as a clear identity marker associated with his educational level and social status.

Finally, the British Asians in Chapter 8 tell very different London stories from those found in Chapters 5–7, and they do so for several reasons. First, Aisha, Tahir and Geet are the children of migrants as opposed to migrants themselves, and in two cases, they were born in London. Given their experience of having lived in London as children and adolescents, their relationships with multicultural London cannot be viewed in the same way as the relationships of the other migrants in this book with London. Despite Aisha's and Geet's positioning to the contrary, London has to be considered the closest thing to home that these young adults have. Second, they belong to the largest recognised ethnic minority group in Britain, which is known as British Asians. As I observed above, although there may be more SSLs than the census estimates and Japanese and French people are coming to London in high numbers at present, none of these groups is yet a part of ongoing discussions of multiculturalism in London in the way that British Asians are. For example, there is no mention of these three migrant groups in Winder (2004), an otherwise comprehensive text that I have cited extensively in this book. Third, within their larger definition as ethnic British Asians, all three are strongly associated, both by themselves and by others, with a recognized ethnolinguistic community in London: Urdu/Punjabi-speaking Pakistani for Aisha and Tahir; Gujarati-speaking Indian for Geet. However, these associations are embraced to very different degrees by the three. On the one hand, Aisha and Geet engage willingly with their associated communities, although Geet's engagement is far more family-centred while Aisha's contacts work at the family, London and transnational levels. Meanwhile, Tahir seems to engage just enough with the Pakistani community to keep his parents happy, just enough for them to leave him alone.

As regards their bi- and multilingualism, in particular their practices in the different languages that make up their repertoires, Aishia, Tahir and Geet again vary considerably. Aisha seems 'at home' in Urdu as a community language and English as an all-purpose social and educational language. She eschews Punjabi as 'rude' and old fashioned, putting all her effort into speaking Urdu, as the medium through which she conserves family and community ties. Tahir, by contrast, has a limited command of both Urdu and Punjabi, and he does not even differentiate one language from the other. English is by far the dominant language in all aspects of his life. Geet shares with Aisha the claim that his first language is not English. However, he maintains Gujarati solely as a family language, seeing English as the language of education and eventually, professional advancement.

What do these stories tell us about migrant identities in the early 21st century?

The four sets of stories show migrants at different points on the scale ranging from expatriates to full-fledged immigrants, manifesting varying degrees of cosmopolitanism and transnationalism. They also show how in the telling of their stories, migrants bring to the fore different subject positions based on language, nationality, ethnicity, race, gender, social class and the communities of practice to which they can claim membership. Revisiting some of the findings from Chapters 5 to 8, I now explain how.

The Japanese graduate students discussed in Chapter 5 are five individuals who initially intended to spend one year in London as students on an MA course. They arrived in London as well-educated English language teachers from solid middle-class backgrounds in Japan, one of the wealthiest countries of the world. In this regard, they are 'middling' (see above) and privileged 3C migrants, like the Americans, Australians and fellow East Asians (from Taiwan, South Korea and Hong Kong), who are well received in Britain as what might be termed 'model sojourners': they are perceived as migrants who will add to the local economy while taking little back, and cause no problems while in the country.

However, beneath this broad-brush label as model sojourners, there are differences among the five as regards the individual sociohistorical baggage that they brought with them to London and how they lived the city once they arrived. On the one hand, there are three students – Motoko, Akira and Naomi, who had extensive cosmopolitan experience, acquired through years of living abroad in English-speaking countries during their childhood and adolescence. On the other hand, there are late cosmopolitans – Mie and Yukiko – who did not spend any time abroad until they were young adults. Interestingly, the former group experienced their sojourn in London more as expatriates than transnationals. Their previously acquired cosmopolitanism served to make their stays more comfortable, but they were never tempted to stay on after they had finished their studies. By contrast, the late cosmopolitans – Mie and Yukiko – seemed to be on the path to become something akin to immigrants, having lived in London for five and four years, respectively, at the time of writing.

Motoko, Akira, Naomi, Mie and Yukiko positioned themselves nationally and ethnically as Japanese. However, they also manifested a strong affiliation to the English language, as a means of exploring alternative gendered subject positions. All claimed to feel more assertive and freer to say what they wanted in English. Echoing authors such as Mori (1997), Akira, Mie and Yukiko even described the Japanese language as a kind of straightjacket for women. This type of language identity, of course, could be invoked anywhere in the English-speaking world and is not specific to life in London. Nevertheless, Motoko, Akira and Naomi did attribute to London a special status, as a city where they did not feel foreign. And for their part, Mie and Yukiko explicitly stated that it was the only place they wanted to live at present. There is, therefore, a strong identification with London in their stories.

The four French teachers in Chapter 6 are also well-educated individuals from solid middle-class backgrounds in one of the wealthiest countries of the world. However, they tell stories of a very different type of migration. Taking advantage of their European citizenship to live and work as they please in London, all four are representatives of a rising European identity which is emerging in the wake of the 1993 Maastricht treaty. This EU citizen identity is for the moment far more about relaxed geographical borders and the removal of legal impediments on free movement, albeit with limitations (Martinello, 2000). However, it also opens up the prospects of a deeper sense of belonging as Europeans (Bauböck, 2002; Croucher, 2004). For the moment, however, Maastricht simply allows for a form of transnationalism to exist in combination with more classical expatriate and immigrant subject positions.

Thus the stories told by Lise, Nancy, Laure and Chantalle ultimately are about how they live their lives in close contact with France and the extent to which they invoke French expatriate or immigrant-like subject positions in their talk about their lives in London. In their stories, there is an ongoing struggle around the question – 'Do I stay or do I go?', which is resolved in very different ways by all four. On the one hand, there is Lise, who eventually leaves London, but does not return to France, preferring instead to go to Kenya to work in an international school. On the other hand, there are Nancy and Laure, who despite their expressed intentions to leave London, had not actually done so at the time of writing. Meanwhile, Chantalle, the most anglophile of the four women, was to leave London in March 2005, following her boyfriend (and future husband), who had been transferred by his company to Hong Kong.

In their stories, Lise, Nancy and Laure invoke a strong sense of French national identity that they believe marks them as different from other Londoners. This difference is related to various aspects of their lives, such as what they buy and consume, their socializing habits and above all the French language. As I noted in Chapter 2, national identities are socially constructed, consensuated forms of understanding oneself as a member of a large collective known as French, Japanese, Colombian and so on. In this sense, Lise, Nancy and Laure drew on idealizations of putative worldviews and habits assigned to 'the French' and 'the English'. Thus, the French do not engage in the kind of reprehensible behaviour that the English do, such as drinking to get drunk or eating bad food. And, they do not allow their public services to decay or abandon rigour in education. The French subject position adopted by these three women is therefore as much about who they are as who they are not.

Chantalle, by contrast, adopts a slightly different tack as regards her national identity. On the one hand, she too claims a strong French identity and says that she socializes almost exclusively with French nationals, such as Lise, Nancy and Laure. However, she tends to value more what she identifies as 'English' than the other three. Of course, her position is different from the other three, given that she is set to marry a British Chinese man from London.

In the case of Spanish-speaking Latinos in Chapter 7, the stories told show a range of language, social class, ethnic and migrant subject positions, with Javier representing the most negative profile. Given his lack of marketable skills and his poor English, Javier is doomed to a marginal economic existence in London. He cannot improve his work situation because he lacks the English language skills that would allow him to do so. However, he does not have time to study English because he works for so many hours. Javier lives his life primarily in a Spanish-speaking world, which at least allows him to maintain a strong affiliation to a Colombian national identity. However, he does not position himself as a part of a larger SSL community in London. Indeed, he tells the story of an individual, trying to eke out an existence in a dog-eat-dog labour market and send remittances back home. To sum up, Javier lives the limited and limiting expatriate experience of so many labour migrants around the world with few prospects for socio-economic advancement.

By contrast, Luis tells an altogether happier and more optimistic story. This is in no small part to do with the fact that he is a well-educated person from a middle-class background in Cuba, with a European phenotype that allows him to pass unnoticed on the streets of London. His London story is one of an individual who has been able to move from job to job at his leisure. And although he is not moving up the social ladder, or making a lot of money, he seems quite happy with the quasi-bohemian existence that has seen him leave a desk job to become a plumber during the time that I have been writing this book. While not rejecting his Cuban background, Luis seems uninterested in maintaining a strong Spanish language identity. Indeed, he has made a great deal of effort to improve his English and to approximate his communication norms to the dominant English-speaking culture around him. However, he claims that he does not want to become 'English' in any way; rather, he prefers to project a kind of citizen-of-the-world subject position both in his interview and in informal contacts I have had with him. At the time of writing, he has lived in London for some seven years and he shows no signs of leaving.

Finally, Carlos's story is of the former philosophy lecturer in Colombia who moves from being an extended visitor in London to something more akin to an immigrant, as he settles into family life in London and attempts to improve his employment situation. Like Luis, Carlos arrived in London as a well-educated migrant. However, his language skills did not allow him access to the kind of white-collar employment he was accustomed to in Colombia. Indeed, Carlos's story is one of an extreme form of 'declassing' as he moved from academia to supervising cleaning crews. London therefore has meant a major readjustment to his sense of social class on the job. In a nutshell, the same social and cultural capital that served him so well in Colombia has been detrimental to the development of strong bonds with his colleagues at work. In response to this situation, Carlos has developed a transnational identity as an educated Spanish speaker who, at least in his social life, associates with people he sees as more like himself, that is Spanish-speaking professionals from a range of different countries where Spanish is the dominant language (e.g. Spain, Argentina, Chile). At the time of writing, Carlos shows every sign of staying in London for the foreseeable future. He has moved to a better job and has managed to bring to London his two children from his first marriage.

In Chapter 8, the children of migrants from Pakistan and Kenya adopt different subject positions related above all to transnationalism. Indeed of the four cases examined here, this is the one that most resembles the focus of literature on transnationalism in the US (e.g. Cordero-Guzmán, Smith and Grosfoguel, 2001). In that literature, researchers examine the extent to which the concept of transnationalism, as opposed to assimilation, best captures the ways in which the children of migrants live their lives. In Chapter 8, Preece presents three very different approximations to the transnational ideal.

Aisha positions herself as a balanced transnational: although she was born and raised in London, she maintains very strong links with her Pakistani heritage. She manages this balancing act via her expertise and strong affiliation to Urdu, the language she inherited from her mother. She keeps up with cultural events in Pakistan to some extent, through the Urdu-mediated media and reading, but the heart of her transnationalism is her ongoing contact with her extended family both in Britain and in Pakistan. Still, her transnational identity comes across as highly controlled and it appears that this is the way Aisha prefers matters. On the one hand, there is an idealization of Urdu as a feminine language, easy for her to identify with, which stands in direct contrast to Punjabi, which she brands as a masculine and perhaps even backward language. On the other hand, her Pakistani subject positions are somewhat limited, primarily family-related in nature. Ultimately, in the majority of her activities, and in the majority of the communities of practice in which she can claim membership (those related to leisure activities, work and education), far more British subject positions come to the fore. These British subject positions can be seen in Aisha's command of the nuances of British culture (recall her expertise and occasional affiliation to 'ladette' culture) and the English language.

Standing in direct contrast to Aisha's transnational balancing act is Tahir, who lives an altogether more British existence, albeit one played out against a strong Pakistani background. Like Aisha, Tahir has had a good deal of contact with Pakistani culture and his languages of inheritance, Urdu and Punjabi, in his lifetime. However, unlike Aisha, he has not developed any sense of self mediated by Pakistani culture or language. Indeed, he sees family pressure in the direction of transnational cultural maintenance to be tiresome and he has never enjoyed his trips 'back home'. As Preece notes, he is far more comfortable with his male British Pakistani peers, with whom he shares a 'laddism' wrapped up in popular youth culture. Indeed, it seems that he would like to be left alone and allowed to be a free agent living his life as a Londoner.

Finally, Geet presents a very different profile from Aisha and Tahir. First, he was born not in London, but Kenya, where he was part of the Gujarati-speaking community, which had begun to leave Kenya in the late 1960s (see Chapter 3). Having arrived in London at the age of eight, he therefore has a stronger claim to a non-British homeland than Aisha or Tahir. However, as his Kenyan birthright and homeland is denied him (as an Asian, he can never be a 'real' Kenyan), he has inherited a diasporic Gujarati-mediated Indian identity. Such an identity allows him, to some extent, to live his life as a transnational in London, maintaining Gujarati as his home language and watching Bollywood films with his family. However, in common with Aisha and Tahir, just about all of his activities and the communities of practice in which he can claim membership are English mediated, and English has become the language in which he does the most identity work. In common with Tahir, he aspires to 'cool' masculine subject positions, heavily oriented to and influenced by popular culture. However, he has not been as successful as Tahir has in projecting such subject positions. Indeed, as Preece notes in Chapter 8, he is not accepted as 'cool' by the likes of Tahir and he seems to be having problems establishing a stable sense of self in the hurly-burly of London life.

What do these stories tell us about London as a global city?

In Chapter 3, I cited nine criteria which a city must meet if it is to merit the name 'global city'. Four of these criteria were economic in nature, stating that global cities are essential command centres in the world economy; the locations of high-powered service industries and centres of international finance; the sites of development and innovation in the service industries and international finance; and markets for developments and innovations in the service industries and international finance. One criterion concerned culture, that is the extent to which a city is the site of culture industries and innovations in these industries. Another was about population, namely that global cities are the centres of metropolitan areas exceeding 10 million inhabitants. This book does not deal with any of these criteria directly; however, it has dealt with the remaining three criteria presented in Chapter 3, which read as follows:

1. Global cities are the sites of multiple and massive migrations of people from all over the world.
2. Global cities are diverse in every sense of the word: ethnically, racially, religiously, culinarily, culturally and so on.
3. Global cities have reached a point in their development that they are de-nationalized as regards lifestyle and points of reference (London is not *really* England (or Britain), New York is not *really* America and Paris is not *really* France)

Regarding the first criterion, I have argued in Chapter 3, and attempted to show in Chapters 5–8, that London is the destination of many migrants on the move in the world today. These migrants might be like Javier in Chapter 7, that is low skilled labour migrants performing services that more established Londoners do not want to do. Or they might be like Naomi, Akira and Motoko in Chapter 5, Conradson and Latham's (2005) wealthier '*middling* transmigrants', spending a year in London as students.

Regarding the second criterion, the stories presented in Chapter 5–8 show how current migrations, in combination with the intensive inflow of people from all over the world in the decades after the Second World War, have made London one of the most ethnically and linguistically diverse cities in the world. Indeed, if we are to judge by the various references to national/ethnic groups in books such as Winder (2004), press articles such as Benedictus (2005) or websites such as the 'United Colours of London', we see that in addition to the Asians, Spanish-speaking Latinos, French nationals and Japanese nationals discussed in this book, there are many national/ethnic groups which can count more than 10,000 residents in London. From Africa alone, Ethiopia, Ghana, Kenya, Nigeria, Senegal, Somalia, South Africa, Sudan, Uganda and Zimbabwe would easily fall into this category. Indeed, the breadth and depth of London's diversity is rivalled only by Paris and New York.

Finally, regarding the third criterion – that global cities are cities that have reached a point in their development that they are de-nationalized as regards lifestyle and points of reference – I think that the stories presented in this book make this point well. In all cases there is a sense that London somehow is not the same as England (or even Britain). The French nationals and Japanese nationals, in particular, made it clear on different occasions that they could not conceive of living anywhere else in Britain besides London. And it is hard to imagine Carlos or Tahir living anywhere but London.

I must say that walking the streets of London, I often get the impression that the city has seceded from the nation state called Britain. And I begin to ask myself if London is perhaps no longer a city, but a kind of reinvention of the city state, such as those which arose in Italy during the European renaissance. As John Merriman (1996) notes, the city states of the Italian renaissance were societies unto themselves, with political, economic and cultural autonomy. Notwithstanding its role as recognized political capital of Britain, containing within its borders all of the centralized administrations of the British government, London is progressively emerging as a kind of free-standing city state, independent of Britain. At first glance, the analogy of the city state might seem exaggerated. However, the idea has been around for some time. In a book about London, written over 70 years ago, Harold Clunn wrote that London 'has outgrown the population and dimensions of a capital and has become a nation of itself, busier and more populous than many sovereign states that fill a considerable space on the map of Europe' (Clunn, 1932: 7; cited in Eades, 2000: 24). In addition, as Eades notes, when political referenda on devolution (i.e. the transfer of power from the national government to local authorities) were held in Britain from 1997 onwards, they were held in the traditionally recognized nations within Britain – Northern Ireland, Scotland and Wales – as well as London.

London was thus treated as different from the rest of England and, in a sense, as a self-determining national territory within the UK.

The stories told in this book add to my feeling that London is an island unto itself, perhaps even the global city par excellence. The Japanese graduate students, the French foreign-language teachers, the Spanish-speaking Latinos and the second generation Asian university students all go about their business, contributing to the ongoing multicultural and multilingual stew that is London. However, as they make their contributions, they seem to do so oblivious to the members of other ethnolinguistic groups or indeed, often to those who would be considered to be co-members of their own groups. Thus, although there is a great deal of talk today about communities – ethnic, racial, national and so on – in the case of so many Londoners it is difficult to gauge exactly what membership in said communities actually means. There is also a great deal of talk about the number of languages in London. One very often hears or reads statements such as: 'There are 80 different languages spoken in this borough'. However, as the stories in this book illustrate, being bilingual or multilingual can mean many different things as regards, the inheritance of, the affiliation to and the expertise in the different languages that purportedly make up an individual's repertoire (Leung, Harris and Rampton, 1997). Both the borders around and the demarcations within ethnolinguistic groups are at best fuzzy.

This fuzziness as regards the ethnic and language identities of so many Londoners is perhaps the secret of London as a global city. It is, in effect, a multicultural and multilingual city with little or no superordinate coordination or internal definition. Its multicultural and multilingual identities, therefore, are constructed not from order, but disorder.

Notes

1 Globalization and migration

1. An exception to this general trend is to be found in Robin Cohen's (1995) edited collection, *The Cambridge Survey of World Migration*. This ambitious volume contains contributions from over 25 different countries and is, as a result, less Eurocentric in outlook.
2. There is also a case for a third settlement option, the 'differential exclusionary model', historically practised in different ways by countries such as Germany, Austria, Switzerland and Japan (Castles and Miller, 2003). In countries adopting this model, the reigning philosophy as regards citizenship is *ius sanguinis* (literally, 'law of blood'), which means that, in principle, one can only be a citizen if there is a bloodline by which one descends directly from other citizens. It should be noted, however, that in practice *ius sanguinis* is never applied so rigidly that it is absolutely impossible to obtain citizenship without a direct bloodline. Thus, Turkish immigrants can obtain German citizenship and Korean immigrants can obtain Japanese citizenship, albeit in both cases with greater strictures than would apply in countries with an *ius soli* (literally, 'law of land') policy.
3. But see Brubaker (2005) for some cautionary comments about 'the application of ... diaspora to an ever-broadening set of cases[,] ... essentially to any and every nameable population category that is to some extent dispersed in space' (Brubaker, 2005: 3), which he argues would empty the term of any meaning.

2 Multiculturalism and identities

1. However, it was Ernest Renan (1990 [1882]), writing a century before the authors cited in this section, who first problematized the concept of nation in such terms. He called the nation 'daily plebiscite', dependent for its existence on the individual's sense of belonging to a self-defined community whose members share a past, a present and a future.

3 The global city and the history of migration and multilingualism in Britain and London

1. Here I will not bother with possible differences between 'world' and 'global' in such discussions. Jörg Dürrschmidt (2000), however, argues that there is an important difference between the two. While the term 'global city' shows an 'emphasis on the city as the centre of financial and other related transactions', the term 'world city' shows an 'emphasis on the presence of the world in one city, of the world-mindedness of those cities' (Dürrschmidt, 2000: 13). In my view, Dürrschmidt's distinction makes sense if one sees the

term 'global' as restricted to economic issues. However, as I see 'global' as encompassing a wide variety of forces and flows (see Chapter 1), the term 'global city' can take on board both a city as financial centre and as 'world-minded'.

2. Over 20 years ago, Anthias (1984) estimated that there were 200,000 Greek Cypriots in Britain.

3. According to the *Oxford English Dictionary* (2001), the word derives from the Urdu word (via Persian) *laškar* (*laškari*) originally used to refer to soldiers and later to sailors.

4. The reader should note that in my coverage of 'languages in London besides English', I will focus exclusively on languages spoken outside the British Isles which have been brought to London by migrants with no previous links to Britain. Thus, I am excluding national languages such as Welsh and Gaelic as well as Romani, the language of gypsy communities across Europe.

5. As we will see in Chapter 5, the vast majority of registered Japanese residents are in London, associated with either business tenures of 1–10 years or university studies. It is hard to imagine that very many of these Japanese residents would not qualify as proficient speakers of Japanese.

5   Japanese graduate students in London

1. I am grateful to Masami Yoshida for having provided me with this information.

2. An exception is Robin Cohen (1997), who states that as of the mid-1990s, the 'official' figure stood at 45,000. However, he goes on to explain that this figure included only those Japanese who had registered with the embassy in London, before venturing that 'the total is likely to be about 90,000' (Cohen, 1997: 159). Although Cohen cites no sources to support his claim, he is unique in positing the existence of a substantial undocumented presence of Japanese nationals in Britain and London.

3. Two examples illustrate this broad range. During the academic year that one of my informants, Naomi, was in London as a student, she put her 14-year-old daughter in English-medium international school from September to March before sending her back in time for the beginning of the Japanese school year in April. By contrast, while visiting Japan in 2002, I met a 27-year-old woman who told me that she had lived abroad, with no interruptions, from the age of three to the age of 18.

4. See also earlier publications, such as White (1988) and Goodman (1990).

5. See Eckert (1989) and Heller (1999) for interesting accounts of life in North American secondary schools and Miller (2003) for an account of immigrant children adapting to primary school education in Australia.

6. For an interesting and very different view of *akogare* among Japanese women studying in Sydney, see Piller and Takahashi (2005).

6   French foreign-language teachers in London

1. The PGCE is the qualification required of prospective teachers by most schools in Britain.

2. Although it should be noted that the Jewish populations of Europe had by this time been involved in migrations of this kind for centuries.

3. Prior to asking Lise and the other three informants about how they would place themselves on this scale, I explained what I meant by 'expatriate' and 'immigrant' in the same terms I used in Chapter 2 to define these two concepts.
4. The CAPES (*Certificat Pédagogique pour l'Enseignement Secondaire*) exam is a civil service exam that must be passed by anyone who aspires to be a teacher in the French educational system.
5. Resistance is a matter of not only distancing oneself from particular local ways and norms, but also actively invoking what are perceived by the individual to be better alternatives. Compromise, by contrast, refers to a conciliation, whereby the individual not only accepts local ways and norms, but also appropriates them.
6. Interestingly enough, far worse than any anti-French sentiment were anti-German manifestations. Nancy, Laure and Chantalle have all at one time or another taught German and all three have had to endure Nazi salutes (e.g. *Zieg Heil!*) and tired references to 'the war'. Indeed, on one occasion, Laure was accosted by a student at a bus stop who called her a 'Nazi'.

7   Spanish-speaking Latinos in London

1. In this chapter, all excerpts originally spoken in Spanish will be presented as follows: an English translation is provided first in normal script, followed by the original Spanish in italics. English translations are an attempt to capture what was said in Spanish in an English that is as natural as possible. In some cases, this process has led to noticeable morphological changes: for example, on a couple of occasions singular forms in Spanish have been changed to plural forms in English because in this way the utterance sounds more natural in English. All translations have been double checked with a professional English/Spanish translator.
2. By 'informed source', I mean an individual whose working life makes him/her privy to information unavailable to the general public or official organisations (e.g. The Office for National Statistics). This information is only partially backed up by empirical work, if at all, and therefore must be accepted with reservations. Nevertheless, the three individuals cited here – the Peruvian Consul General, a local priest and a refugee worker – all tell a very similar story. Given that they do not generally move in the same professional circles, this coincidence of viewpoints lends credilbity to their estimates.
3. Of the three cases discussed in this chapter, two – Javier and Carlos – would likely be classified as mixed race in census terms. Given his European appearance, Luis would be classified as 'Other White'.
4. To be precise, Luis has 'indefinite leave to remain', with which he can live in London for an unlimited period of time.

8   British Asian undergraduate students in London

1. A pseudonym.
2. This is a Labour Government initiative to increase the number of university graduates by attracting entrants who either have no history of higher

education in their families or live in areas where a low proportion of the population are graduates.
3. Pilgrimage to Mecca that Muslims are required to make at least once during their lifetime, provided that they have the financial means and are in sufficient health.
4. Tahir defined 'rough' as ideas which earn respect because of their simplicity and ingenuity.
5. Area of London which has had many immigrant communities over many centuries and is currently home to South Asians migrants, the lives of whom were recently explored in Monica Ali's (2003) novel, *Brick Lane.*
6. A pseudonym.

9 Taking stock: Where to London?

1. In addition, there is by now an established literature on Caribbean and South Asian immigrant experiences in Britain, documented by authors such as Shusheila Nasta (2002) and James Proctor (2003), and exemplified by novelists ranging from George Lamming (1954) to Andrea Levy (2004) and G.V. Desani (1948) to Monica Ali (2003).
2. But see Raj (2003), who focuses on middle-class British Asians, as well as the special issue of the *Journal of Ethnic and Migration Studies* (Vol. 31, No. 2, March 2005), for which Conradson and Latham (2005) is the introduction.
3. Or, more precisely, they claimed to avoid such contact away from work, as Yukiko was working in the Japanese hair salon and Mie would eventually take a job in a Japanese school.

Bibliography

Adams, J. *The Teaching Force and the Recruitment and Retention of Modern Languages Teachers* (London: Institute for Policy Studies in Education, University of North London, 2000).

Adia, E. *Higher Education: The Ethnic Minority Student Experience* (Leeds: Heist Marketing Services for Universities and Colleges, 1996).

Ager, D. *Ideology and Image. Britain and Language* (Clevedon, UK: Multilingual Matters, 2003).

Albrow, M. *The Global Age: State and Society beyond Modernity* (Cambridge: Polity, 1996).

Alexander, R. *Other Primary Schools and Ours: Hazards of International Comparison* (Coventry: CREPE, University of Warwick, 1996).

Ali, M. *Brick Lane* (London: Doubleday, 2003).

Ali, S. *Mixed-Race, Post-Race: Gender, New Ethnicities and Cultural Practices* (Oxford: Berg, 2004).

Alibhai-Brown, Y. *Mixed Feelings: The Complex Lives of Mixed-Race Britons* (London: The Women's Press, 2001).

Alladina, S. and V. Edwards (eds) *Multilingualism in the British Isles*, volume 1 (London: Longman, 1991a).

——. (eds) *Multilingualism in the British Isles*, volume 2 (London: Longman, 1991b).

Alsop, R., A. Fitzsimons and K. Lennon. *Theorizing Gender* (Cambridge: Polity, 2002).

Anderson, B. *Imagined Communities: Reflections on the Origins and Spread of Nationalism*, 2nd edition (London: Verso, 1991).

Anthias, F. 'Some issues affecting Greek Cypriots in Britain: An ethnic profile', in M. Roussou (ed.) *Greek Outside Greece: A Profile of a Greek Speaking Community in Contemporary Britain* (London: National Council for Mother Tongue Teaching, 1984) pp. 4–8.

Anwar, M. *Continuity and Change in the Lives of Young Asians* (London: Routledge, 1998).

Appadurai, A. 'Disjuncture and difference in the global cultural economy', in M. Featherstone (ed.) *Global Culture: Nationalism, Globalization and Modernity* (London: Sage, 1990).

Arnold, M. *Culture and Anarchy: A Essay in Social and Political Criticism* (New York: Bobbs-Merrill, 1882/1971).

Atkinson, R. *The Life-Story Interview* (London: Sage, 1998).

Atkinson, P., A. Coffey, S. Delamont, J. Lofland and L. Lofland (eds) *Handbook of Ethnography* (London: Sage, 2001).

Baker, P. and J. Eversley (eds) *Multilingual Capital* (London: Battlebridge Publications, 2000).

Baker, P. and J. Kim. *Global London* (London: Battlebridge Publications, 2003).

Baker, P. and Y. Mohielden. 'The languages of London's school children', in P. Baker and J. Eversley (eds) *Multilingual Capital* (London: Battlebridge Publications, 2000) pp. 5–60.

Basch, L., N. Glick Schiller and C. Blanc-Szanton. *Nations Unbound: Transnational Projects, Postcolonial Predicaments, and Deterritorialized Nation States* (Langhorne, PA: Gordon and Breach, 1994).

Bauböck, R. 'Political community beyond the sovereign state, supranational federalism, and transnational minorities', in S. Vertovec and R. Cohen (eds) *Conceiving Cosmopolitanism: Theory, Context and Practice* (Oxford: Oxford University Press, 2002) pp. 110–36.

Baugh, A.C. and T. Cable. *A History of the English Language*, 5th edition (London: Routledge, 2002).

Bauman, Z. *Modernity and Ambivalence* (Oxford: Polity, 1991).

——. *Community* (Oxford: Polity, 2001).

Baumann, G. *Contesting Culture: Discourse of Identity in Multi-Ethnic London* (Cambridge: Cambridge University Press, 1996).

——. *The Multicultural Riddle: Rethinking National, Ethnic and Religious Identities* (London: Routledge, 1999).

Bell, D. *The Coming of Post-Industrial Society* (New York: Basic Books, 1973).

Benedictus, L. 'Special Report: What is Britain', *The Guardian*, 21 January, 2005. Available at: http://www.guardian.co.uk/britain/article/0,2763,1395543,00.html.

Benhabib, S. *The Claims of Culture: Equality and Diversity in the Global Era* (Princeton, NJ: Princeton University Press, 2002).

Bennett, T. *Culture: A Reformer's Science* (London: Sage, 1998).

Berger, P. and P. Luckman. *The Social Construction of Reality* (London: Penguin, 1966).

Bhabha, H. *The Location of Culture* (London: Routledge, 1994).

Billig, M. *Banal Nationalism* (London: Sage, 1995).

Binnie, J. *The Globalization of Sexuality* (London: Sage, 2004).

Bird, J. (1996) *Black Students and Higher Education: Rhetorics and Realities* (Buckingham: SRHE and Open University, 1996).

Bleich, E. *Race Politics in Britain and France: Ideas and Policymaking since the 1960s* (Cambridge: Cambridge University Press, 2003).

Block, D. 'Social constraints on interviews', *Prospect* 10/3: 35–48 (1995).

——. 'Problematizing interview data: Voices in the mind's machine?' *TESOL Quarterly* 34/4: 757–63 (2000).

——. 'Foreign nationals on PGCE in modern languages course: Issues in national identity construction', *European Journal of Teacher Education* 24/3: 291–312 (2001).

——. 'Destabilized identities across language and cultural borders: Japanese and Taiwanese experiences', *Hong Kong Journal of Applied Linguistics* 7/2: 1–19 (2002).

——. 'Convergence and resistance in the construction of personal and professional identities: Four French modern language teachers in London', in S.A. Canagarajah (ed.) *Reclaiming the Local in Language Policy and Practice* (Malwah, NJ: Lawrence Erlbaum, 2005).

Borg, P. *Promoting Internationalization in Japan: The Role of Jet Programme*, PhD thesis in progress (Institute of Education University of London).

Bourdieu, P. *Language and Symbolic Power* (Cambridge: Polity, 1991).

Brah, A. *Cartographies of Diaspora: Contesting Identities* (London: Routledge, 1996).

Brice-Heath, S. *Ways with Words* (Cambridge: Cambridge University Press, 1983).

Broadfoot, P. and M. Osborn. *Perceptions of Teaching: Primary School Teachers in England and France* (London: Cassell, 1993).

Broadfoot, P., M. Osborn, C. Planel and K. Sharpe. *Promoting Quality in Learning: Does England Have the Answer?* (London: Cassell, 2000).

Brubaker, R. 'The "diaspora" dispora', Ethnic and Racial Studies 28/1: 1–19 (2005).

Buckley, S. *Broken Silence: Voices of Japanese Feminism* (Berkeley, CA: University of California Press, 1997).

Butler, J. *Gender Trouble: Feminism and Subversion of Identity* (London: Routledge, 1990).

——. *Bodies that Matter: On the Discursive Limits of Sex* (London: Routledge, 1993).

Byram, M., A. Nichols and D. Stevens (eds) *Developing Intercultural Competence in Practice* (Clevedon, UK: Multilingual Matters, 2001).

Cameron, D. 'Rethinking language and gender studies: Some issues for the 1990s', in S. Mills (ed.) *Language and Gender: Interdisciplinary Perspectives* (London: Routledge, 1995) pp. 31–44.

——. 'The language–gender interface: Challenging co-optation', in V. Bergvall, J. Bing and A. Freed (eds) *Rethinking Language and Gender Research* (London: Longman, 1996) pp. 31–53.

——. 'Performing gender: Young men's talk and the construction of heterosexual masculinity', in S. Johnson and U. Meinhof (eds) *Language and Masculinity* (Oxford: Blackwell, 1997) pp. 47–64.

——. 'Styling the worker: Gender and the commodification of language in the globalized service economy', *Journal of Sociolinguistics* 4/3: 323–47 (2000).

——. 'Language, Gender and Sexuality: Current Issues and Future Directions', Plenary address given at the American Association of Applied Linguistics meeting, 1 May 2004.

Campbell-Platt, K. 'Distribution of linguistic Minorities in Britain', in CILT *Bilingualism and British Education* (London: CILT, 1976) pp. 15–30.

Castells, M. *The Rise of the Network Society*, 2nd edition (Oxford: Blackwell, 2000).

Castles, S. and M. Miller. *The Age of Migration*, 3rd edition (London: Palgrave, 2003).

Chamberlayne, P., J. Bornat and T. Wengraf (eds) *The Turn to Biographical Methods in Social Science* (London: Routledge, 2000).

Cheng, Y. 'The Chinese upwardly mobile', in C. Peach (ed.) *Ethnicity in the 1991 Census, Volume Two: The Ethnic Minority Populations of Great Britain* (London: HMSO, 1996).

Coates, J. *Women Talk: Conversation between Women Friends* (Oxford: Blackwell, 1996).

——. 'Thank god I'm a woman: The construction of differing femininities', in D. Cameron (ed.) *The Feminist Critique of Language: A Reader*, 2nd edition (London: Routledge, 1998) pp. 295–320.

——. *Men Talk* (Oxford: Blackwell, 2003).

Coffey, A. *The Ethnographic Self: Fieldwork and the Representation of Identity* (London: Sage, 1999).

Cohen, R. *Frontiers of Identity: The British and the Rest* (London: Longman, 1994).

—— (ed.) *The Cambridge Survey of World Migration* (Cambridge: Cambridge University Press, 1995).

——. *Global Diasporas: An Introduction* (London: UCL Press, 1997).

Conradson, D. and A. Latham 'Transnational urbanism: Attending to everyday experiences and mobilities', *Journal of Ethnic and Migration Studies* 31/2: 227–33 (2005).

Conway, D., A.J. Bailey and M. Ellis. 'Gendered and racialized circulation-migration: Implications for the poverty and work experience of New York's

Puerto Rican Women', in H.R. Cordero-Guzmán, R.C. Smith and R. Grosfoguel (eds) *Migration, Transnationalization, and Race in a Changing New York* (Philadelphia: Temple University Press, 2001) pp. 146–63.

Cordero-Guzmán, H.R., R.C. Smith and R. Grosfoguel (eds) *Migration, Transnationalization, and Race in a Changing New York* (Philadelphia: Temple University Press, 2001).

Coupland, N. 'Age in social and sociolinguistic theory', in N. Coupland, S. Sarangi and C. Candlin (eds) *Sociolinguistics and Social Theory* (London: Longman/Pearson, 2001) pp. 185–211.

Cox, R. 'A perspective on globalization', in J.M. Mittelman (ed.) *Globalization: Critical Reflections* (London: Lynne Rienner, 1996) pp. 21–30.

Croucher, S.L. *Globalization and Belonging: The Politics of Identity in a Changing World* (New York: Rowman and Littlefield, 2004).

Daley, P. 'Black-African: Students who stayed', in C. Peach (ed.) *Ethnicity in the 1991 Census, Volume Two: The Ethnic Minority Populations of Great Britain* (London: HMSO, 1996).

Davies, B. and R. Harré. 'Positioning and personhood', in R. Harré and L. van Langenhove (eds) *Positioning Theory* (London: Sage, 1999) pp. 32–52.

Delanty, G. *Community* (London: Routledge, 2003).

De Mente, B.L. *Japanese Etiquette and Ethics in Business* (Chicago: Contemporary Books, 1994).

Dempsey, R. and J.C. Lema. *La comunidad colombiana en Londres* (Peterborough, UK: Open Channels, 1998).

Derrick, J. *The Language Needs of Minority Group Children* (London: NFER, 1977).

Desani, G.V. *All About H. Hatterr* (London: Aldor Press, 1948).

Du Gay, P. *Consumption and Identity at Work* (London: Sage, 1996).

Dürrschmidt, J. *Everyday Lives in the Global City: The Delinking of Locale and Milieu* (London: Routledge, 2000).

Eade, J., T. Vamplew, and C. Peach. 'The Bangladeshis; The encapsulated community', in C. Peach (ed.) *Ethnicity in the 1991 Census. Volume 2: The Ethnic Minority Populations of Great Britain* (London: HMSO, 1996) pp. 150–60.

Eades, J. *The Politics of Community: The Bangladeshi Community in East London* (Aldershot, UK: Avebury, 1989).

——. *Placing London: From Imperial Capital to Global City* (Oxford: Berghahn Books, 2000).

Easton, S. *The History of the Modern World*, 3rd edition (New York: Holt, Rinehart and Winston, 1970).

Eckert, P. *Jocks and Burnouts: Social Categories and Identity in the High School* (New York: Teachers College Press, 1989).

——. *Linguistic Variation as Social Practice: The Linguistic Construction of Social* (Oxford: Blackwell, 2000).

Eckert, P. and S. McConnell-Ginet. *Language and Gender* (Cambridge: Cambridge University Press, 2003).

Estebanez, S. 'The Spanish speech community', in S. Alladina and V. Edwards (eds) *Multilingualism in the British Isles* (London: Longman, 1991) pp. 241–54.

Faist, T. *The Volume and Dynamics of International Migration* (Oxford: Oxford University Press, 2000).

Farr, M. 'Home or away? A study of distance travelled to higher education 1994–1999', *Widening Participation and Lifelong Learning* 3/1: 17–25 (2001).

——. *Ethnolinguistic Chicago* (Mahwah, NJ: Lawrence Erlbaum, 2004).

Fishman, P. 'Conversational insecurity', in D. Cameron (ed.) *The Feminist Critique of Language* (London: Routledge, 1990) pp. 234–41.

Fishman, W. 'Allies in the Promised Land: Reflections on the Irish and the Jews in the East End', in A.J. Kershen (ed.) *London: The Promised Land?* (Aldershot, UK: Avebury, 1997) pp. 38–49.

Flusty, S. *De-Coca-Colonization: Making the Globe from the Inside Out* (New York: Routledge, 2004).

Foner, N. 'Transnationalism then and now: New York immigrants today and at the turn of the twentieth century', in H.R. Cordero-Guzmán, R.C. Smith and R. Grosfoguel (eds) *Migration, Transnationalization, and Race in a Changing New York* (Philadelphia: Temple University Press, 2001) pp. 35–57.

Foucault, M. *The History of Sexuality. Volume One: An Introduction* (Harmondsworth: Pelican, 1981).

——. *The History of Sexuality. Volume Two: The Use of Pleasure* (Harmondsworth: Viking, 1986).

——. *The History of Sexuality. Volume Three: The Care of the Self* (Harmondsworth: Viking, 1988).

Fouron, G.E. and N. Glick Schiller. 'The generation of identity: Redefining the second generation within a transnational social field', in H.R. Cordero-Guzmán, R.C. Smith and R. Grosfoguel (eds) *Migration, Transnationalization, and Race in a Changing New York* (Philadelphia: Temple University Press, 2001) pp. 58–86.

Fraser, P. 'Africans and Caribbeans in London', in N. Merriman (ed.) *The Peopling of London* (London: Museum of London, 1993) pp. 51–61.

Friedman, J. 'Globalization, transnationalization, and migration: Ideologies and realities of global transformation', in J. Friedman and S. Randeria (eds) *Worlds on the Move: Globalization, Migration and Cultural Security* (London: I.B. Tauris, 2004) pp. 63–88.

Friedman, J. and S. Randeria (eds) *Worlds on the Move: Globalization, Migration and Cultural Security* (London: I.B. Tauris, 2004).

Friedmann, J. 'The world city hypothesis', *Development and Change* 17/1: 69–93 (1986).

Friedmann, J. and Wolff, G. 'World city formation: An agenda for research and action', *International Journal of Urban and Regional Research* 6: 309–44 (1982).

Frosh, S., A. Phoenix and B. Pattman. *Young Masculinities: Understanding Boys in Contemporary Society* (Basingstoke: Palgrave, 2002).

Fryer, P. *Staying Power: The History of Black People in Britain* (London: Pluto Press, 1984).

Fuentes, C. 'La frontera de cristal', in C. Fuentes (ed.) *La frontera de cristal: Una novella de nueve cuentos* (México: Alfaguara, 1995) pp. 185–211.

Gao, B. *Japan's Economic Dilemma: The Institutional Origins of Prosperity and Stagnation* (Cambridge: Cambridge University Press, 2001).

Gee, J.P. *Social Linguistics and Literacies: Ideology in Discourses*, 2nd edition (London: Falmer, 1996).

Gellner, E. *Nations and Nationalism* (Oxford: Blackwell, 1983)

Gentil, B. 'La population française immatriculée à étranger est en forte hausse', *INSEE Première* No. 919 Août: 1–4 (2003).

Giddens, A. *The Constitution of Society: Outline of the Theory of Structuration* (Cambridge: Polity, 1984).

——. *The Consequences of Modernity* (Cambridge: Polity, 1990).

——. *Modernity and Self-Identity: Self and Society in the Late Modern Age* (Cambridge: Polity, 1991).

——. *Runaway World: How Globalization is Reshaping Our Lives* (London: Routledge, 2000).

Giles, H., R.Y. Bourhis and D.M. Taylor. 'Towards a theory of language in ethnic group relations', in H. Giles (ed.) *Language, Ethnicity, and Intergroup Relations* (London: Academic Press, 1977) pp. 307–48.

Gilpin, R. *Global Political Economy* (Princeton: Princeton University Press, 2001).

Gilroy, P. *The Black Atlantic* (London: Verso, 1993).

——. *Between Camps: Nations, Culture and the Allure of Race* (London: Allen Lane, 2000).

——. *After Empire* (London: Routledge, 2004).

Glick Schiller, N., L. Basch and C. Blanc-Szanton. *Towards a Transnational Perspective on Migration: Race, Class, Ethnicity, and Nationalism Reconsidered* (New York: New York Academy of Sciences, 1992).

Glinert, E. *The London Compendium* (London: Penguin, 2003).

Goodman, R. *Japanese 'International Youth': The Emergence of a New Class of Schoolchildren* (New York: Oxford University Press, 1990).

Gouldner, H. and M.S. Strong. *Speaking of Friendship* (New York: Greenwood Press, 1987).

Hall, S. 'The question of cultural identity', in S. Hall, D. Held and T. McGrew (eds) *Modernity and Its Futures* (Cambridge: Polity, 1992) pp. 273–326.

——. 'Fantasy, identity and politics', in Carter, E., J. Donald and J. Squires (eds) *Cultural Remix: Theories of Politics and the Popular* (London: Lawrence and Wishart, 1995) pp. 63–9.

——. 'Introduction: Who needs "identity"?', in S. Hall and P. du Gay (eds) *Questions of Cultural Identity* (London: Sage, 1996) pp. 1–17.

Hammersley, M. and P. Atkinson. *Ethnography: Principles in Practice*, 2nd edition (London: Routledge, 1995).

Hannerz, U. *Transnational Connections* (London: Routledge, 1996).

Harré, R. and L. van Langenhove. 'Introducing positioning theory', in R. Harré and L. van Langenhove (eds) *Positioning Theory* (London: Sage, 1999) pp. 14–31.

Harvey, D. *The Condition of Postmodernity* (Oxford: Blackwell, 1989).

Held, D. 'Culture and political community: National, global, and cosmopolitan', in S. Vertovec and R. Cohen (eds) *Conceiving Cosmopolitanism: Theory, Context and Practice* (Oxford: Oxford University Press, 2002) pp. 48–58.

——. *Global Covenant: The Social Democratic Alternative to the Washington Consensus Democracy and the Global Order* (Cambridge: Polity Press, 2004).

Held, D. and M. Koenig-Archibugi (eds) *Taming Globalization: Frontiers of Global Governance* (Cambridge: Polity, 2003).

Held, D. and A. McGrew (eds) 'The great globalization debate: An introduction' *The Globalization Transformations Reader* (Cambridge: Polity Press, 2000) pp. 1–45.

——. *Globalization and Anti-globalization* (Cambridge: Polity Press, 2002).

Held, D., A. McGrew, D. Goldblatt and J. Perraton. *Global Transformations: Politics, Economics and Culture* (Cambridge: Polity, 1999).

Heller, M. *Linguistic Minorities and Modernity: A Sociolinguistic Ethnography* (London: Longman, 1999).

Henley, N. *Body Politics: Power, Sex and Nonverbal Communication* (New York: Simon and Schuster, 1986).

Hewitt, R. 'Language, youth and the destabilisation of ethnicity', in C. Palmgren, K. Lovgren and G. Bolin (eds) *Ethnicity in Youth Culture* (Stockholm: Stockholm University, 1992) pp. 27–41.

Hey, V. *The Company She Keeps: An Ethnography of Girls' Friendship* (Buckingham: Open University Press, 1996).

Hirst, P. and G. Thompson. *Globalization in Question*, 2nd edition (Cambridge: Polity, 1999).

Hobsbawm, E. *Nations and Nationalism since 1780: Programme, Myth, Reality* (Cambridge: Cambridge University Press, 1990).

Holmes, C. *John Bull's Island: Immigration and British Society* (Basingstoke, UK: Macmillan, 1988).

Holmes, J. 'Doing collegiality and keeping control at work: Small talk in government departments', in J. Coupland (ed.) *Small Talk* (London: Longman, 2000) pp. 32–61.

Holmes, J. and M. Meyerhoff (eds) *The Handbook of Language and Gender* (Oxford: Blackwell, 2003).

Hoogvelt, A. *Globalization and the Postcolonial World*, 2nd edition (London: Palgrave, 2001).

Jacobs, J. *Edge of Empire: Postcolonialism and the City* (London: Routledge, 1996).

Japanese Information and Culture Centre, Embassy of Japan (London, August 2004).

Johnson, J.M. 'In-depth interviewing', in J. Gubrium and J. Holstein (eds) *The Handbook of Interview Research* (London: Sage, 2001) pp. 103–19.

Johnson, F. and Aries, E. 'The talk of women friends', in J. Coates (ed.) *Language and Gender: A Reader* (Oxford: Blackwell, 1998) pp. 215–25.

Jordan, B. and F. Düvell. *Irregular Migration: The Dilemmas of Transnational Mobility* (Cheltenham, UK: Elgar, 2002).

——. *Migration: The Boundaries of Equality and Justice* (Cambridge: Polity, 2003).

Joseph, J. *Language and Identity* (London: Palgrave, 2004)

Kanno, Y. 'Bilingualism and identity: The stories of Japanese returnees', *International Journal of Bilingual Education and Bilingualism* 3/1: 1–18 (2000).

——. *Negotiating Bilingual and Bicultural Identities* (Clevedon, UK: Multilingual Matters, 2003).

Kearney, C. *The Monkey's Mask: Identity, Memory, Narrative and Voice* (Stoke-on-Trent, UK: Trentham, 2003).

Kelsky, K. *Women on the Verge* (Durham, NC: Duke University Press, 2001).

Kershen, A. 'The Jewish community in London', in N. Merriman (ed.) *The Peopling of London* (London: Museum of London, 1993) pp. 138–48.

——. 'Huguenots, Jews and Bangladeshis in Spitalfields and the spirit of capitalism', in A.J. Kershen (ed.) *London: The Promised Land?* (Aldershot, UK: Avebury, 1997) pp. 66–90.

King, A.D. *Global Cities: Post-Imperialism and the Internationalization of London* (London: Routledge, 1990).

Kinginger, C. 'Alice doesn't live here anymore: Foreign language learning and identity construction', in A. Pavlenko and A. Blackledge (eds) *Negotiation of Identities in Multilingual Contexts* (Clevedon, UK: Multilingual Matters, 2004) pp. 219–42.

Kress, G. and T. van Leeuwen. *Multimodality* (London: Edward Arnold, 2001).

Kubota, R. 'Japanese culture constructed by discourses: Implications for applied linguistics research and English language teaching', *TESOL Quarterly* 33/1: 9–35 (1999).

——. 'The impact of globalization on language teaching in Japan', in D. Block and D. Cameron (eds) *Globalization and Language Teaching* (London: Routledge, 2002) pp. 13–28.

Kyriacou, S. and Z. Theodorou. 'Greek Cypriots', in N. Merriman (ed.) *The Peopling of London* (London: Museum of London, 1993) pp. 98–105.

Labov, W. *The Social Stratification of English in New York City* (Washington, DC: The Center for applied Linguistics, 1966).

——. *Principles of Linguistic Change: Social Factors* (Oxford: Blackwell, 2001).

Lakoff, R. *Language and Woman's Place* (New York: Harper & Row, 1975).

Lamming, G. *The Emigrants* (London: Michael Joseph, 1954).

Lave, J. and E. Wenger. *Situated Learning: Legitimate Peripheral Participation* (Cambridge: Cambridge University Press, 1991).

Le Page, R.B. and A. Tabouret-Keller. *Acts of Identity: Creole-based Approaches to Language and Ethnicity* (Cambridge: Cambridge University Press, 1985).

Lessinger, J. 'Class, race, and success: Two generations of Indian Americans confront the American dream', in H.R. Cordero-Guzmán, R.C. Smith and R. Grosfoguel (eds) *Migration, Transnationalization, and Race in a Changing New York* (Philadelphia: Temple University Press, 2001) pp. 167–90.

Leung, C., R. Harris and B. Rampton. 'The idealised native speaker, reified ethnicities and classroom realities', *TESOL Quarterly* 31/3: 543–60 (1997).

Lévi-Strauss, C. *Structural Anthropology* (New York: Basic Books, 1963).

Levy, A. *Small Island* (London: Review, 2004).

Linde, C. *Life Stories: The Creation of Coherence* (New York: Oxford University Press, 1993).

Linguistic Minorities Project (X. Couillard, M. Martin-Jones, A. Morawska, E. Reid, V. Saifullah Khan and G. Smith) *The Other Languages of England* (London: Routledge & Kegan Paul, 1985).

McMahill, C. 'Self-expression, gender, and community: A Japanese feminist English class', in A. Pavlenko, A. Blackledge, I. Piller and M. Teutsch-Dwyer (eds) *Multilingualism, Second Language Learning, and Gender* (New York: Mouton De Gruyter, 2001) pp. 307–44.

MacMaster, N. *Racism in Europe* (London: Palgrave, 2001).

Martin-Jones, M. and K. Jones (eds) *Multilingual Literacies: Reading and Writing Different Worlds* (Amsterdam: John Benjamins, 2000).

Martinello, M. 'Citizenship of the European Union', in T.A. Aleinikoff and D. Klusmeyer (eds) *From Migrants to Citizens: Membership in a Changing World* (Washington, DC: Carnegie Endowment for International Peace, 2000).

Maswood, J. (2002) *Japan in Crisis* (London: Palgrave, 2002).

Mathews, G. *Global Culture/Individual Identity: Searching for a Home in the Cultural Supermarket* (London: Routledge, 2000).

May, S. *Language and Minority Rights* (London: Longman, 2001).

Merriman, J. *Modern Europe: From the Renaissance to the Present* (London: W.W. Norton, 1996).

Merriman, N. (ed.) 'The invisible settlers: From prehistoric times to the Huguenots', *The Peopling of London* (London: Museum of London, 1993a) pp. 28–47.

——. (ed.) *The Peopling of London* (London: Museum of London, 1993b).

——. (ed.) 'Latin Americans in London', *The Peopling of London* (London: Museum of London, 1993c) pp. 149–53.

Miller, J. *Audible Difference: ESL and Social Identity in Schools* (Clevedon, UK: Multilingual Matters, 2003).

Mishler, E. *Storylines* (Cambridge, MA: Harvard University Press, 1999).

Modelski, G. *The Principles of World Politics* (New York: Free Press, 1972).

Modood, T. and T. Acland (eds) *Race and Higher Education: Experiences, Challenges and Policy Implications* (London: Policy Studies Institute, 1998).

Modood, T., R. Berthoud, J. Lakey, J. Nazroo, P. Smith, S. Virdee and S. Beishon. *Ethnic Minorities in Britain: Diversity and Disadvantage* (London: Policy Studies Institute, 1997).

Mori, K. *Polite Lies: On Being a Woman Caught between Cultures* (New York: Henry Holt, 1997).

Mouer, R.E. and Y. Sugimoto. *Images of Japanese Society* (London: Kegan Paul, 1990).

Nanton, P. 'The Caribbean diaspora in the Promised Land', in A.J. Kershen (ed.) *London: The Promised Land?* (Aldershot, UK: Avebury, 1997) pp. 110–27.

Nasta, S. *Home Truths: Fictions of the South Asian Diaspora in Britain* (London: Palgrave, 2002).

Nederveen Pieterse, J. *Globalization and Culture. Global Mélange* (Oxford: Rowman and Littlefield, 2004).

Norton, B. 'Non-participation, imagined communities and the language classroom', in M. Breen (ed.) *Learner Contributions to Language Learning* (London: Longman, 2001) pp. 25–43.

Ong, A. *Flexible Citizenship: The Cultural Logic of Transnationalism* (Durham, NC: Duke University Press, 1999).

ONS (Office for National Statistics) 2001 census (London: ONS) http://www.statistics.gov.uk/census2001.

Owen, D. 'The other-Asians: The salad bowl', in C. Peach (ed.) *Ethnicity in the 1991 Census, Volume Two: The Ethnic Minority Populations of Great Britain* (London: HMSO, 1996) pp. 181–205.

Oxford English Dictionary Online (Oxford: Oxford University Press, 2001), http://dictionary.oed.com.

Palmer, A. *The East End: Four Centuries of London Life* (London: John Murray, 2000).

Pang, C.L. *Negotiating Identity in Contemporary Japan: The Case of the Kikokushijo* (London: Kegan Paul International, 2000).

Papastergiadis, N. *The Turbulence of Migration* (Cambridge: Polity, 2000).

Parekh, B. *Rethinking Multiculturalism: Cultural Diversity and Political Theory* (London: Palgrave, 2000).

Parker, D. and M. Song (eds) *Rethinking 'Mixed-Race'* (London: Pluto Press, 2001).

Peach, C. (ed.) 'Introduction' *Ethnicity in the 1991 Census, Volume Two: The Ethnic Minority Populations of Great Britain* (London: HMSO, 1996) pp. 1–24.

Perlmutter, H.V. 'On the rocky road to the first global civilization', *Human Relations* 44/9: 897–920 (1991).

Perrons, D. *Global and Social Change: People and Plans in a Divided World* (London: Routledge, 2004).

Pes, J. 'The Spanish in London', in N. Merriman (ed.) *The Peopling of London* (London: Museum of London, 1993) pp. 179–84.

Petras, J. and H. Veltmeyer. *Globalization Unmasked: Imperialism in the 21st Century* (London: Zed Books, 2001).

Phillips, M. *London Crossings: A Biography of Black Britain* (London: Continuum, 2001).

Phillips, M. and T. Phillips. *Windrush: The Irresistible Rise of Multi-Racial Britain* (London: HarperCollins, 1998).

Pichler, P. 'The Construction of bicultural femininities in the talk of British Bangladeshi girls', in J. Cotterill and A. Ife (eds) *Language Across Boundaries* (London: Continuum, 2001) pp. 25–46.

Pilkington, A. *Racial Disadvantage and Ethnic Diversity in Britain* (London: Palgrave, 2003).

Piller, I. and K. Takahashi. 'A passion for English: Desire and the language market', in A. Pavlenko (ed.) *Emotions and Multilingualism* (Cambridge: Cambridge University Press, 2005).

Portes, A., L.E. Guarnizo and P. Landolt. 'The study of transnationalism: Pitfalls and promise of an emergent research field', *Ethnic and Racial Studies* 22/2: 217–37 (1999).

Preece, S. and J. Godfrey. 'Academic literacy practice and widening participation: First year undergraduates on an academic writing programme', *Widening Participation and Lifelong Learning* 6/1: 6–14 (2004).

Proctor, J. *Dwelling Places: Postwar Black British Writing* (Manchester: Manchester University Press, 2003).

Puri, J. *Encountering Nationalism* (Oxford: Blackwell, 2004).

Raj, D. *Where are You From? Middle-Class Migrants in the Modern World* (Berkeley, CA: University of California Press, 2003).

Ramdin, R. *Reimaging Britain: 500 Years of Black and Asian History* (London: Pluto Press, 1999).

Reich, R. *The Work of Nations* (New York: Vintage, 1991).

Reicher, S. and N. Hopkins, *Self and Nation* (London: Sage, 2001).

Renan, E. (1990 [1882]) 'What is a nation?', in H.K. Bhabha (ed.) *Nation and Narration* (London: Routledge, 1990) pp. 8–22.

Richards, B. and A. Yamada-Yamamoto. 'The linguistic experience of Japanese preschool children and their families in the UK', *Journal of Multilingual and Multicultural Development* 19/2: 142–57 (1998).

Ritzer, G. *The McDonaldization Thesis* (Thousand Oaks, CA: Sage, 1998).

——. *Enchanting a Disenchanted World: Revolutionizing the Means of Consumption* (Thousand Oaks, CA: Sage, 1999).

——. *The Globalization of Nothing* (Thousand Oaks, CA: Sage, 2004).

Roberts, B. *Biographical Research* (Buckingham: Open University Press, 2002).

Robertson, R. 'Glocalization: Time-space and homogeneity-heterogeneity', in M. Featherstone, S. Lash and R. Robertson (eds) *Global Modernities* (London: Sage Publications, 1995) pp. 25–44.

Robinson, V. *Transients, Settlers and Refugees: Asians in Britain* (Oxford: Clarendon Press, 1986).

——. 'The migration of East African Asians to the UK', in R. Cohen (ed.) *The Cambridge Survey of World Migration* (Cambridge: Cambridge University Press, 1995).

——. 'The Indians: Onward and upward', in C. Peach (ed.) *Ethnicity in the 1991 Census. Volume 2: The Ethnic Minority Populations of Great Britain* (London: HMSO, 1996) pp. 95–121.

Román-Veláquez, P. *The Making of Latin London: Salsa Music, Place and Identity* (Aldershot, UK: Ashgate, 1999).

Rosen, H. and T. Burgess. *Languages and Dialects of London School Children* (London: Ward Lock Educational, 1980).

Rosenau, J.N. *Turbulence in World Politics* (Brighton: Harvester Wheatsheaf, 1990).

Rubin, L. *Just Friends: The Role of Friendship in Our Lives* (New York: Harper Row, 1985).

Rubin, H.J. and I.S. Rubin. *Qualitative Interviewing: The Art of Hearing Data* (Thousand Oaks, CA: Sage, 1995).

Sakai, J. *The Clash of Economic Cultures: Japanese Bankers in the City of London* (New Brunswick, NJ: Transaction, 2004 [2000]).

San Eufrasio, A. 'Luz al final del Metro', *Canta y Camina* 71 (Septiembre–Octubre): 4 (2003).

Sassen, S. *The Global City* (Princeton, NJ: Princeton University Press, 1991).

——. *The Global City*, 2nd edition (Princeton, NJ: Princeton University Press, 2001).

Seidman, I. *Interviewing as Qualitative Research: A Guide for Researchers in Education and the Social Sciences*, 2nd edition (New York: Teachers College Press, 1998).

Siegle, L. 'Vive les rosbifs', *The Observer Magazine*, 16 January: 20–7 (2005).

Simmel, G. 'The Stranger', in K. Wolff (ed.) *The Sociology of Gerog Simmel* (New York: Free Press, 1950) pp. 401–8.

Solomos, J. *Race and Racism in Britain*, 3rd edition (London: Palgrave, 2003).

Sowell, T. *Migrations and Cultures: The World View* (New York: Basic Books, 1996).

Spence, L. *Third Country Nationals Living in London 2000/01: A profile of Londoners who have non-EU nationality based on analysis of Labour Force Survey data*. Data Management and Analysis Group Briefing 2003/6 (London: Greater London Authority, 2003).

Spivak, G. *The Post-Colonial Critic: Interviews, Strategies, Dialogues* (London: Routledge, 1990).

Stiglitz, J. *Globalization and Its Discontents* (London: Penguin, 2002).

Storkey, M. 'Using the schools' language data to estimate the total number of speakers of London's top languages', in P. Baker and J. Eversley (eds) *Multilingual Capital* (London: Battlebridge Publications, 2000) pp. 63–66.

Sugimoto, Y. *An Introduction to Japanese Society* (Cambridge: Cambridge University Press, 1997).

Sword, K. 'The poles in London', in N. Merriman (ed.) *The Peopling of London* (London: Museum of London, 1993) pp. 154–62.

Tannen, D. *You Just Don't Understand: Men and Women in Conversation* (New York: William Morrow, 1990).

Tizard, B. and A. Phoenix. *Black, White or Mixed Race: Race and Racism in the Lives of Young People* (London: Routlege, 1993).

Touraine, A. *Pourrons-nous vivre ensemble, égaux et différents?/Can We Live Together?* (Paris; Editions Fayard/Stanford, CA: Stanford University Press, 1997/2000).

Tsuchiya, M. *Bilingualism and Socialisation in Childhood: A Case of Japanese Children in the UK*, PhD thesis in progress (Institute of Education University of London).

Tylor, E.B. *Primitive Culture: Researches into the Development of Mythology, Philosophy, Religion, Language, Art and Custom* (Boston: Estes and Lauriat, 1874).

United Colours of London, http://www.bbc.co.uk/london/yourlondon/ unitedcolours/, accessed 1 November 2004.

Vertovec, S. 'Conceiving and researching transnationalism', *Ethnic and Racial Studies* 22/2: 447–62 (1999).

Vertovec, S. and R. Cohen (eds) *Conceiving Cosmopolitanism: Theory, Context and Practice* (Oxford: Oxford University Press, 2002).

Visram, R. *Asians in Britain: Four Hundred Years of History* (London: Pluto, 2002).

Wallace, C. 'Local literacies and global literacy', in D. Block and D. Cameron (eds) *Globalization and Language Teaching* (London: Routledge, 2002) pp. 101–14.

Weedon, C. *Feminist Practice and Poststructuralist Theory*, 2nd edition (Oxford: Blackwell, 1997).

Weil, P. and R. Hansen (eds) *Towards a European Nationality, Citizenship, Immigration and Nationality Law for the EU* (London: Palgrave, 2002).

Weiner, A. *European Citizenship Practice: Building Institutions of a Non-State* (Oxford: Westview Press, 1999).

Wenger, E. *Communities of Practice* (Cambridge: Cambridge University Press, 1998).

Wengraf, T. *Qualitative Research Interviewing* (London: Sage, 2001).

West, C. 'When the doctor is a "lady" ', *Symbolic Interaction* 7/1: 87–106 (1984).

Whelehan, I. *Overloaded: Popular Culture and the Future of Feminism* (London: Women's Press, 2000).

White, M. *The Japanese Overseas: Can They Go Home Again?* (New York: The Free Press, 1988).

Whitehead, J. and A. Taylor. *Teachers of Modern Foreign Languages: Foreign Native Speakers on Initial Teacher Training Courses in England* (Bristol: Faculty of Education, UWE, 1998).

Williams, R. *Keywords: A Vocabulary of Culture and Society* (London: Fontana, 1976).

Winder, R. *Bloody Foreigners* (London: Little, Brown, 2004).

Wong, B. *Ethnicity and Entrepreneurship: The New Chinese Immigrants in the San Francisco Bay Area* (Boston: Allyn and Baker, 1998).

The World Bank, http://devdata.wordlbank.org.

Yamada-Yamamoto, A. 'Statistical overview of Japanese children in the UK and language environment survey', in A. Yamada-Yamamoto and B. Richards (eds) *Japanese Children Aboard: Cultural, Educational and Language Issues* (Clevedon, UK: Multilingual Matters, 1998) pp. 17–26.

Yamada-Yamamoto, A. and B. Richards. *Japanese Children Aboard: Cultural, Educational and Language Issues* (Clevedon, UK: Multilingual Matters, 1998).

Yashiro, K. 'Japan's returnees', *Journal of Multilingual and Multicultural Development*, 16/1&2: 139–64 (1995).

Yoshida, M. *The Impact of Globalisation upon UK Higher Education with Special Respect to Japanese Study Abroad*, PhD thesis in progress (Institute of Education University of London).

Yoshino, K. *Cultural Nationalism in Contemporary Japan: A Sociological Enquiry* (London: Routledge, 1992).

Index

230